This book is dedicated to

Mrs. Frances Ryan

a lady of extraordinary skills
whose friendship and help I appreciate greatly
and without whom this book could not have been written

and to

Fiona, Heather and Morag

the best daughters that any father could have

****

With all best wishes —
from the author!

The Psychic Investigators Casebook

Vol. 2

Arl. A. Lawrie

By
Archibald Lawrie

authorHOUSE™

1663 LIBERTY DRIVE, SUITE 200
BLOOMINGTON, INDIANA 47403
(800) 839-8640
WWW.AUTHORHOUSE.COM

First published by AuthorHouse 02/23/05

ISBN: 1-4208-3666-8 (sc)

Printed in Scotland.

Cover design by

Mr. Alfredo de los Ojos
WEBSITE
WWW. PSYCHIC-INFO.COM

The above website has been brought into being to enhance
the pleasure of the readers of this series of books as well as to
widen their knowledge of all the author's books.
It contains photographs and pictorial images that can be better
presented to the reader on a screen and should be looked upon
as a helpful addendum to the books.
Unless the website gets overwhelmed by requests, readers will
be able to seek advice and help from the author on existing
psychic problems.

Electronic Format
Please know that the book itself is available in electronic format
from the publisher.

****

CLIENT CONFIDENTIALITY

As most accounts in this book deal with private families
encountering psychic happenings within their own homes I have
concealed their true identities by using pseudonyms where they
asked me to do so.
I assure readers that NO CHANGES of any kind have been
made to the actual accounts.
These happenings did take place: they are real.

****

OPINIONS and **CONCLUSIONS**

As the Scottish Society for Psychical Research holds
no corporate views on psychical matters
all opinions and conclusions expressed in the books
and the website
are those of the author

CONTENTS

FOREWORD

This book is the second in a series of paperbacks that are designed for light and yet educational reading on the little-understood topic of the supernatural.

It is by virtue of their containing *genuine and first-hand* accounts of the paranormal *during our lifetime* that makes them stand out from other books, for book-shops are full of 'spooky tales from spooky castles'. The trouble with such tales is that most of them are traditional by nature and nobody quite knows if they are true or otherwise.

There is no such problem with this series for I, personally, have been closely connected with each and every case that I have recorded for you. I see no point in presenting you with accounts that I cannot personally vouch for, for if anything is needed when researching the paranormal, that something is *THE TRUTH.* Psychical research cannot move forward on Hollywood fantasy, half-truths or imagined happenings.

Neither can such important research move forward on spasmodic or isolated cases. Cases must come forward in such numbers that they can be compared and contrasted and suitably logged and recorded. Having dealt, firsthand, with nearly five hundred cases in five years I think that I can rightfully claim that I now have enough information before me to be able to make comparative judgements with reasonable accuracy.

Sadly, psychical research is in its early infancy: in fact it is currently almost an unrecognised science but the reasons for that are so complex that I must deal with them in another publication. After more than twenty years of personal research I know enough to be able to tell you with complete confidence that at the moment modern science has neither the knowledge, motivation nor the instrumentation to launch paranormal investigation in any meaningful way.

The only current way left open to us, therefore, to gain reliable information on the paranormal world is through the services of *reliable* psychic mediums. As you will see, I have been blessed over the years with the company and help of one such medium, 'Francesca'.

x

CHAPTER 1

RIGHT PLACE – WRONG TIME

The Case of the Popping Corks
Old lady – Older Companions
Nastiness Lingers

You can demolish a property, you can remove all the bricks and mortar but you'll never shift the memories that once lay within the confines of that property! They are there for keeps and that means for hundreds and even thousands of years.

I know that because I meet these memories along with my talented medium friend, Francesca, almost every week in life when we are called in by some puzzled or even traumatised family to evaluate precisely what they have lurking within their home. They believe, for the most part, that something is in the wrong place at the wrong time …but Francesca and I know that something is in the **right place** but at the wrong time.

It is up to us to find what is there and to arrange for it to go and I now record for you three cases where we did precisely that.

****

The Case of the Popping Corks

"It's like waking up in the middle of a domestic scene of someone else's making," said Monica as she tried to described the noises that seemed to be all around her when she would sometimes wake at intervals during the night. She and her partner Bernard had invited me into their home after she had put up with quite a variety of strange noises over a period of nearly two years. I don't usually like lists but perhaps that is the best way of dealing with the variety of sounds that Monica heard.
There were,

1) Cracking or crackling noises very close to her head.
2) By December 2003 this was superseded by a sound near the bedroom window as if someone was rubbing his hands together every now and again.
3) Then came a flapping sound at times… like someone wafting either a dusting cloth or sheets of paper ("or perhaps even bird's wings?" Monica thought).
4) This was often accompanied by a noise similar to what one might get if one held up a sheet of thick paper in one hand and repetitively flicked the fingers of the other hand against it. This often happened *behind* Monica's head.

Now it gets interesting for the "big smoochy kisses" (Monica's words) also began being heard somewhere to the back of the victim's head during the night although there was no attempt at any physical contact by whoever was making them.

5) And at the time of my first visit, this last noise that I am about to mention was the most common of all and that was most definitely the popping of tightly fitting corks as they were drawn forcefully out of bottles. I say, "most definitely" for Monica could think of no other sound with which that could be confused.
6) This householder also made it clear that there appeared to be an invisible cat (or similar small animal) that walked up and down over her bed on many nights, sometimes even settling itself comfortably down to one side of her. When she "shooed" it away it usually took a telling and went.

Monica's partner, Bernard, worked overseas quite a lot and even when he was at home he snored so loudly (Monica told me) that the couple had separate bedrooms. Thus it was that Bernard never had the opportunity to discuss a noise with Monica at the moment of its occurrence, although he never at any time cast doubts on her account of these mystery noises. He just accepted what his partner told him as he had no reason to doubt her word.

At some particular point in such a case as this, a time comes when enough is enough and the breaking point came for Monica when she was alone in the house in April 2004. Then it was that a sound that she said sounded like a "high pitched female note" could be heard in the "favourite spot for spooks" by the window. It was then that she found my phone number and told me her tale.

By mid May Francesca, (the world-class medium lady with whom I work), a student of the paranormal called Maureen and myself all visited the house that was about one mile north of Edinburgh city center and close to the old city port of Newhaven. By luck that evening we met Bernard as well, for he was on leave at that time: something that Monica was very glad about for many reasons. We got straight down to work without coffee or the niceties of life and on this occasion I thought it wise for Monica to read out for us the notes that she had so kindly prepared.

At personal level I was worried about our medium Francesca that evening for she told us that she had been notified about a sudden family bereavement not an hour previously and I wondered whether I should not have insisted that she remain at home to quietly grieve and to be with her husband. As it turned out, this marvellous lady benefited I think by having something to involve her lively and active mind that evening, other than letting it dwell on the sad and sudden loss of a good friend. I noticed no diminution of her great abilities and that showed her to be a true professional. But I knew that already!

Francesca bowed her head for a moment or two and moved into one of her 'mini-trance' states. At such times this talented lady seems to flick continuously in and out of the here-and-now as she connects to the information-gathering mode of the spirit world. When you look at her, however, during this time there are often no hints that she is in any altered state ….although I know she is.

"You are experiencing all these things in your bedroom which, I think, must be at that side of the apartment," she said to Monica, pointing to the rear of the building. "Can we go through there to take a look at that bedroom?" Francesca, I realised at once, had already picked up upon something or other but what was it?

I watched as this lady looked out of the bedroom window into the courtyard and gardens below as if visually searching for some specific building or landmark.

"What was on this site before the apartments were built?" she asked and was told that a large old house had been demolished to make way for the present block of houses. Francesca then went on to tell us that the building that occupied that site *before that previous building* had been a sort of hostel for seamen when they landed ashore in the Edinburgh port of Newhaven. The hostel had been a substantial size and had been of several floors to accommodate all the seamen involved. The man in charge at the time when it interests us, Francesca told us, was a Mr. Nesbit (or Nisbit?) and it was his presence that was being felt in that apartment for his office had been on the second floor. This had been, therefore, at exactly the same height above the ground as was Bernard's and Monica's second-floor home.

As soon as our medium bowed her head and meditated upon the situation I saw her hands move in front of her. I noticed how the fingers of her right hand seemed to be 'writing' invisible words on the palm of her left and I knew that she had been taken over to a degree by the spirit persona of Mr. Nesbit.

"What are you writing down?" I asked softly in her ear.

(My job during our visits to clients is to move the entranced medium down the correct mental line in order to come to definite conclusions .....for mediums can go off at tangents when in trance. It was my task to keep Francesca's mind focused on specific points. Often when in this altered state she does not know what she, herself, is doing. She might well have been totally unaware that her right hand was writing invisible words on the palm of her left. It was my job to point this out to her and move the whole scene forward.)

"It's their names," she said as she explained that each seaman had to produce documentation from his captain to prove that he was a bona-fide sailor in need of accommodation upon land. The information that the man gave was noted and recorded in a very large book and then the seaman himself had to sign an agreement about the rules that he was expected to abide by when at the hostel. This part of the process, Francesca said, *(speaking as Nesbit)* was difficult for such men as they could neither read nor write. She said that any scratching noises heard by Monica were the "signing" of the papers involved, for the men could only draw a strong dark line across the paper with an unusual writing implement.

My ears pricked up!

"Will you please focus your mind in on that unusual writing implement and tell us what it looks like please? Watch a sailor using it on the paper, Francesca!"

Frances paused for a moment,

"Oh, it's a thick, black stick and it looks like wood".

I knew at once what it must surely be …..a stick of charcoal and I quite understand the audible nature of making such 'signatures' for the scraping of charcoal upon a thick sheet of paper does indeed make a very loud and scratchy noise.

Francesca told us how Mr. Nesbit was quite a character. No doubt he had to be in order to control dozens of landed sailors on his premises! He would have to run his establishment with an iron hand too I'd imagine. She told how he would often take payment for board and lodging by accepting bottles of naval rum that would probably be smuggled ashore from the ships in the harbor. It was the opening of such rum bottles that Monica was hearing around her head during the night hours.

(I must remind my readers that when an entity decides to make himself known to humans many years after he was alive, he brings back with him the things that he once held dear or at least by which he was surrounded. That is as true for his bottles of rum and the cats as for his personal papers and records of the coming and going of his seamen lodgers.)

The cats (for there were several, Francesca said,) belonged neither to the premises nor to Mr. Nesbit himself. They were cats of the area or the alleyways and chose to congregate in the hostel. Perhaps they were given tidbits of fish from the seafarers (who, themselves must have stunk of fish) and, of course, there would always be a roaring fire in the main room of the hostel during the colder winter weather, I'm sure. Yes, the 18th century felines in the Trinity area of Edinburgh were obviously in some sort of pussy heaven!

All human beings have various degrees of sensitivity to the paranormal and Francesca and I came to the conclusion that

Monica probably had more than average capacity for linking herself to the other world…although she would never know of that ability before the above incidents. While we told her that the very fact that the above details had been uncovered might be enough, of itself, to remove those leftovers of the past, she should attempt NOT to dwell mentally on any of the above things. We informed her that if she found herself thinking of Mr. Nesbit, his rum bottles and the cats she should at once turn her mind purposefully to other thoughts, for to dwell on him mentally would only serve to strengthen his ability to make his way back into our world …and neither Monica nor Bernard would like that to happen.

*(Remember the little ghost boy from page 101 in Volume 1 of The Psychic Investigators Casebook? Well, he came back when one of the cleaners in the Medical Center began to think that she was missing his company. We had to move him on **for a second time** because of that but I am pleased to tell you that he has remained away for the past couple of years. Entities who have been sent "to the light" can come back sometimes of their own volition or sometimes by being unwittingly "strengthened" by careless thoughts of some human being. During the Second World War there was a saying in the UK that, "Careless talk cost lives!" With entities, the saying might be, "Careless thoughts can bring entities back into our lives once again!")*

We never did get an explanation of the high-pitched voice heard by Monica that she said sounded, "female". I'm sure, however, that it does not need a lot of imagination to think of who such a visitor to the hostel might be.

****

I made a point of asking Francesca to inform "Mr. Nesbit" that his time had been and gone and that this area of the earth's surface now belonged to Monica and her partner and that he should leave them and their home in peace. However, even as we were going out of the door of the apartment I felt that we had not heard the last of Mr. Nesbit and that proved to be correct for in mid-August I got another phone call from the householder followed by a second call of utter alarm a few days later.

The first call said that this lady had begun, once more, to feel small air movements on her bare arm as she awoke from sleep. It was as if someone was perhaps blowing gently on her arm to wake her up or moving an invisible "something" next to her to create air movement. A "swishing" noise was also reported along with more "paddy paws" being felt on the bed.

At that point I said that I would return to make a visit as soon as Francesca returned from her summer holiday and I suggested that Monica keep her bedroom light and her radio on for the time being.

The second, more frantic phone call that came in from this lady about a week later, told how the illumination from the main bedroom light had indeed "slowed down" the psychic incidents to almost zero but soon Monica was sleeping with only a small bedside light shining and it was then that things began to happen more strongly.

On August 18th she described the following,

1) The localised air movement on her arms, still.
2) A flapping noise around her that might have been frantic turning of large paper pages **or** the flapping of a bird's swing. Even the shaking that a dog gives itself when removing rainwater from its coat was considered a possibility. And unexpectedly, from my viewpoint as a researcher, she also told of,
3) A small orange/red spider that she thought she saw moving in several places close by her. She had seen it several times on her arm and it had also been seen on her pillow where it "just disappeared through the cloth" when Monica challenged it. Actually Monica used the words, "several red spiders" initially until we worked out that it might just be **one** visual thing seen in several different positions. Naturally, this good lady was very, very upset as she recorded this last event with me: she thought that there was at least a chance that her mind had caved in completely under the strain and that she was now hallucinating wildly.

I was pleased to be in a position to reassure her that nothing of the kind was happening to her but that what she had seen was an exceedingly interesting and somewhat rare event. She had witnessed, I believe, what is known as a "spirit light". These are most often encountered in near-dark situations and are usually about the size of an average garden pea. I have previously recorded them in four distinct colors (I have no idea why there is a color difference!) red, green, blue or yellow/white or minor variations of those colors. They appear to "float" around a room or in an area close to a living person and often move very close indeed to their intended "target".

(In fact I mention in another publication, one of my earliest cases where a woman in Dunfermline, Fife, Scotland was so used to several of such red spirit lights floating around her that she just accepted their presence as something almost normal and unrelated to other psychic activity which took place in her house. Towards the end of my examination of the case I told her my thoughts on such lights and her reply was, "So that is why they come close and have a good look at me every now and again!")

I think that that little light was very probably doing precisely that with Monica. It may well have been having a good look at her as she slept.

That, of course, begs the question,

"What are such lights?"

Regretfully, I must tell you that nobody knows for sure what these things are ….except that they are of psychic origin. I myself treat them as if they are some sort of "nucleus" of a deceased person…a sort of condensed, wandering memory but I have no scientific reason for such a thought. Treating them as that certainly seems to work and so I will continue to do so until I gain evidence to the contrary. After all, we have to begin somewhere in this spirit-light research business.

(Researchers might like to know that such spirit-lights have been known for centuries in Scotland at least. There are records of them being seen "all the time" in a house in the Pends area of St Andrews in Fife and the name given to them in the 18th century were, "burbelangs". I rather like that name but for international use like in this publication I'll have to stick with, "spirit-lights".)

Francesca and I did manage to visit Monica in late August and we found her apprehensive but not overtly alarmed. We knew, when we last left her, that she would find it difficult to switch her mind off completely from what was in her house in spite of the fact that that was necessary to "push" Mr. Nesbit back into the psychic world where he really belonged.

The problem that we were then encountering was that while Mr. Nesbit himself was not in fact giving Monica any ongoing problem, his strong personality (in psychic terms) was still around and enabling secondary spirit memories to enter our world 'in the background' so-to-speak through his presence. We would have to re-contact both that man and any other entity who was generating unrest in the house. We already knew a lot about Mr. Nesbit, the popping of corks (which had now gone) and the seamen who lived in the old hostel on the site but we had not really gone into the mysterious flapping noise and the air movement in depth and that was what Monica was now experiencing. I therefore asked Francesca to move into trance and to home in on the source of the flapping for there seemed to be some sort of second spirit entity present…..which is not at all unusual for spirit entities can congregate as groups just as we humans can. There is often a central character surrounded by minor characters.

The medium's head went down and her breathing deepened and then it normalized again about thirty seconds later.

"I'm getting the personality and the memories of a little girl who stayed in the area all her life for I also see her as an old woman here as well as a young child. I feel that the flapping business revolves around her in some way."

"Right then, Francesca," I said, " Would you please go back into that scene again and find out initially at what point in her life the flapping took place, what it actually was and why it still presents us with a problem in 2004."

Again the lady's head bent down and she was soon murmuring in a trance state,

"A girl…a little girl. Stupid parent ..wanted to punish her. Often the same punishment…locked in a little room. Oh such a tiny room! What a tiny room, no more than a cupboard actually.

Goodness! There is a bird in there! What a big bird….it's a seagull, a great big seagull. It's frightened out of its wits and the girl is crying and yelling because she hates it flapping in her face. She screams and yells and the bird get even more panicky and flaps more……."

I ask Francesca to "return to us, return to Edinburgh in the year 2004" and she raises her head and shakes it to once again become the Francesca that I know.

"Phew!" she says with relief, "I had a poor girl there who was frightened out of her mind with a flapping bird."

"Yes, Francesca, Monica and I know already for you were enunciating well."

(Very often a medium does not know what she has (has not) said when in trance and that was the case here. I feel it only right that part of my task is to keep her updated in what she has said to us when she has been mentally 'elsewhere'.)

I was about to ask our medium to move the girl away to where she should be but I could see that Francesca was getting further knowledge as she sat in the armchair opposite me. She addressed Monica directly,

"Do you have some sort of glass ornament with some sort of twisted blue stripes in the glasswork …and have you moved such an ornament off a windowsill somewhere in this house?"

I looked across at Monica to see her jaw dropping and her mouth open with surprise. I awaited her answer with interest for I knew that Francesca's question must be linked to the little girl and the bird but I could not think how.

"Well, actually," said the surprised householder, "I did have such an ornament on the windowsill in the bedroom but as that was where there was the flapping noise I thought I'd take that fragile item down and store it in a cupboard just in case the bird's wings knocked it off the ledge."

(A researcher's job is to look for clues all the time and this last sentence immediately illustrated to me just how real the bird must have seemed to Monica!"

That told me a lot of things, of course. Not only did it vindicate Francesca's words but it showed me that Monica took all these things very seriously: the bird in her mind was almost a real bird capable of knocking over glass ornaments!

The medium then went on to say that the spirit lady, in the persona of the little girl who she had once been, took great delight in admiring the ornament on the windowsill and was so, so disappointed when Monica had removed it from view.

(That appears to tell us that we humans can conceal physical items from the psychic world which runs counter to what I have found elsewhere. I think that this business needs further investigation for last year I met a similar situation where a spirit-being knew that a glass paperweight had been put in a certain drawer but he left me with the impression that he could not see it there and, as in Monica's case he asked for it to be put on display in the usual place.)

I now realised the method by which we had to move forward here and, strange to say, I also realised that we now had a lever to use if we had to "draw up a contract" with the psychic world. We had a 'bargaining chip' so to speak, for believe it or not that is sometimes handy to have if an entity is reluctant to go towards the light.

"Francesca, would you make contact with the persona of the little girl and tell her that the episodes with the bird are over and done with and that she now has nothing to fear. Ask her to leave this house and move to the light in order to leave Monica in peace but tell her also that Monica will replace the glass ornament on the window ledge should she ever wish to see it again …but on the strict understanding that she does not alert Monica to her presence!"

(The possibility that some sort of "contract" can be drawn up with the supernatural world must seem very strange to my readers but I have used this mechanism on several occasions with great effect. Strange to say, I cannot think of a single example of a spirit person breaking such an agreement. Perhaps a spirit person's word is 'their bond'?)

The medium put her mind to the task and after about a minute I saw a broad smile cross her face as she "awoke" from trance. (This was, in fact, to be the first of two smiles that day.)

"That looked like fun!" I said, smiling across to a puzzled Monica for psychical research is not all 'doom and gloom'.

"It was the little girl," explained Francesca, "She showed herself to me hopping and skipping up a cobbled street and disappearing into the distance while she waved 'Goodbye' with her hands. I thought it rather sweet."

I too thought it 'sweet' but it also prompted thoughts in my head for while there is much symbolism used by the psychic world I did not know whether the 'going-up-the-street' business was sheer symbolism or had the girl used some scene from her childhood of so long ago. Did such a scene still exist in her complete memory bank (which I knew that if it did, it was still totally available to her as a spirit person) and had it been projected for the benefit of Francesca. Which ever it was we will now read about a similar 'effect' that I feel sure is pure symbolism …for it can be little else.

Having moved the girl away from the property I now wanted to put something to Mr. Nesbit…who I thought might still be lurking in the background so-to-speak because Monica's dwelling mentally upon him may have brought him back to a degree. I wanted to tell this spirit man that he must move away (again) and this time take his fellows with him. I therefore voiced this opinion to Francesca and asked that she re-contact him if he was around in order to put such thoughts to him.

A little way through the trance a big smile came over the medium's face for a second time that day, and a little laugh began as she awoke.

"And what on earth was all that about?" I asked. Even Monica, I noticed, was smiling this time.

"He's going all right but it was the manner of his going that amused me for he showed me a man (presumably himself) playing a musical pipe and walking along a dockside with hundreds of rats behind him like the Pied Piper!"

I thought it rather clever of Mr. Nesbit and suggested to the other two ladies that, being a seaman he also might have considered that he was leading the rats (alias his minor fellow spirit-people) away from a sinking ship (the ghost hostel for sailors that is now no more).

To date we have had no further communication from Monica or requests for more help so I conclude that all is now quiet in this property. A good result I think for a rather interesting case.

****

Old Lady – Older Companions

Many of us make the mistake of confusing the bodily disabilities of the aged with their mental capacities. Severe old age is not necessarily synonymous with total collapse of the mind. That fact was forcefully brought home to me in mid November 2003 when I was invited by a close relative of Ruby to evaluate statements made by that old lady regarding spirit people she claimed were around her most of the time.

Part of the problem appeared to be that Ruby, whose ninetieth birthday was merely a week away, lived in a sheltered housing complex and that was run by a warden. This meant that the dear lady was living within her own suite of rooms and was probably being looked after well enough but her state of mental stimulation was unknown to a degree. Was she, for example, having many visitors or was she perhaps shut away from the world until the weekend when, hopefully some relations would arrive to talk with her. I certainly could not answer those questions and so I had to go gently into the situation when I was asked to talk with Ruby to find out just who or what she had in her apartment that she claimed was supernatural. The relative who asked me to make that evaluation was the only relative to take Ruby seriously when she said that she could see this person or that person suddenly appear or disappear …and at times by merely moving straight through her bedroom wall. All the others relations seemed to think that poor Aunt Ruby was definitely sinking into the pit of mental decay.

Jane was the only relative who took what Ruby said as the truth so Francesca and I met Jane at her home in central Edinburgh in the early afternoon and we drove 25 miles south to a lovely little border town to meet Ruby. After a mental and verbal tussle with a "tough cookie" female warden who didn't seem to like the way that Jane pressed the entry bell we entered the tranquillity of Ruby's apartment. It was neat, tidy and comfortable but I could see immediately that this lady was frail although when she began speaking she spoke clearly and coherently although softly.

"Jane tells me that you've come to see about the lady with the grey hair that is often tied at the back of her head when she visits me," she started.

"Yes, I'd love to hear about her and all the other strange visitors you get from time to time," I continued.

"Well, she's the main one but she doesn't always have her hair tied back you know: sometimes she just has it hanging down….. especially when she is working away at the floors."

"What does she do on the floor?" I enquired genuinely.

"Oh, she scrubs away at them. Always, she scrubs and scrubs and I'm so afraid that sooner of later she'll damage the carpets by all that scrubbing. Every night almost, she scrubs away at the rugs and she uses a sort of silver-coloured implement in the process. I don't know what that can be although I try to get a good look at it I seem to fail each time."

This told me that not only was Ruby observant but that she was honest: she had clearly stated what she was seeing and did not give way to the temptation to make up a name or function for this "silver-coloured" tool she had seen. That was a good beginning for I could see that I was going to get the truth out of this old lady, albeit the truth as she saw it.

I thought I'd move the conversation forward,

"There are other people who come and visit you from the spirit world also I believe?"

"Oh yes, lots of them! There is always a big boy or young man hanging about the place and sometimes I see him with a younger boy. They don't hurt me or anything but I often get a shock when I find them in the kitchen or whatever before they disappear through the wall. Sometimes I feel that they see me and sometimes I feel that they don't know I am there at all."

Ruby went on to tell of events, like the opening of drawers, which she attributed to her apparitions but I did not go down that route for at ninety years old this lady would be quite prone, I imagine, to doing things and then forgetting about the fact that she'd done them.

Jane and Francesca were sitting opposite Ruby and I. Jane was just listening and observing while I noticed that the medium was keen to tell us something and so I led the way in for that.

"Francesca, what can you tell us about things so far?"

She looked at Ruby and asked,

" Did you ever see that lady with a cup in her hand?"

"No, just a strange silver thing."

Francesca went on to explain, looking at Ruby,

"O.K., I know your spirit visitor had a lot to do with cups for she lived in an old house which once stood on the site of this housing complex and she told people's fortunes by reading the pattern of the tea-leaves left in their cups after the tea had been drunk. She made her money by telling fortunes in this way and she was well thought of for her skills. It was her way of making money although some of her family worked in a nearby cloth mill of some sort."

Ruby seemed to find hearing Francesca difficult so the medium, at that point, wisely moved and sat right next to her.

After some prompting by me and deep thought by the medium, Francesca came up with the name of the spirit lady who made money by reading cups. Mary O'Neill was the apparitional grey-haired cup-reader while her son was apparently called James. They belonged to around the year 1910 we were told and then she said that she believed that James had died by hanging. She did not specify whether this young man had hanged himself by accident or as an act of suicide or, perhaps, had even been executed by the state for murder but that traumatic revelation was the only one of that nature that afternoon and was therefore meaningful to me.

(Dedicated researchers should know that often when there are multiple entities found in a certain location there is at least a possibility that the whole assembly has been triggered into existence by a dominant single entity. That "trigger entity" is trapped in memory here on earth due to a psychic problem of some kind and that very entrapment somehow allows further entities to move back to be around him. The process may be somewhat similar to that of "drop-in communicators" who seize upon an existing connection with our world to make themselves known to us. I have also come across what I can only call "psychic–bonding" whereby one of a pair of entities is so closely associated with a second entity that he disables the second's ability to move towards the final resting place for that entity in the great memory system. In other words one entity can enforce "earth-entrapment" on a

second even if they hate and loathe each other. What a terrible fate! To be trapped for eternity with someone you hate!)

As you will soon see, by the end of that afternoon I had come to the conclusion that the hanging of young James may well have been the nucleus of the haunting. I believe it was his presence that dragged back his mother and her clients, his home, his friends and even his pets.)

Having spoken about the reading of the cups by Mrs. O'Neil, deceased, Francesca then moved down that line by saying to Ruby,

"I see it gets pretty busy in here sometimes. I see Mrs. O'Neil brings her clients along with her at times."

"Tell me about it!" exclaimed the old lady. There isn't a day passes but they are all over the place: sometimes even men come along but always several women. They seem to be sitting down on chairs that I don't see and drinking tea. Sometimes I think I recognise someone who appeared from a previous week and sometimes it seems to be new people who appear."

"Like the two ladies in the corridor out there?" said Francesca, indicating the entry point to the livingroom. (That really took me by surprise!)

"Yes! You've met them then?" Ruby said, almost as if they were 'real' people. "They are often out there but no one believes me, you know."

"I do!" replied the medium, "We passed them on the way in and they both have dark blue coats on and are laughing together…."

"Yes! And they are holding cups of tea," added Ruby.

"Indeed they are!" responded the medium who knew for sure by now that Ruby was indeed telling the truth.

I glanced at Jane and she seemed very content with what she was hearing for it vindicated her decision to invite us in to prove that Ruby was not in the slightest way going mad.

"And how about the dogs?" Francesca asked of Ruby.

"Now, them I don't really like at all. The bigger hairier one that hangs around with James always seems to keep sniffing at me but the smaller one never seems to come near me."*

Again this told me that Francesca and Ruby were both seeing the same things for which I was very glad. Jane and I smiled at each other again.

*(This dog-sniffing business, I'll have to have a longer and deeper think about from the psychic science point of view. While I am quite happy that the entity dogs, like the entity spirit people see us and probably hear us when they choose, I was unaware until that day that spirit dogs (and spirit people) can also **smell** us. I see no reason why they cannot: I just have never come across it before now.)*

Now a few things of interest and puzzlement came up…like the fact that the demolished house where Mrs. O'Neil had once lived had no internal doors, just openings between rooms. One wonders whether this was due to poverty or what?

Could they have been taken off and used as fuel? I have come across that before.

While interesting, such things did not move us ahead in our task that once more was coming to the fore.

I'm not any sort of trained psychologist or psychiatrist but I saw our conversation heading for a big problem. It was becoming more apparent by the minute that Ruby had been telling the truth all along and that was a salient fact in the whole business. That really meant that while she might receive few human visitors during the majority of the week she most certainly was witnessing the coming and going of a vast amount of visitors from a world beyond ours and that was giving her a definite interest in life. What none of us knew was whether she was somehow equating the two groups. She had a fine TV set in her apartment for her entertainment but were her supernatural visitors some sort of add-on to this? Did they, in her eyes, have a friendship or entertainment factor perhaps for her?

To remove her TV set would be a cruel act that no one would consider doing but perhaps if we removed her spirit visitors that might be considered a similar act of deprivation as she had been with her phantoms for certainly a year or more and had certainly expressed no fear of them. Francesca, at one point had made a direct reference to the possibility that Ruby might be thoroughly scared by her visitors from a world beyond ours but she categorically denied having any fear at all of them.

"Ruby", I said, "Do you want rid of your ghost, Mrs. O'Neil and all the other people? Do you want her to stop scrubbing your rugs each night?"

"Oh, yes, yes," came the unequivocal reply, "I'm sure she must be ruining my rugs. It's time it all stopped!"

I looked at both Jane and the medium and they knew exactly why I was taking this line of questioning. In turn, gently and in their own way the other two asked the dear lady if she really wanted her "friends" from the other world turned away and each time the answer was "Yes".

This triple positive response meant that I therefore had little option but to explain aloud to Mrs. O'Neil that she would be asked to go and then I handed over to Francesca to put the request to the spirit world on my behalf.

*(Researchers should be quite clear that my own verbalisation of the request would undoubtedly be heard by Mrs. O'Neil as in the case of Old Granny Broon, discussed in this same book. In fact my mental formulation of the request would be known to her even prior to my actually vocalising it. Strange though it may seem, entities have access to your thoughts before you do! That is why you have no option but to be honest with them: you will never be able to trick them into a situation. In this case I invited Francesca to take part at that point once more for two reasons. Firstly I always ask that to make it look right from the clients' point of view for they **expect** the medium to take action. In this case, however, we had an unusually large number of entities to be "moved back" and I, myself, thought that strong mediumistic capacity should be employed as well as my verbal request to them to 'back off'. Just for once we might have to "drive" the entities back as opposed to the usual way where we "request them" to move off.)*

Francesca's head tilted back as she entered a light trance-like state and her eyes closed. I could hear her breathing change. Usually this part of the proceedings takes but a few moments… perhaps thirty seconds… but more and more time went past. One minute….this was rare. Two minutes …. now as her spiritual "minder" I was beginning to look at her more closely for I consider myself to be responsible for bringing her back to our world in a safe and sound way.

I thought I'd give it another half minute before intervening and we were fast approaching that point where I felt I should step into things when Francesca's head nodded gently and then tilted forwards in a relaxed way.

"Right, Francesca, you are back in our world again. Just come back gently to us. You are with Archie and Jane and Ruby in Ruby's apartment."

The lady's eyes opened slowly and she looked around and blinked as if she was coming out into the light from some dark tunnel.

"Phew, phew, I was well away there!" she said softly as she twisted her head to loosen her tense neck muscles and then she turned and asked me,

" I didn't float off my seat did I? I felt I was about to float upwards just at the end."

"No, Francesca, you didn't float but you were "away" for a long time."

"I was totally surrounded by the brightest of bright lights: it was all around us!"

I knew then that the spirit people had been moving on and that the duration of the entranced removal session had been commensurate with the large numbers of spirit entities involved. Ruby might well be very much alone now although sometimes, as I told Jane, there is a sort of "psychic hiccup" that takes place a few days after which seems to be a final "goodbye" gesture by the psychic world. I do not know enough about psychic mechanics to understand what that final blip represents or how it is generated.

Jane was happy, not only because her own thoughts on the state of Ruby's acute mind had been correct (and her other relatives wrong!) but that the old lady's wishes had been carried out. Francesca and I were not so sure that this would be in the long term interests of the lady concerned and we both thought, as we drove back to Edinburgh, that sooner or later Ruby might pine for her mysterious friends. We both knew that spirit people can and **do return** upon the mental volition of we humans. After all, we had had to contend with that at a Health Centre in 2002 when a little ghost boy returned because a cleaning woman so missed his company! He had to be gently "pushed back" into the spirit world for a second time.

Let's hope this doesn't happen with Ruby.

****

Nastiness Lingers

By 2003 the new Royal Infirmary of Edinburgh was up and running and replacing the out-dated premises that had initially been close to the center of town in the capital city of Scotland. Those new hospital buildings were constructed on the outskirts of the city at an area known as "Little France" but it is not the new and expensive buildings that we now take an interest in but a tiny stream that flows through the grounds.

"Mickey's Burn" (i.e. Scots for "Mickey's stream") flows eastwards through the hospital grounds but before it gets there it once flowed through a golf course until the developers decided that houses could produce more income than golf courses and so it now flows between people's houses. Separating those new houses from the hospital is a main road that runs south, linking Edinburgh to northern England and while that road has now long been superseded by a modern motorway that runs close by, it is still there. We therefore have a sort of intersection where a main road from the past and a swiftly flowing stream cross each other at right angles. For the reason of ease-of-access, it was at such points that wise men in the middle ages built either mills or castles and this, we now know, was no exception. There is today, however, not the slightest indication at all that there had ever been any building at that site and I'd be pleased to see some map or other drawn up during those far-off times showing us what exactly did stand there.

If there had been a ruin there at some point in time then the stones of it had been completely transported away and used for the construction of some other building ...or perhaps a boundary wall. I must stress to you that when we passed that point in the car looking for Roann's house, we had no optical clue at all that there had ever been a mill there but yet we found that such a building must have been there once we'd listened to Francesca's deliberations later that evening.

It was only thanks to a phone call from Roann, who was a secretary in a local High School, that I ever stumbled across that site in the first place. Not that she phoned to talk historical talk to me but she phoned as a very distressed lady who was being "got at physically and sexually on a nightly basis by something from the other world".

Once we'd driven over the bridge that straddled Mickey's Burn, Roann's small house was right there; in fact it was built in actual physical contact with another house which was even nearer the stream than Roann's was. By the end of the evening that fact worried me quite a lot for I knew that whatever we found in one house would almost certainly be in the other property also…but more of that later.

As this was the second client whom we had been called out to that evening we did not sit down to a cup of coffee although we had been offered one but we got straight into the factual part of the evening. I asked Roann to recount to us what she had told me privately on the phone and she did so in as delicate way as she could for this poor lady had been sexually attacked by an entity on quite a number of occasions and over a period that covered several years. She, like many others in her situation, had not been able to bring herself to discuss her dreadful secret with others for fear of ridicule and so it was a relief in a way that she could talk about things to people who not only knew and understood her problem but people who had met and cured similar cases in previous years. (see, for example, page 179 of Volume 1, The Psychic Investigators Casebook).

(For those who have not purchased this earlier volume, I must tell you that some spirit entities take upon themselves the characteristics of sexual molesters. This is mainly because they had those characteristics during their lifetime here on earth or had, perhaps, become "women-haters" due to some unfortunate chain of events during their lifetime. Unlike some forms of ghosts, these loathsome spirit individuals don't "re-enact" happenings that took place decades or even centuries before but seize upon living human females in the guise of invisible sexual perverts in order to have their way with them after having stalked them visually for some time. Remember that the members of the psychic world can see what they wish to concerning our world as and when they want to. These poor women victims, therefore, are got at in various sexual ways and it often does not seem to matter whether

they have or do not have a happy and normal relationship with either a husband or partner. I know of a case in Glasgow (2001) where such an entity attacked a woman in the presence of her husband. Such an event surely demonstrates the determination of this type of spirit entity. I must stress most forcefully that such attacks are very genuine and are not merely sexual fantasies of some sort generated by "sexually deprived" women. The correct name for such an unpleasant spirit male entity is an "incubus" (sometimes spelled "incumbus") and there is, in fact a female equivalent although I, personally, have never come across one. It is particularly unfortunate for the women concerned that the presence of such a thing as an incubus is not recognised either by science or even by the majority of psychologists or psychiatrists. These latter two categories mentioned find it more convenient to believe that the female victims of such events are poor deluded and deprived sex-mad creatures who need medical attention and drugs from their pharmacies in order to lower their sexual drives. In fact, the truth of the matter is that incubuses (incubii) are out there and always will be but few girls are brave enough to come forward to people like Francesca and I to seek help. Roann did and she was saved from further nightly trauma and embarrassment!)

Francesca got right to the hub of the matter immediately and told us that the house we were presently in had been built upon the site of an ancient building that had completely disappeared. At that point in the evening there had been no mention of an old mill at all but I got the immediate impression of such a thing although I said nothing to interrupt the flow of words from our medium. *(I must tell readers that my own meagre psychic abilities are often greatly...and temporarily... enhanced when I am in the presence of Francesca. This present case was one of those times.)*

"The large structure was on three floors and looked as if it belonged to the Middle Ages or thereabouts," the medium said. There were local people who came daily and worked in the premises and her mind immediately moved to the upper floor of the building which she said was deeply covered in straw. It was at that level in the building that some terrible thing had taken place that had eventually resulted in the haunting of Roann and her home.

It was at that point that I cut in for I wanted Francesca herself to establish whether this building had, or had not, been an old mill and to do that I carried out a practice that I often use with her when she is moving into and out of trance situations.

"Francesca, I want you to imagine yourself standing outside this building and looking around," I said and then paused as she took up that mental attitude.

(This procedure is, of course, very similar indeed to the processes used in hypnotism and one must wonder what the connection is. I discovered many years ago that I could control a medium in a trance situation in a manner identical to the way I could control a client under hypnotism. See also the "Psychic Investigators casebook", Vol. 1, page 241.)

"Do you see any water around you?"

"Yes, there is a stream."

"Well, I want you to walk about thirty paces upstream from the building and then turn and look back at it then tell me what you see." There was a slight pause.

"I see that it is an old stone mill of three floors and has only the smallest of windows in its walls!" She did not actually say that she saw the water-wheel that drove the whole process but the very fact that she said the word "mill" confirmed my own thoughts on the matter and that pleased me, of course. Now the mind of this clever medium moved again to the upper straw-covered floor and a small window that threw a little light into that upper room for there was a girl there, Francesca said, and she was facing a nasty man who had somehow trapped her in that upper room. I asked the medium to describe the man and she said,

"The others (?) know that he does not belong here. He comes from the mines and while he has worked locally he is more used to working in tin mines.

(There were only coal mines in this part of the country to the best of my knowledge and the nearest tin mines were probably 80 miles away.)

He is a very dirty man and the smell coming from him is abominable, truly abominable! *(Francesca turned away her head and made a grotesque face. You will notice too that she used the present tense i.e. "is". We can therefore see that this indicates to us that things are very real for this medium when she is in one of her mini-trance states. She really HAS moved back in time! She really is "THERE"!)* And his clothes are little better than rags. He is hiding his face from me *(spiritually speaking)* because he knows that I am enquiring into what he is about to do to a young girl who is in the room with him. He is not allowing me to see any features on his face at all!"

We all watched in horror and silence as Francesca's own hands moved up to her own throat and wrapped around it. I personally watched acutely and almost fearfully. For some moments she actually appeared to be strangling herself for her fingers were actively grasping her own throat and pressing deep into the flesh and then we could see her head twisting from left to right and back again several times. At that point I considered that the medium's own hands (if not her whole self) were possessed by the killer and that he might be re-enacting the initial murder. As you can imagine, as Francesca's "minder" when she was in that trance state I was keeping a watchful eye on her just in case the hands around her neck over-tightened themselves. *(Strange isn't it that I had to at least consider at that point that this lady's own hands did not actually belong to her....and might thus attempt to strangle her!)* Matters changed very swiftly and almost in a split second Francesca seemed to be more the victim than the killer for her hands now appeared to be fighting off something invisible and I concluded that she then might be possessed by the entity of the young girl victim who was being strangled to death by this evil stranger. In hindsight I have come to the conclusion that Francesca was, perhaps, being alternately taken over by first the young girl and then by her attacker and then finally by the girl once again.

(For the benefit of the researchers amongst my readers I must tell you that such a thing is completely possible by the "rules" that govern the relationships between the psychic world and the human world. A medium "opens herself up" to a spirit entity and almost "invites" him or her to take over (part of) her mind. Once the mind is opened up to one particular entity there is always the possibility that a second ...or third...entity might enter. This may have taken place in this case. You might also like to know that in cases of possession where a particular victim of this affliction does NOT purposefully open his or her mind to a spirit entity

we very often find several entities finally "inhabiting" the victim. Possessed persons are rarely inhabited by merely a single spirit entity. After the initial "take-over" process by a single entity rarely does the process end there and several entities end up in the same body….taking turns, as it were, for control. Believe it or not there can actually be in-fighting between the invading entities as to which of them should be in control of the "body" that they have seized! You might also like to know that various parts of the body can be taken over by separate entities in a simultaneous way. The strangest case I have heard of is one where a victim of possession was in hospital for an operation and under anaesthetic and while the victim was correctly anaesthetised the possessing entity was not! And he let the surgeon know it.)

Finally, Francesca released her grip on her own neck and slowly came back into 'our' world once again and began to tell us a harrowing tale about the struggle between the girl and her assailant. The victim fought against the man she said and tried again and again to get up to a tiny window that was just above her in order to escape through it …although that would mean her falling many feet to the ground. At each attempt, however, he pulled her back down from the window ledge and set about attacking her once more until she was finally overcome and strangled. Sad to say, the fiend made his getaway and so justice was never, in fact, done. I know that because I asked that particular question of Francesca.

I also asked our medium, for the sake of Roann, if she would at least attempt to get over to the murderer that he should leave Roann strictly alone….particularly now that we knew what he had been up to. The lady closed her eyes and later re-opened them.

"He still does not want to acknowledge my presence!" she said, "But I told him anyway that he had to back-off from this young lady of the 21st century and I think he understood."

I think perhaps he did, for this case took place many months ago and although Roann has my phone number she has not been in contact again. I take it, therefore that she sleeps peacefully in her bed these days.

CHAPTER 2

MURDER MOST FOUL

Gassed !
The Tunnel
The Hanged Man

Sometimes we human beings are not very good at getting along with each other and in a few cases we get on so badly that we wish the other party would die or at least disappear forever. Fortunately, not many of us realistically consider murder as a way of ridding ourselves of a problem but yet in two of the above cases that was the method employed. It is interesting to note that in the first case I believe that one of the two (undetected) murderers was actually alive until very recently.

In the third case we believed at first that a murder had also taken place until we found out that half way through the hanging process sense had prevailed so perhaps a better title for that case might have been, "The Partially Hanged Man".

****

Gassed!

It strikes me that we all have different levels of psychic awareness. Perhaps that is why members of one family feel themselves forced out of their own home by something which they claim is both unseen and nasty while the family who purchases the house from them does not. One family flees the house while the next occupants feel nothing strange at all and live there quite happily. Is that a case of "ignorance is bliss" or has family number two just got no psychic awareness? In other words, the paranormality involved might be there all the time but it takes the presence of that special someone to bring it to the fore. Only time and research will furnish a definitive answer to this obvious question.

I raise the point because a branch of a famous firm of travel agents in a town in West Central Scotland recruited a new member of staff in October 2002 and the psychic abilities of that person might have had something to do with the case I now lay before you.

The lady in question, who I'll call Margaret, was not only widely travelled herself ...surely an asset to any travel agency... but she had all the skills necessary for the day to day work required of her.

At first things were just fine for not only did Margaret fit in well with the existing staff but she always played her full part in all the hard work required of a busy travel agency. By the time the pre-Christmas stress began to set in so did some mysterious happenings. At first nothing seemed too alarming and Christmas tensions were always blamed for any discord in the office. Various items would seem to move, unseen, from desk to desk and some things would seem to disappear completely only to turn up again at the very place where they were last seen. It seemed almost as if someone was playing pranks, except that they were always so busy that there was just no time for anyone getting up to nonsense. Up till that point events could, perhaps, be classified as "troublesome" but then just a few days before the Christmas holidays things got serious.

Some of the girls in the office were claiming to be getting touched by something invisible. Some were also hearing voices whispering to them at the same time as they were being touched when they went downstairs to the staff toilet in the basement and this was taken very seriously because it was happening with such regularity. They eventually became so alarmed that they started to go down to the toilet area in pairs and I'm sure psychologists might claim that it sounds very like so-called "typical female hysteria" brought on by pre-Christmas stress.

It wasn't!

Things got worse and chill blasts both in the main, larger upstairs office and the basement kitchen area were added to the list of mysteries and then a black shadow began moving between the desks and amongst the staff. Somehow it was thought that

Margaret seemed to be the focal point of the activity but this was never proved.

If there was a "crunch day" it was a couple of days before Christmas Day when two things happened. Firstly the black shadow turned into a black cloud of such a density that it partly obscured one member of staff from the others as she sat at her desk. And as if that was not bad enough, overnight, coffee and sugar were removed from two jars in the basement kitchen area (which themselves seemed not to have been moved from the shelf in any way, I was assured) and sprinkled on the floor in a strange pictorial manner. That was near the foot of the stairs and in the general area of where the worst of the downstairs activity had been centred. In order to complete this unusual sugar/coffee picture, the lids of both jars were laid out as circular "eyes" in a strangely elongated and grotesque face.

I fully understand that is easy to say that some girl was merely getting up to pranks but if the skeptics amongst you will just give me a few more minutes I'll show you that it all has meaning.

Because the mystery picture so "spooked out" the staff, not one of them would clean up the sugar and coffee granules and rather than pass that spot they actually all began using the toilet in the shop next door. Surely that in itself must indicate the genuineness with which the girls looked upon things.

The fact that no one would clean the picture off the floor was a blessing in disguise for me because when I was eventually called in, I was able to photograph the image from several angles on Sunday 29th December. Details will be given later.

(Dedicated researchers should know that while it is somewhat unusual for the psychic world to make pictures for our benefit, it is not unknown (although I've never heard of a sugar and coffee collage before). Such a thing is merely an attention-seeking device and quite within the powers of the world of supernature.)

There is no doubt in my mind that the male manager had a very difficult job on his hands, for normally reliable girls were permanently "on edge" and saying all sorts of strange things and reacting very differently from normal. He must have wondered whether the proximity of Christmas had anything to do with such behaviour and he also must have wondered about the accuracy with which the girls were constructing the travel plans for the clients.

The coffee and sugar picture along with the black cloud incident just put him over the edge because he, himself, in the privacy of his inner office had seen and heard nothing: to him it was all a lot of ridiculous female nonsense.

Now comes the fun!

Enough was enough and after lunchtime on that last day he stormed out of his small back office into the larger main room and began ranting and raving at his staff about their childish approach to the strange things that were taking place around them.

"There is no such thing as the supernatural!" he bellowed and then it happened!

Behind him all hell was let loose: there were bangings and thumpings as through the open door the staff watched open-mouthed as all his desk drawers shot out of their usual places and ended up in a messy, upturned pile in the middle of his floor!

The agency was closed virtually instantaneously.

Thank God for Christmas and the holidays!

It was during this Christmas break that I got the phone call from Margaret to see what could be done: to see what could be found out about the origin of the disturbance.

The Area Manageress was brought into things and she was wise enough to at least consider that something paranormal might be taking place and so it was decided that she should open up the office at 10am on Sunday so that my medium friend, Francesca, and I could join her and Margaret in an investigation.

If that investigation went well then on Monday morning the premises could open once again and the staff could move back into the normal business routine. The Area Manageress was keeping her fingers very tightly crossed.

It was a foul day, weather-wise, but we were there for 10am.

The office was like most such offices, bright and warm and efficient-looking. Not the sort of place that one might associate with the supernatural. I got around to thinking how much easier my work would be if I could tell by merely looking at a premises whether there was an entity there up to some tricks!

Taking off our wet coats we hung them over spare chairs as the Area Manageress and Margaret told us what they knew of the business. It was clear that at least the staff thought that the haunting was genuine even if Francesca and I were not at that moment in a position of being able to confirm (or deny) that possibility.

"Let's go down to the basement and start there," I suggested to my medium, "For that seems to be the place that really spooks the girls out".

(I find that while the intuition of others is not always correct it often pays to listen well to it as a possible shortcut into a situation.)

Thinking that it would be wiser to leave the two members of staff upstairs in the main office so that their presence would not influence our deliberations we asked if we could go down into the basement by ourselves to start with.

We did not have to go far to get to grips with matters for as I moved down the stone steps which led into the basement I could see in the bright fluorescent lights the kitchen floor below. There, right at the foot of the steps and slightly to the right and into the kitchen proper was the sugar and coffee picture. The description that I had been given was not wrong: the picture was indeed grotesque! It was larger than I had imagined too for it must have measured two and a half feet tall and three feet across. I remember looking down on it as I took out my camera and thinking that it was more like a mask than a drawing of a face.... particularly because of the large, round red eyes. As you will see later, that turned out to be truer than I could ever have guessed.

We had also been told that even although none of the girls would touch the image, it appeared to be slowly disappearing by itself: Margaret had said in the initial interview that it had fewer features to it now than it had the previous day and that some of the coffee and sugar seemed to have disappeared, leaving it a "weaker" less pronounced picture. Of course we had to take the word of the staff on that one but I did look to see if there were any signs of mice present which might have enjoyed a free Christmas lunch of lovely sugar crystals. There was, in fact, no sign of rodent activity whatever.

(This "disappearing trick" with the sugar and coffee is par for the course I'm afraid. While we humans are used to having physical items permanently present in a place unless someone

actively takes them away from it, that is not the case with the psychic world. Things there come and go for reasons that we do not understand and by means that don't conform to our scientific principles...that is as we currently understand them. That is particularly true of psychically induced images on photographs and video and audio tapes. Those come and go and change almost as the other world pleases and we can't do a thing about it. It certainly makes research very difficult if the thing you are looking into is there one minute and gone the next. Sometimes I am left wondering if that is why the psychic world removes an image or an object...to prevent us from carrying out a detailed examination of it. See Volume One for further details of this type of phenomenon.)

Francesca, who was behind me, inched her way around me as I took a few photos from different angles for record purposes and she moved into the kitchen area proper. She walked quietly around close to the "face" just getting the feel of the place and attempting to sense what was around her from the psychic aspect. There had been a rather grisly murder quite close to the rear of this building some years before when a poor girl was killed and then concealed in a large drain that served the apartment block above us. This story from the past had come into the deliberations of the staff when they had attempted to explain the situation to each other.

"In spite of what we've been told about that girl," said Francesca, "I'm only getting a man down here in spirit. I have no murdered girl here with us!"

(Potential psychic investigators should know that it is good to listen well to all information from all sources but, as an unbiased investigator, you dare not base conclusions upon any single piece of information from any source at all. You merely use it to further your investigations. If it all fits in somewhere by the end of the case so be it but if it has to be thrown out because it has nothing to do with the case then that is fine also. Eventually, as you will see, the murdered girl had nothing at all to do with the case in hand and her spirit was not to be found anywhere in the building.)

At that point the medium then elaborated and went on to say,

"I am, however, getting some sort of connection between the man who is causing all the bother and a girl........"

I saw Francesca pause in her monologue: she raised her eyebrows and began looking very surprised,

"I'm being told that this new girl I am hearing about is the youngest sister of the main character of this whole business. It seems to concern a man and his sister."

There was another pause as I stood beside Francesca, who was now standing with head bowed quietly mouthing words that I could not hear as she spoke to someone I could not see.

"There is something rather not nice about this whole business. Let's take a walk around this basement area to see what we'll find." I think that at that point Francesca was taken very much by surprise by what she was picking up from the psychic world and wanted a 'mental break' to adjust to the new situation that she found herself in.

I moved past the image on the floor and followed Francesca through one of several quite large storage rooms which made up this basement area and into a warren of interconnecting rooms which lay beyond, each with a very low ceiling. There were files and folders everywhere on the shelves all around us. These were obviously the past day-to-day records of the travel agency and seemed to be everywhere. The basement, as I said before, was well lit and had bright and well-painted walls even if the ceilings were low so there was nothing overtly "spooky" about the place.

There was a strange sort of chute running from a sealed entry point on the sidewalk above, which came down into the main area of this basement and I was later to learn that this was a chute for meat as the shop above had once been a butcher's shop before it had been turned into a travel agency.

I kept looking around myself to memorize the layout of this warren as I followed the medium and soon found myself at the end of a short corridor with no way out. I was for turning back but Francesca, I noted, did not have the same intention and she moved a few steps this way and that in the restricted area sniffing the air.

"Do you smell *the* gas, Archie?"

It was the phraseology that struck me immediately rather than the actual words.

She had *not* said to me, "Do you smell gas, Archie?" but had put in that tell-tale word, "*the*". That meant to me that she was already smelling gas and merely wanted me to know that fact. That assumption proved to be correct.

While I am cursed with below-average hearing, I have an excellent sense of smell and so I sniffed the air carefully but could not detect the slightest whiff of gas.

"No Francesca, I smell no gas." I said, eyeing up all the myriad of pipes and plumbing which ran around the place. I could see no piping that was usually associated with a gas supply.

"We're talking psychically about gas, aren't we?" I said.

"Yes!" came the reply.

The lady moved right into the corner of that tiny area,

"This is where it happened I'm being told," and then the story began coming to us from the other world through this marvellous woman.

"He's an awful man! Just awful! A tiny, undersized nasty bit of goods! He's a thief, an inveterate liar and is perpetually up to no good. If he himself is not stealing then he's attempting to sell goods which have been stolen by others."

"What's his connection with this place?" I asked. "Get from him why he was on these premises, Francesca."

Again the head was bowed down and the medium's lips moved gently.

Eventually the head came up again and I got the answer to my question,

"This was a pub at one point in its history...and comparatively recently too, perhaps in the 1950s and before it became a butcher's shop."

The story then came out steadily and it was this:-

The weedy little man was the elder brother of a girl who had married a well-made athletic fellow who owned (or was tenant of?) the building when it was a pub.

Whether the little man had some sort of financial share (or even controlling interest?) in the running of the pub I do not know but he felt so secure in his position in the building that that is where all his illegal dealings were centred. There was a small back room (which was presently the office of the travel agency manager) where the man spent much of his time, drinking with his like-minded fellows and no doubt hatching various plots for carrying out local robberies and the like.

Francesca said that she could actually see him playing various games of chance there, including card games and he was well known for the cheating that he carried out. He was not even a liked man in the eyes of his fellow rogues apparently and I can easily understand why. He used to lend money too and if the person to whom it was lent did not pay up then, because of his diminutive stature, he was forced to pay bigger men to lay claims on his clients for speedy repayment.

All this went on for a series of years and the man's sister and brother-in-law (as well as the others who used that pub) were forced to accept the situation until they could stand it no longer. Eventually the worms turned, as the saying goes.

When the crunch came, the man was lured down to the basement area at the end of that short passage. We do not know on what pretext, but he came. There, in those days, was a gas oven of some sort (perhaps for making food for the pub?). Francesca tried to describe it but found difficulty because she said that she had never seen a gas oven like it. She said that even in those days in the 1950s it must have been terribly old-fashioned.

Anyway, old-fashioned or not, it worked and Francesca described how the well-built barman grabbed his brother-in-law and pushed his head into the gas oven while the man's own sister turned on the gas and then stuffed "something that looked like a towel" into the space above the man's head to keep the gas from escaping out into the room itself. After a few minutes of struggling it was all over and the man was dead and the neighbourhood had got rid of a villain.

The medium was understandably quite overcome with emotion by the end of her story and so I did not press her regarding the disposal of the body...although she did say that there had been no great problem concerning that aspect of the death.

Now that we knew about the unpleasant man and the manner in which he had been killed we walked slowly through the basement rooms again towards the kitchen area with a view to going upstairs once more. We only got the length of the room before the kitchen, however, when Francesca stopped suddenly in her tracks.

"The man is talking to me again!" she said as she stood in a listening pose with her head tilted to one side....almost as if listening to a far-away human voice.

"He says that if only he had had his gas-mask with him that day he would not be dead now."

Remembering that he had been one of the generation who had to carry a gas-mask with him day in and day out during the second world war I understood his allusion to a gas-mask but I did not know whether to take the words that had been relayed to me through the medium in jest or not. Then he said to Francesca with a degree of urgency apparently,

"Look at the picture on the floor! You will see me in my gas-mask and you will see the sister who killed me also: I added her later."

This was indeed a revelation and Francesca and I moved into the kitchen area again and stood looking down at the picture on the floor with renewed interest.

"My God!" I said, "It *is* a face in a gas-mask. No wonder we thought it a rather strange, elongated face with completely circular eyes. Now let's see if we can find the sister's face here somewhere."

We both scanned the image with our eyes from top to bottom and it was I who found the missing face first. It was rather small (three inches tall and two inches wide) and had been drawn somewhat crudely in the chin area of the main drawing but it was there for everyone to see once you knew what you were looking for. It looked as if it had been done as a secondary afterthought and certainly after the main drawing had been done by scattering sugar and coffee to form the main image.

I kept thinking that if I had not had this clever medium with me that day I would never have come up with the idea that the picture was of a man in a gas-mask: it would have seemed too far-fetched to mention to anybody..... even if I had had the wit to think of it....but yet that was the clue to the whole thing.

Together we looked at what must be the strangest picture that I have ever seen for one last time and then we went upstairs and told the whole story to the Area Manageress and Margaret. Naturally enough they shot downstairs again to re-assess the sugar and coffee picture that no one had dared to sweep up and, sure enough, they too agreed with the verdict that it was of a man in a gas-mask with a minor image on the chin area.

While those two were still pondering the facts in the basement Francesca and I ventured upstairs and into the smaller back office where the manager usually worked...that was until his drawers had all shot out onto the floor! He had never gone back!

"Oh yes!" said the medium, "This is where the nasty little man spent a lot of time. His memory is very strong here and, boy, was he a powerful personality mentally. Always wanting to boss other people about......."

"Well, he bossed his sister and her husband around once too often, I reckon," I interjected.

Francesca described lots of things from the time of the man in that room. There were card games and gambling and a game that this lady had no knowledge of and so she said to me,

"Archie, I see them playing a game I don't understand. They're using a rough block of wood with lines of holes along its length and in the holes are small bits of wood like golf-tees. They keep moving these about for some reason."

I smiled at the accurate description and told Francesca that they were probably playing cribbage: a game more traditional to England than Scotland. It was there too that she said that she was watching him cheat during a game of cards and there was an enormous amount of swearing and drinking to excess taking place also.

We heard the others coming up the stairs again and so we joined them in the main office and added the latest information to what we had already told them.

While we can never say that an entity has gone from the premises for good we both felt that what the entity had wanted had now been achieved on his behalf: he had arranged things so that the story of his last minutes in this life had been made known to others and was no longer a secret.

The travel company involved seemed happy enough with the result of our visit. They opened up again as normal after the Christmas holidays and to date we have had no further request from them to go back to visit that place.

Was justice done, I ask myself? We must leave it to others as to whether a prosecution of the guilty parties is even a possibility fifty years after the event, especially when much of the evidence that would have to be led by the Prosecuting Counsel would have to come from a world beyond ours.

****

The Tunnel

I cannot think of an occasion when Francesca and I went out together on a possible case without me at least having prior information upon where we were going and what we might well encounter. On May 10th, 2003 things were different for we headed west out of Edinburgh and along the motorway towards the town of Falkirk without ever knowing what it was we were being called upon to investigate.

"This may be a non-event, Francesca," I confessed. "I sure hope that I haven't wasted your entire Saturday afternoon."

It all began because friends with an interest in the paranormal, Alan Bryan and his wife Angie had seen an account in their local newspaper about a couple who had apparently been spooked out by encountering a ghost of some sort in a tunnel. I can't think how but while Alan mentioned that a tunnel was involved he failed to tell me any more and certainly nothing about the couple or the fact that they claimed to see a ghost. Apparently my friends had initially attempted, through their local newspaper, to contact the elusive couple but with no success. That was when their thoughts turned to Francesca and myself.

We got to Alan's house at the appointed time and left almost immediately in their car for that mysterious tunnel. I was exceedingly patient as we drove through the countryside for I did not even ask what kind of tunnel it was that we were heading for although I was somewhat alarmed to find ourselves getting closer to a place where I knew there were several railway tunnels: no one was going to get me into a working railway tunnel! I need not have worried for the car stopped about a mile from the railway tunnels and we were invited to start walking up a hill. By this time, the lack of knowledge about the whereabouts of the destination was becoming a bit of a good fun puzzle.

It was quite a climb but the panoramic view when we looked back was well worth the effort for the valley of the river Forth stretched out before us on a sunny Spring afternoon. However, we did not come either to see lovely views or laze in the sun, which in any case was about to disappear behind a large dark thundercloud.

Over the next rise I saw what we had come for and was very surprised to see in front of us at that elevation ….a canal! I always thought that canals flowed through valleys and not half way up hillsides: apparently I was wrong. I knew then that we had been brought to see a canal tunnel and said so to Alan. He merely smiled in order to keep the mystery going and ushered us along the gravelled tow-path where strong draft horses had once upon a time drawn heavy barges full of industrial goods, coal and farm produce to the towns of the Scottish Central Lowlands. We rounded the next corner and then we saw it......the gaping mouth of a large tunnel carrying the canal deep into and then through the hill in front of us.

"How long is it?" I asked, pointing to the cave-like entrance in the distance where I could see vegetation dangling down as if to conceal it all. "It's about quarter of a mile long or so I believe," said Angie. "We used to play in there when we were children."

Now merely a hundred yards of path lay between us and the entrance but Francesca stopped and looked up and to the left of our goal. Her eyes were focused on the flat shoulder of the hill into which the tunnel burrowed. I knew how this woman's mind worked and I immediately realised that something of a psychic nature had come to her notice.

"What is it, Francesca?" I asked as the other two also stopped and turned.

"I don't suppose you'll see it, any of you, but there is a black motor bike with an attachment coupled to the side of it to take another person. (she had forgotten the more usual phrase for such a thing ...... "A motor bike and sidecar"). It doesn't belong to this world anymore but I'm being told it has something to do with a dreadful happening in the tunnel beneath."

Wow, my admiration of Francesca's abilities never ceases!

Just at that very moment and before we could put any questions to this medium on this chance discovery the heavens opened and enormous spots of rain began hurtling down so we ran as best we could to the tunnel mouth and got there a lot wetter than we had wanted. As the whole sixty miles of canal system had been completely upgraded at tremendous expense as part of a much larger environmental and recreational project, I was pleased to see that fluorescent lighting had been installed along the tunnel length. In spite of this I noted that the towpath that ran through the tunnel and which is regularly used by cyclists and walkers still seemed somewhat dim at the centre of the first 500 yard stretch. It must have been exceedingly dim at the center of its length prior to the installation of those modern lights. Anyway, we walked in by about 30 yards and stood in a little cluster just sensing the overpowering feeling of the place. Water dripped and trickled from the curving stone roof and at one point near us it cascaded downwards from a circular hole that appears to have been drilled upwards into the stonework...perhaps to relieve the hydraulic pressure of rainwater gathering just above the tunnel roof.

For a bit I purposely said nothing at all to Francesca but let her stand there absorbing the atmosphere of the place while I chatted away to both Alan and Angie. I could see that our medium was picking up something but what? We clustered around her now and with no other members of the passing public near I said,

"Are you sensing something? Has it to do with that motor cycle?"

"The answer is "Yes" to both questions!" was the reply, "But first I must tell you that a little bit past that second light on the far wall of the tunnel there is a psychic black shape of a person moving in and out of the rock face: he's watching us and he knows we are here to discuss him." We all looked but I think that only Francesca saw anything. She then embarked upon a silent "conversation" with the entity who seemed to be only about 25 yards away. We stood on the single tow path which, from our entry point, was on the left of the waterway which filled the remaining breadth of the tunnel all along its length.

We all watched Francesca's movements and reactions to things unheard by us.

Her head tilted to the left and her right hand went up to touch the right hand side of it, just above her ear,

"So that's where he hit you," we heard her say then,

"You'd come all the way from Glasgow, forty miles away! Why?"

There was a pause as we watched the mediums lips move although no words came out, then,

"He's showing me his hand but it is clenched: it is holding something I know."

"Ask him to open it to let you see what he has brought to show you," I urged and in a second Francesca spoke to us again.

"He's moving his hand towards me and he is opening it," she said. "Oh, he's got dice in his hand! He's showing me four dice! I think he wants to tell us that his journey was necessary because of something to do with gambling."

Alan and I looked at each other,

"Settling a gambling debt perhaps?" He shrugged his shoulders and asked,

"Can you get a name?"

"I already have it," said Francesca. "He tells me that he is Brian May aged about forty and now he is saying openly that he was killed in this tunnel, murdered.......I think perhaps in the early 1950's."

Again there was a pause in the proceedings for we were all pondering the facts that had just come to light but then the medium started to speak once more.

"How strange!" said Francesca, "Now I'm being shown a picture of a wood-yard that I know is not far from my own home." She was obviously puzzled but that lasted only for an instant for the entity was speaking to her telepathically once again.

"Oh I see!" she exclaimed, "Now he's telling me that he has never had a proper burial: he wants a wooden coffin made for the proper burial of his body. He says it was never found and has remained concealed under the water for more than half a century. His murder has never been recorded he says."

"We'd like to know where his murderer came from, Francesca," I said. "Ask him to point in the direction of where he lived or lives."

We watched as the woman's body began to slowly rotate.

She stopped in a certain position and spoke,

"I'm being told to turn around and to face in this direction if I want to know where his murderer came from." She was facing North-east.

I must admit to feeling a very sudden and deep sense of sadness at that point and wondering if the others were sensing it too. It seemed dreadful that a man could come a distance to that spot only to be murdered and have his body so well concealed that his killer could never be brought to justice. The fact that the dark psychic shape was still moving slowly out of and into the stone wall at the far side of the water meant to me that his remains were at that side of the tunnel and not at the towpath side. If that was so, then the murderer who killed his victim on the towpath must have jumped into the water (which was usually only about four feet deep in that canal system) with the body. He must have carried it to the far side and weighted it down with stones. In those days and with no lighting in that dreadful place the only fear that the killer might have had would be that the passing barges might so stir up the water that the corpse would be dislodged from beneath the stones and float to the surface. However, from the killer's viewpoint things could not have gone better, for in that dark cavern the barges which go very slowly at the best of times would be going even slower in the darkness thus causing the minimum water turbulence. My guess is that the body lay there undisturbed until refurbishment and dredging of the canal took place about the year 2000. Then the dredging machine would work its way along the canal bottom scraping up the mud and rubbish as it went and putting it onto an accompanying barge for dumping later at some landfill site no doubt. Could it possibly be that the poor man's bones were unknowingly swept up in that manner and now lie with other canal mud at some site close by?

I think there is need for further inquiry here!

Will police records show a missing man from Glasgow by the name of Brian May?

What happened to the motorcycle and sidecar? Was it stolen by the murderer or did it end up in a scrapyard somewhere?

Those were the kinds of questions that we were all going to be asking as we drove back home that afternoon.

One last thing took place in the tunnel itself. As a grand finale, Alan decided to photograph the actual spot where the murder might well have taken place. There was a large indentation in the rock wall of the towpath that was exactly opposite to the spot where Francesca saw the black shape moving from the wall. At that very place someone might well have hidden in readiness to pounce upon some unsuspecting victim. As the two female members of the party had no desire to wander a further 30 yards or so into the tunnel, Alan and I therefore went forward by ourselves and having taken several shots by flash photography (both by digital and standard cameras as part of a further experiment) we turned and walked slowly back towards the ladies and the tunnel mouth again. It was then that I noticed Francesca looking anxiously back at us as we were approaching her.

"What's up Francesca?" I asked when we caught up with her.

"Neither of you saw it then?" came the reply.

"Saw what?" I said.

"The tall column of swirling white mist which was following you a few seconds ago?"

I whipped around in the hope of getting a glimpse of a psychic event but too late.

"It moved back across the water and into the wall before you reached us," Francesca said.

****

I will now mention something that might have nothing at all to do with any of the above but because of its strangeness and timing I'll put this little tale before you and let you be the judge. My including it in this book is really based upon the fact that at times mediums *(and I don't claim to be one)* take upon themselves the bodily attributes experienced by the entity often around the time of the death of that entity.

As I lay in bed that night after returning from the tunnel incident and before going to sleep, I suddenly became aware of water coming out of my right ear! I could not say that the volume might be called a trickle but it was definitely a steady drip, drip, drip and had to be mopped up by a handkerchief that became rather wet. I had no sense of either pain or discomfort and I had not just had a bath or a shower so I have no idea whatever as to where that water came from. When it was happening, logic told me that I must be suffering from some sort of infection of the ear and I mentally prepared myself for a very sore ear the following day...and perhaps even a journey to the doctor. I am pleased to say that the following morning there was no infection, still no pain and everything was totally normal. More than a year has passed and I still have no idea whatever as to why water started to come out of my right ear that evening. It had never happened before and it has not happened since. Whether it had anything at all to do with the case that had just been investigated I have no idea but it is right that psychic investigators take full cognisance of everything that take place around them and analyses it. In relating this small and inexplicable incident to you I believe I am being true to my calling.

****

My interest in this canal tunnel seemed to spread around somehow and a member of the public e-mailed me with the following information that I now give as shortened verbatim. The young man's walk through the tunnel with his friends was obviously at a time before the new and recent lighting was put in.

"As we walked into the tunnel we discussed who should go first and I ended up as the last member of the group to enter.

About half way up the tunnel I stopped to tighten my jacket and laces and asked my friend Barry to stop while I did so. Unknown to me he did not hear and just kept walking on.

I finally looked upwards and to the front of me where I saw in the gloom someone wearing a long coat and a flat cap on his head. I thought that Barry had put a hat on perhaps because of the drips of water which were falling from the roof and I walked behind "him" talking as we moved forward but then got a very strange feeling as if I was being watched by someone. I called out to the person in front (still thinking that it was Barry) but I was completely ignored and then the figure suddenly turned and disappeared into the wall.

At that point Barry shouted back to me, "Are you still down there?" Then I realised that I was far from my friends and ran to catch up with them in a very frightened mood. When I got to them they asked me who I had been talking to and that was the first time I mentioned a ghost. I was very scared although I did not believe in ghosts then."

The writer then tells of a second recent visit to the tunnel where he felt the presence of something but saw nothing. Naturally, his first adventure may have had a bearing upon his attitude to his second visit and so should be discounted as any sort of "evidence".

The following story may be of interest also although I cannot vouch for it however and in any case it took place in a second tunnel that was about a mile further west from the tunnel mentioned here.

The canal in question follows a line parallel to a Roman wall called "Antonine's Wall", after the General who ordered its construction to keep the warlike Scots out of the territory which was to be known later as England. The Roman wall and the canal are merely yards apart in places and at one point there is actually a new tunnel leading the canal under that famous wall. During the recent construction of that new tunnel that leads the canal to the world-famous and revolutionary Falkirk Wheel (an enormous engineering device that bodily lifts boats from a lower canal to a higher canal) the tunnel-diggers reported several times that they saw a mysterious figure dressed as a Roman Centurion.

Two canal tunnels with two different ghosts! You must admit it's different!

Addendum

My friend Alan contacted the Strathclyde Police as to whether a man called Brian May had been reported missing in the 1950s but the police said that they were not in a position to give such information. He also discovered the whereabouts of the material that had been dredged from the canal bottom at the time of its renovation but that material had been sealed into concrete chambers because it was thought that harmful chemicals from the past had been lying on the base of the canal bed. It would therefore seem that the victim's bones (if they still existed) might now therefore lie in a totally inaccessible place ……a rather sad ending to an interesting account!

****

The Hanged Man

When you buy an old house for a lot of hard cash and start renovating it lovingly, the last thing you want to hear from one of your new neighbors is that a rather unpleasant suicide took place in your main room many years before. The story that my friend got from his neighbor was that a bank manager of the 1940s or 1950s who lived in the property had run off with a gigantic sum of money from his local bank and upon being found out had committed suicide. He had done this by hanging himself with a rope from one of the large wooden and hinged internal shutters that could swing out to cover the window of the main room of the house.

While my friend found himself in this unhappy situation as a new owner of the property he never actually let me know precisely, at that point, what it was that displeased him. I was never told then of any details of the "shutter business" but some time later he sent me photographs by e-mail of a party that he had held in his house and in the very the room I have described above.

As you might imagine, I am sent quite a lot of spooky photos by people at times. Some of these are rather interesting and some are not but when I saw Mark's digital photos I sat bolt upright at my computer. There before me were not only the more usual orbs of various types but I could also see some very clear images of the upper halves of two men and one woman on the woodwork of the right hand pillar which supported a shutter in a large room. It is important to note that I only learned later that Mark had only seen the orbs and NOT the three figures on his photos. As I had only rarely seen human torso images of such clarity I was very excited at what I had been sent but unfortunately I had to rush off to a lunchtime meeting with someone important and so I closed my computer down and looked forward very much to coming back to it in mid afternoon to re-examine these photos.

By 2.30pm I had opened up my PC again and, with great excitement, I shot straight into the file that I had open before lunch. DISMAY is not a word strong enough for what I felt for there wasn't the slightest sign of a single human being on the very photograph that I had been looking at earlier. Whoever those people were, they had just plain disappeared! The orbs were still intact I noted, but the people were nowhere to be seen and there were no strange marks or blemishes in the woodwork of the shutter pillar which I could have accidentally mistaken for people. Where they had been a few hours before was just plain ordinary beige-coloured wood!

Because I knew that I really had seen those images merely a few hours before I was still excited for it meant that there was true paranormal activity in the house and also emanating from it. I decided to phone up my friend and tell him that perhaps the rumour about that bank manager hanging himself might be true although I knew that he was dreading the correctness of such a thing. In our conversation he confirmed that the photo had indeed been taken in the same room as the supposed suicide and he sounded rather mentally down about the whole business so I suggested that the best way forward might be to bring in a medium and have a good, thorough look at what psychic things did (or did not) lie within his property. I pointed out to him, as I do to most clients, that it is only after we get to know the whole story that we can move forward and then make decisions as to what should be done to better matters.

It was therefore decided that I should visit his house in the company of Francesca and this was to be done on Monday, July 14th 2003.

At 7pm that evening we drove up the steep hill leading to Mark's house in Oldburgh only to find that the turn into his driveway was going to be such a tight turn that I said to my companion that we'd just park in the street behind the house.

As I swung the car around the corner to the back of the house Francesca suddenly gave a little jump of surprise and exclaimed,

"Oh, there's a mine or tunnel or something like that here: I've just felt its presence! Did they mine coal or whatever in this part of the world?" I told the lady that I was pretty sure that there was no mining activity around that area of Fife as the geology of the area was not right for such a thing and the conversation died away naturally.

I had no thoughts at all about such a thing and even yet I have no idea what connection, if any, that tunnel had with the property we were about to visit. The fact that Francesca had detected it without any prompting, however, was very interesting to me and as you will see in the addendum to this account, it leads to a second story in its own right.

We stood before a large door of a large house and were soon ushered in by Mark who led us to that main room and then went off to get a nice selection of tea, coffee and wine for us all. My medium wasted not a second of time for, while our host was gone and without my asking it of her, she moved quickly towards the right hand shutter at the window.

"I'm being drawn to this," she said, "I'm being told that it is of importance to us this evening!" And that surprised me greatly for I knew for sure that she knew nothing at all about this house, far less that something had taken place concerning a shutter.

This was the very shutter on the photograph that Mark had sent me earlier by e-mail so I'm sure you will understand that I looked at it as if my very life depended upon it. No, there were no markings at all upon the woodwork.

Just at that very point and with us both examining the shutter, our host returned and said,

"Oh, you've told Francesca about the shutter then?"

"Oh no I haven't!" I said emphatically, "**She** has told **me** about the shutter."

We sat down and sipped away at our coffee and as the shutter had somehow made its own way into our conversations I felt it only fair to ask Mark to tell our medium what exactly he knew of the tale of the thieving bank manager. It transpired that his story came from neighbors who no doubt had heard it from other neighbors when they had moved into the area years before. Alarm bells began ringing in my head when we were told that the sum involved was truly gigantic by today's standards. Two million pounds ($3,000,000) was mentioned, which in the 1940s, say, would be perhaps forty million pounds today. As the man in question had, in all probability, merely been a branch manager of a tiny country bank which catered for perhaps a few thousand people, that part of the story was obviously false.

Anyway Francesca was soon to discover another completely different tale about this hanging which I am sure, though stranger, is probably closer to the truth.

"Right, Francesca, let's get down to moving into the psychic world and getting some information for Mark."

The dear lady relaxed her head and let it fall forward as she closed her eyes. Soon there were tiny and indecipherable murmurings coming from her mouth and her head was nodding every now and again as if she was either acknowledging something from that other world or agreeing with something that was being telepathized to her. Her information came in staccato bursts,

"Small, broadly built man…. Some sort of priest or church minister but one who had not been ordained in any way. No, definitely not a "real" minister but he lived in this house and this house was bought with the express purpose of housing people such as himself and his family. He had a real daytime job but was also someone who preached the word of God."

At least some of that tied in with what Mark knew. The mystery man connected with that shutter appeared to have been what we call a "lay-preacher" nowadays, so that it was quite possible that he was a bank manager throughout the week but a preacher on the Sunday.

"Book, book!" mumbled the medium in her altered state. "There is a book. It's still here and it's got all the names."

It slowly came out that, quite apart from being a lay preacher, the man was also a petty money-lender of some sort and kept a book of all the deals he was doing. This, Francesca said, was still on the property somewhere in 2003 even although the house had been severely knocked about due to a whole series of renovations

"Quarrel!" said Francesca, "Family quarrel…. A land deal of some sort…. documents and papers on the table….one hundred guineas! They keep repeating it, 'A hundred guineas! A hundred guineas!'"

She went on to explain that a man and a woman who were related to the podgy little man were trying to force money out of this relative. It appeared that the three of them had made some sort of verbal agreement to buy a piece of land and that each of them was to put into the joint fund a certain amount of money.

The share expected from the bank manager was this sum of one hundred times a guinea (that was an old form of money exchange used until about 1960 that was one hundred pounds plus one hundred shillings) which we might understand better today as £105. The man was stubborn and seemed unwilling to part with the money (even if he had it) but the other man and his wife (?) were just as stubborn and they all struggled physically as a rope was flung around the neck of the man who would not pay.

(I find it interesting that someone had actually brought along a rope for the very purpose of scaring the man for I cannot believe that a length of rope just happened to be present in that main room on that particular evening)

The woman's husband was a taller and perhaps stronger man for the smaller man soon had the rope around his throat. This came across very dramatically from Francesca who sat close beside me on the settee for by now her head was tilted back and her mouth open, her tongue was a little way out and she was obviously gasping.

"Uh, uh!" she barked as her left hand clasped the front of her throat as if trying to pull a rope away from it while her right hand was high in the air over her head, obviously holding onto a rope or similar. Her hand was jerking up and up again and again as it held tightly onto some invisible rope which was strangling her. It was clear that whatever had taken place in that house was not merely a moment's rashness: it was a concerted attempt at a hanging that was being re-enacted before our very eyes. It may never have been an attempt to hang him *to the point of death* but it was certainly a lengthy attempt to get the man to sign a document. Every now and again Francesca seemed to become the woman rather than the victim.*(which is not uncommon in mediumship as the case entitled "Nastiness Lingers" shows).*

"Sign, Sign!" she demanded. "One hundred guineas!"

More "Uh, uh, uh!" came from the lady from my right with her hand clasping her own throat. She had once again become the victim but no words needed to be spoken for Mark and I watched what was truly the representation of someone being hanged by the neck.

Eventually the medium's hands both slid downwards until she sat relaxed but gasping on the settee.

"Come back to us Francesca!" I said gently to her, "Come back to 2003. You are safe and well and with Archie and Mark. Come back to us. You feel good and you feel relaxed!" I treat her at such a time as if she is returning from some sort of hypnotic trance *(which might be nearer to the truth than many of us understand)*.

The lady sipped from her cup of tea, which was somewhat cold by now, as I asked her almost tentatively,

"Did they hang him to the point of death?"

I wanted to know whether we had a murder on our hands when initially I had considered that we might be looking into the possibility of a suicide.

It was with a bit of relief for Mark more than myself when she replied,

"No, he didn't die but they carried their frightening prank a lot further than even they had initially intended. They got a fright as well as their victim!"

That part of the story ended there and the mood in the room lightened up for a bit. Francesca was still getting all sorts of impressions from the past though.

"Are you trying to get both parts of the house under one ownership again then?" she asked which made Mark look up suddenly for he had never told her that the house had been split into a major and a minor part.

"Well, yes, actually," he said, "If I could get the money together I'd like to buy the other people out and make the house one whole unit again. Then he added,

"How did you know it had been divided in two, in any case?"

The medium then told a strange story about a married couple who appeared to have lived in early part of the 1900s (although that is by no means certain) where the man had been a lay preacher while his wife had not held the same ideas as he did at all. Francesca thought that they were called Mr. and Mrs. Anderson and she knew that they lived very separate lives but under the one roof. He was a tall gangly man while she was a small-built lady and while he lived in the smaller apartment to one side of the main house, she lived in the larger portion. Mark had a little circle of candles set out on the top of a wood-burning stove in that main room and that is what triggered her thoughts on the Andersons the medium said. The lady of the pair held regular seances with her lady friends in that room with a circle of candles ringed around it to give a circle of light which no doubt generated a lot of atmosphere also. She was understandably absolutely paranoid that her husband might come home at some point and discover what she and her friends were doing. Whether he lived in the same part of the house or not, he was a man of the church who must have been totally against such "demonic practices". I must admit to rather liking the wife's bravado over the whole matter.

The above episode does illustrate, however, that the house had been divided in use rather early on even although it was not split legally into two homes until much later.

We still don't know the identity of the person who was the *victim* in the "bank manager" incident or its date and I even wonder whether the Andersons were the people responsible for his hanging. I just don't know but I do know that the three images which I saw on that original photograph sent to me by Mark resemble the descriptions given of Mr. and Mrs. Anderson and a small chubby man.

As a final courtesy, Mark showed us over the house upon which he had spent so much time and money and every now and again Francesca told us that she felt this presence or that presence. Of course a house of that age must have had a lot of people and a lot of events attached to it.

The main thing, however, for its current owner was that there had not been a suicide on the premises. Perhaps the people of that little town were given to spreading and maintaining rumours, for we came across a second rumour that day and one that was generally held by virtually the entire local community ….and that was about the "Monk's Tunnel". That was said to lie large and long somewhere under the whole little town and lead to an old monastery which lay at one end of the built-up area.

I would have dismissed that as a total nonsense if Francesca had not given a jump that evening at 7pm as we were about to park the car. The words now ring in my ears even yet,

"Oh, there's a mine or tunnel or something like that here: I've just felt its presence! Did they mine coal or whatever in this part of the world?"

It sure makes you think!

****

I thought that I had finished with this tunnel business in July 2003 but in November 2004 it came to the fore again for at a weekend conference in Perth (Scotland), where I was an invited lecturer, I came across a most knowledgeable geomancer, dowser and ley-line specialist. (i.e. someone who takes an interest in the energies that flow through the surface of the earth). Mr. David Cowan impressed me by giving me answers to questions that had long disturbed me and these were always reasoned and logical. *

As there was at least a possibility that the energies used by the psychic world to produce phenomena like apparitions and poltergeist activity were being drawn from the earth's geomagnetic forces Mr. Cowan and I decided to work together occasionally for reasons of research.

As he considered that a good percentage of human illness could be accounted for by the victim living over a particularly unpleasant energy-spot we decided that we would visit two very unfortunate families on November 2nd where most members of the family were seriously ill and in a concurrent way. As Mr. Cowan would be passing through the town of Oldburgh where the tunnel had been detected by Francesca through her psychic abilities, I wondered whether he might be interested in meeting me there and attempting to locate that same tunnel by his own dowsing methods. I am pleased to say that he readily agreed although he did add that "tunnel-finding" was not any sort of speciality with him.

We met as arranged and walked up the steeply sloping street where Francesca and I had been the previous year and there we encountered the two crossroads that the medium and I had driven over in an attempt to locate the house to which we had been invited to in 2003. It was rather fortuitous that I had forgotten which of the two junctions had actually been crossed by the supposed tunnel structure for now I could not accidentally give away its location to the dowser. The talented man walked this way and that with his simple metal dowsing rod in his hand and in next to no time had picked up some subterranean structure that he said was of a "tunnel-like nature" and that it appeared to be running diagonally across the road and under gardens at both sides. Whatever the void was, it appeared to be about one metre wide and travelling at a shallow angle across the face of the hill upon which so many houses were built.

We could see by the line it was taking that at the top end it would cross the street again just beyond the road junction and so we walked uphill and turned the corner and sure enough there it was …still travelling diagonally uphill. We followed it until it did two things simultaneously: part of it seemed to continue under a large house while Mr. Cowan felt that some sort of chamber had collapsed in some way thereby making the earth-energies that he was picking up travel in a whole hotch-potch of muddled directions.

At that point he said that he felt he could do no more to assist our research but as far as I was concerned I though he had increased my knowledge greatly. He had independently confirmed by dowsing methods something that Francesca had accidentally discovered the previous year by the truly psychic methods of mediumship. This, of course, made me wonder what the relationships must be between dowsing and psychic mediumship if the presence of the same **hidden** item can be picked up by both methods. If anything, it strengthened my initial thoughts that dowsing (like hypnotism) is actually some form of psychic mediumship. There is obviously a lot of work to be done on this topic but I can see that the researching of this type of thing will be easier than much of the research that must be undertaken in other parts of psychic work.

****

(* Many times Francesca and I are invited into "haunted" homes after the family have previously called in some dowser who

claims that all the problems of the family will disappear if they allow him to drive copper stakes into the surrounding land and pay him a handsome fee for the privilege. The story is always the same: namely that while the whole "copper-stake business" works for the first few weeks things soon return to their normal unpleasant and haunted state and thus Francesca and I are sent for. Mr. Cowan explained straight away that copper stakes have an initial ability to "absorb and dissipate" negative energies that can depress a household but that they become "saturated and overwhelmed" by such energies and soon become useless. He suggested that a large stone placed in front of the property by a method of precise calculation would split the energies and force them to pass left and right of the house then re-bond behind the house before travelling on their way again.)

Addendum

Mark has now changed his place of work and has actually sold his house at a considerable profit but before he did so he told me that he discovered that the Mr. Anderson mentioned in the case had been a well recognised literary man and had in fact been the main author of one of the a series of famous books. These well known books were entitled, "The Statistical Accounts of Scotland" and were produced every so many years after painstaking research by the writers. In fact Mr. Anderson had become so famous that a street in the town had been named after him. Funnily enough that street was the one where the tunnel had been detected!

CHAPTER 3

HISTORICAL HELP

The White Hart Inn
Maybole Castle
The Mysterious Monks
Mr. Robert Burns

The public in general usually associates spiritualist mediums with telling fortunes through reading the position of tea-leaves in teacups or with assisting people to communicate with deceased relatives.

What a gross under-use of such unbelievable powers!

If I am ever asked what professions would most benefit from looking more deeply at mediumistic abilities I often leave aside the most obvious one ….the pyschiatric care profession, for by 2004 at least some of these people are starting to consider that the spirit world exists and has a bearing upon the problems they face on a day-to-day basis.

The two groups who most consistently under-use the services of mediums are our archaeology services and our crime detection agencies, i.e. the police. For the most part the professionals in those callings cannot bring themselves (in the U.K. anyway) to "lower themselves" to call upon mediumistic talents and abilities that they have never taken the trouble to understand or examine in the first place. In the United States, however, mediums are not only used quite widely in crime detection but some are used so successfully that the gangster underworld has been known to put a price upon a medium's head that has resulted in her murder. That must surely be proof of something!

Archaeology in general is perhaps a little more prone to using the services of a medium and in Volume 1, page 220, you will read of some startling examples of its successful use. It is this aspect of mediumship that I now touch upon here.

The White Hart Inn

CRIME FROM THE PAST AND PSYCHOMETRY

This inn considers, with some justification, that it is the oldest surviving inn in Edinburgh. It is picturesquely situated in the old medieval area called the Grassmarket that lies directly beneath the southern ramparts of the world-famous castle and if you stand outside the White Hart Inn and look up, the castle battlements tower above you.

I know that because I stood on that very spot at 9.30am on 12th December 2003 for I was the first to arrive for a meeting of cameramen, sound men and personnel from the British Broadcasting Corporation. They were there to meet up with Francesca and I to produce a segment for a programme on psychic Scotland which was due to go out on air in the Spring of 2004 and we were all looking forward to the enterprise although not one of us knew what we might or might not find lurking within the walls of that ancient pub.

Perhaps I should have written here, "lurking within its cellars" for it was that part of the premises which was giving rise for concern, psychic concern. Things had been seen and heard by at least three of the staff and some of those things were too recent for comfort, like four weeks recent!

"D.J.", as he preferred to be called was the bar manager who phoned me up. He turned out to be a very pleasant and helpful man and in that initial phone call asked if I could help with a psychic problem which was beginning to "spook out" the staff. The last thing he wanted on his hands was some sort of downing of tools and walking out because of strange things that lurked in the beer cellars and food storage areas of the basement.

To get a bit of privacy for the filming and for Francesca and I to make a psychic sweep of the premises the doors were being kept shut to the general public until about 2pm so there we were all in that olde worlde inn at 10am with cups of coffee and tea in our hands as we watched the film people set up their equipment.

I had been careful to ask Mick, the director, not to give away accidentally any information to Francesca as the day wore on for it was in everybody's interests if she was mentally kept in the dark about all stories of possible haunting or psychic activity.

This arrangement, I am happy to tell you, he scrupulously abided by throughout the whole proceedings.

I felt sorry for Francesca at that point for she was sitting with her cup of tea in her hands killing time in the bar proper as technicians, bar staff and even former bar staff walked past her and descended down the steep stairs into the basement and action so that their stories could be filmed at the spot where they took place. I kept her company and chatted with her but all the while I could see that her mind was already attuning itself to the work in progress,

"Archie, I wish I hadn't seen that painting of Robert Burns above the outside of the door for as soon as I came in I felt his presence *inside* the door." I agreed with this lady that that was now not something that could be brought into our filming that day. In hindsight, however, the point was academic for Burns presence was never again raised to any degree whatever and so I concluded that either he made almost no impact (psychically speaking) on the premises or perhaps Francesca just stopped tuning into his memories altogether. Anyhow, as you are about to see, there were plenty of other things going to take place on that day which would make past memories of even Scotland's national poet pale into insignificance.

Francesca was looking all around herself as we talked and attempted to fill in those empty morning hours,

"There is a man from the world of spirit over there", she said, pointing towards the window looking out to the street in front of the inn, "He's terribly thin but has the most enormously strange nose!"

"Is he prepared to give a name?" I asked.

"Not at all!" came the reply, "But he is somehow linked to another spirit man at the other side of the room. They are both wearing somewhat shabby dark brown coats and neither can be described as tall. They seem rather rough characters and I feel they are well known here and meet here often to discuss things that are very unpleasant."

We stopped the conversation at that point but three hours later, after lunchtime, we moved freely around that bar area and found a drawing of the very same men on an untitled pen-and-ink etching on the far wall. It was one of the bar staff who eventually came across to us as we stood by the picture and told us that the pair were none other than Burke and Hare who were the famous "body-snatchers" of their day. That is, they dug up freshly buried bodies by night and then sold them by day for anatomical research purposes. It was then that we realised that this inn must have been used as a meeting place for those two nasty characters.

(see also the chapter in this book called, " Bodysnatchers".)

It transpired by the end of the day that neither the manager nor his staff had realised up till that point that that pair had any connection with the inn whatever. It all came as a surprise …or perhaps even a "shock" to D.J.!

The film people, who often do things in a non-sequential manner in any case, were initially interviewing and filming Mark, Stephen and Zoe in the basement area because they had reportedly seen and heard strange things down there and then, at long last, came the turn of Francesca and myself to take part. We moved down the very steep and narrow stairway to the basement and looked around. Immediately I could see that Francesca was both surprised and agitated,

"Oh, the whole place is filled with Irish people!" she exclaimed, "And not the kind of Irish people you'd like to meet…. They are all drunk and quarrelling with each other and seem a pretty low form of humanity! *(This was Francesca being totally honest for she, herself, is of Irish extraction.)* This has been the original real bar area of the inn many, many years ago and the better part of the inn had been the floor above this: the place that we, in 2004 now call the bar. I feel that down here in the present basement the floor level is much higher here today that when all those people around us were getting themselves blind drunk." *(This was later confirmed by DJ who had always taken a great historical interest in the pub he managed.)*

Then Francesca described to us in detail a physical fight that she saw going on amongst five men. She said it had begun over a woman called Jean and had got out of hand to such a degree that a small knife had been drawn and a man had been seriously stabbed although he did not actually die of his wounds.

Little was I to know then that we would hear much more of the rogues who frequented this pub and their criminal ongoings.

Keeping our heads down because of the low height of the basement ceiling we moved through the warren of underground rooms until we came to a sort of chute combined with a narrow ladder built into it which was used as a mechanism for delivering barrels of beer down into that cellar area.

"Oh! Oh!" said our medium, almost jumping to one side. "Someone has just thrown a body in through a doorway which used to open onto the street at this point in the past. Oh my goodness," the lady went on in genuine alarm, "The man isn't as dead as his attackers thought he was and two men and a woman and clubbing him to final death as he is lying on the floor. It's obviously a robbery and more!" *(Remember that at this point neither Francesca nor myself realised that the spirit men she had seen upstairs were in the likeness of the infamous bodysnatchers Burke and Hare. If we had known that at the time I am sure we would both have realised that this poor man was being murdered not only for the contents of his wallet but for his very body which would no doubt be sold on to the students of the famous College of Surgeons in the area.)*

We then moved a few feet sideways into a tiny room full of pipes and plumbing and barrels of beer and there we stood in a chilling blast of freezing air. No! The cold air had nothing at all to do with anything psychic but was the result of a refrigeration fan keeping the room temperature down to below 10 degrees C. I tried to stand between Francesca and the blast so that she could concentrate on doing what she had been asked to do …. take us into the happenings of the past.

"There is a little old man at a table down here and he is a nasty bit of work too although I know that he tries to keep himself away from the roughness of the other villains in this place." The medium described a most peculiarly shaped individual who was all physically twisted in some way and quite apart from that he had one leg shorter than the other while his arms looked too small and his hands too big. "He is counting money and putting it into piles for a number of different rogues. It is their share of the proceeds from crime", Francesca said.

I interrupted at this point for I was thinking back to the man who had been bludgeoned to death in the basement room next door,

"Francesca, look at the money on the table and tell us, if you can, where the money came from to be here."

The eyes of the medium closed again and with the chilled air still blasting away at the back of my neck I heard her say,

"They are taking the money from lots of stall-holders. It's a primitive form of extortion or "protection" money!"

(Later that day D.J. showed us a photograph from the 1920's perhaps, of a traditional market and its associated stalls that was held right outside the White hart Inn until almost modern times. It strikes me that this must have been what Francesca was referring to.)

You will hear more later of this little money-counting man with the twisted and mangled left, lower leg but for the moment the people in that area, along with all the cameras, drifted through to another part near a refrigerator where a cook, Zoe, had received a great fright merely four weeks previously.

I saw to it that Francesca stood close to the known spot (although I did not tell her what had taken place there.)

"Do you feel anything here?" I asked.

"I feel someone who is totally out of keeping with this place. He's a well-dressed and tall man and I feel that he might well be a lawyer of some sort as he is holding documents which I am told are of a legal type. He has to do with business and legislation of some kind. I can't think what on earth he is doing down in this squalid basement bar with all those drunken rogues. This is not his scene and he knows it but he has dealings with several people here. He is trying not to make himself known to me! He is almost hiding from me!"

I was becoming steadily more interested in this fellow as the medium spoke and I asked if it were possible to identify this stranger. There was hesitation for a bit and that was quite understandable under the circumstances and then Francesca spoke the unbelievable words,

"He's a Mr. Brodie, a Mr.Deacon Brodie."

I could not believe my ears for our medium had just given us the name of one of the main bodysnatchers of his period and one who is now well known (after the famous trial) as having been an associate with Burke and Hare. This den of debauchery must have been, therefore, one of the main meeting areas where those "Resurrectionists" *(as they were called)* planned their dirty deeds and split the proceeds! What a discovery!

At that point the filming for Francesca was finished for the time being and she returned upstairs for a well-deserved rest and lunch. I, on the other hand, was doomed to stay in the basement for quite a bit longer so that I could interview the staff about their possible meetings with the paranormal while the camera recorded their stories and my reactions to them.

Zoe was the first person to give us her tale and it was particularly meaningful because the events had taken place so recently. She showed us how she had been collecting food from a tall refrigerator and was just closing the door when she found herself face to face with a partial apparition. She said that she knew there was a "top to it" but she didn't seem to see that. What she did see was the figure from the waist down and it really scared her as one can imagine. My readers will now realise that who she saw was none other than Deacon Brodie.

Stephen's tale was completely different although it took place merely twelve feet away from Zoe's sighting. Stephen, a cellarman, had been in that part of the basement changing over a gas cylinder so that the correct gas pressure could push the beer through the pipes then he returned upstairs to the bar to check that the liquids were flowing correctly from the various taps. They did and he was happy with the cylinder change-over......at least for the first five minutes. Then the whole system seemed to shut down and a puzzled Stephen returned to the cellar thinking that he must have inadvertently replaced an empty cylinder of gas with a second nearly-empty cylinder. He found that there was nothing at all wrong with the changeover that he had made. He did find to his amazement, however, that the valve on the top of the new cylinder had not just been screwed off in the last five minutes but so strongly off that he needed a lever to open the valve up again. Stephen might have thought that someone was playing tricks on him except that there was no second person in the inn at that point and in any case the force used to shut the valve must have been very vicious. Anyone playing a trick, he thought, would merely turn the valve off manually and move away. There would have been no necessity by a trickster to use such overpowering force to shut it off.

What Stephen did not know was that the gas cylinder was always located at the very spot where the knife fight mentioned above took place.

Still dealing with gas cylinders being turned off, we mentally move across the same room to a second set of cylinders which were turned off in a similar manner and also with astounding force. That second story, however, came from Mark, a part-time cellarman who worked in the White Hart Inn prior to Stephen being employed there. He had been asked to return to the place of his former employment on 12th December to give evidence to the TV people and he was doing just that. Mark is not a tall man but he is the nearest thing to a barn door that I have encountered for a long time. He must weigh about 20 stones and is physically fit along with it so if he found a valve difficult to turn on again then it really must have been turned off by someone (or something) tougher than he. In fact Mark discovered several fresh cylinders of gas turned off just as Stephen had on quite a number of occasions.

It was not so much his story about the gas that interested me most but his story about the knocking on the walls in the basement. Part of his job was to count up the cash at the end of the day prior to locking it away in the safe and so, on the large mahogany table in the basement, he spread it out and tallied up. While he heard very loud raps on the wall several times during his career in the basement of that inn, the very first time really puzzled then alarmed him. He had been in mid-count after the premises had closed late at night and the manager had gone home leaving him with the only keys to the premises when all of a sudden there was a series of extremely loud raps coming from his right: from the stone wall next to him that must have been about three feet thick. The man was so startled that he left his cash, and hunted around the basement to see how D.J., the manager, could possibly have got into the pub again since he, Mark, had the only key. Then he hunted around in the bar upstairs and then he actually went to the bother of walking out into the street (carefully locking the door after him) and hunting down lanes and alleyways for the elusive D.J. He was not there of course, for he was sitting at home by that time. The puzzled Mark re-entered the inn and went downstairs to continue counting his cash again but the noise returned louder than ever, hammering out from the wall at him in a very meaningful and menacing way. Mark had had enough by that time and abandoning the cash the 20 stone man fled the pub with the speed of a four minute miler. Later, in daylight hours and with company, he tested various knocking through from the room beyond to see what noise came from the wall where he had been sitting. Knock as hard as he could he could not re-generate the kind of noise that came out of the wall that dreaded night. He finally came to the conclusion that the knocking must have been generated from *within* the wall itself…. almost as if someone had embedded a loud speaker just under the plasterwork for that very purpose.

What Mark did not know at that point was that Francesca had already discovered that little old spirit man in the room beyond counting out his ill-gotten gains. It is fascinating, is it not, to think of two people on either side of a thick wall each counting up their money but with 200 years of time separating them. Perhaps the first of the pair took umbrage at the second being around the place and doing the same thing on "his" property…who knows?

PSYCHOMETRY at the White Hart Inn

(Psychometry is the ability that many mediums have to touch items and by contact with them to bring back memories associated with them …..no matter how many years had passed in the meantime.)

By 2pm the public were flooding into this busy city bar for lunch and drinks and by then the filming in the basement had ended.

After the film crew and I had eaten we were able to concentrate on the second part of the event which was something that should, by rights have taken place two days before and in another place. I'm writing now about Francesca's being asked to psychometrise various articles that were found during industrial archaeological reclamation work in an abandoned theatre in Glasgow called the *Britannia*. The items themselves were in the 'lost property' drawer when the theatre closed down in the 1940s and the premises are hopefully about to be given new life once more if funds can be raised for the project. Francesca had undertaken to psychometrise eight articles in that derelict premises but time ran out on the appointed day of the filming and so that work was rescheduled to take place two days later in the White Hart Inn.

With the cameras upon us we sat at a table while members of the public sat at the other side of the room looking on and getting a free demonstration of psychometry. My part in the proceedings was merely to encourage Francesa in her work and, by expanding on her statements, help her mentally to go down the most productive avenues of enquiry. She concentrates so hard on making and maintaining the spirit contact that I have to listen out for clues to linked things: I've got to "read between the lines" so to speak and keep matters moving along a definite line of enquiry. Sometimes when she is in such states of mini trance she can find herself gradually drifting away from the original direction of the line of enquiry that we were following and it's up to me to bring things back on course.

I was handed a large envelope which contained the items to be psychometrised and these I put on the table in front of the lady. Neither of us had seen any of them before that moment. As I remember it, there were various finger rings…perhaps five. There was a lovely cameo brooch which may well have been an expensive item, a small 'cheap and cheerful' brooch with a clover leaf upon it and finally a brass button that looked as if it had come off an old army uniform.

The amount of information held in any physical item when witnessed from the psychometric viewpoint does not depend on its size, value or age but upon the amount of human emotion that surrounded it when it was in the keeping of past owners. Thus as with all psychometric sessions, some items handled by even the best of mediums yield many more emotions and memories than other items and this session that was recorded on camera was no exception to that. You will no doubt be interested in a summary of what was found:-

1) One of the rings had some connection with a military man. We do not know if it was *his* ring or that of someone close to him but his name came up, Robert James Kirkpatrick. It was the only name to come forth during that session and it is the first time that I have heard a three-part name come up for a spirit individual.

2) A second ring brought great sadness with its loss at the theatre for we were told by the spirit lady who lost it that it was a family heirloom that had been in her personal keeping for a long time. Francesca felt the anguish and total sense of devastation that the woman was experiencing through its loss and I realised later that this strongly expressed feeling bore out a theory that I have long held. That theory is that mediums do not get information FROM the item they hold but the fact that they are holding that item enables them to make easiest contact THROUGH it with some great memory system which holds all knowledge, emotions and thoughts.Think about it! If that ring was lost and not recovered (which is the case) then it could never have held the memory of the many days of self-torment that the poor woman endured *after* she lost it!

3) The holding of a third ring brought with it many lovely memories of happy evenings at the theatre ..and beyond its confines too for Francesca saw in her mind's eye, she said, a busy, bustling street with tramcars moving back and forth. At that point I noticed that she was actually humming away to herself with her eyes shut and head swaying back and forth and she had a really happy smile on her face. I asked her if she heard the audience in the musichall *singing* but she shook her head silently as she continued to hum along with them for they all appeared to be *humming* rather than singing along with whatever music was coming from the stage.

4) The psychometrisation of what appeared to be a military button held some unexpected information

because we found that it actually came from a uniform that had been used *on stage*. Francesca had found that the uniform, whatever it was, spent most of its time in a wickerwork hamper and not on the back of a soldier. In fact her body took on the bodily attributes of the man who had worn it on stage and she became temporarily paralysed down her left side…which I found a little alarming although I've had Francesca in a similar psychic state several times previously. I was left wondering whether the man had become paralysed in later life once he had retired or had he actually been a paralysed actor? At this point pressure of time meant that we had to press on with filming other items.

5) The lovely cameo brooch had been lost by a tall, slim, and pretty girl who had secured a velvet scarf around her neck by its means. She must have missed it terribly!

6) Then Francesca put her hand forward and picked up from the table a slim golden ring but immediately put it down again and pushed it away with a gesture of annoyance. I looked at her in surprise and she said that she had pushed it from her as *it had nothing at all to do with what we were doing that day*. With raised eyebrows I glanced past the medium at the director of the film shoot as the cameras rolled and he gave me a look which told me that this was something that he had purposely introduced as a "blind" of some kind to test the medium's abilities to the limit. She had spotted it at once I am glad to say but I was a little sad that her abilities had been queried in such a manner. (After the filming I discovered that the ring actually belonged to a production assistant girl who was with the filming team.)

7) Perhaps of all the items psychometrised there that day I liked best what came forth from the small and battered brooch with the clover leaf. It was a sad little item of low grade metal and perhaps only worth one thousandth of what the cameo cost but oh

what love and innocence Francesca felt coming from it! She felt the rare first love of a teenage girl for her first boyfriend and the reciprocal love that that engendered. It was a simple and pure love and oh how sad it must have been for that girl to lose that cherished item after her young man had saved up long and hard to take her to the local musichall for their first time out together.

****

'Bowed Joseph'

I said that I would return to the tale of the twisted little man who was counting the money in the basement area of the inn and this I now do.

On the day in question we had no idea at all as to who this unfortunately contorted creature might be and due to pressure of time and sheer tiredness at the end of an exhausting day we did not ask DJ or the bar staff who he was. That was probably just as well for I now believe that not one of the staff had any idea as to this man's identity.

About a week later, as chance would have it, a friend of Francesca's lent her a book that she thought might interest her for it had within its covers tales of spooky and historical happenings from old Edinburgh. So it was that in a moment of peace and quiet this good lady flicked over the pages of the book to see what stories of the past lay therein and all of a sudden certain words "jumped out" at her…. "Ill-shapen cobbler"! *(Bodily-twisted shoe-maker).* She read on and as she read more she realised that this might well be the very man whom she saw counting the money at the table in the cellar. Everyone called him 'Bowed Joseph' apparently although he had been christened 'Joseph Smith' and he seemed in adulthood to be a cross between Robin Hood and the Godfather of the local mafia. He would gleefully rob the rich but the proceeds would as often as not be given to the poor who were his fellows …but only to a degree. Francesca had to remind herself that she had found him counting his ill-gotten gains but away from the rabble who were kept at the other side of the wall.

There is a certain type of person who due to his natural charisma, physical good looks or verbal power can gather people around him to follow his causes and even die for him when needed. The tall and handsome come to mind like Robert the Bruce and William Wallace ...with swinging swords and dashing attitude.

There was no way that Bowed Joseph could ever be described as charismatic but he certainly could whip up people's minds and attitudes and it is said that he could gather 10,000 people to his side within half an hour if he had to …..and certainly on one occasion he did precisely that! The story is this:-

There was a severe shortage of flour in Edinburgh at one point and a major flour-stockist in the older part of the city had suddenly started to sell the same amount of flour but at double the price. When Bowed Joseph heard about this he went to the mill owner on behalf of the poorer citizens to ask him to reduce the price to what it had been initially but the man refused. Joseph backed out of the situation without confrontation but within half an hour had had his runners go around all central Edinburgh and soon a mob of nearly ten thousand people stormed the mill and removed every last grain of flour. Such was the power of this little twisted man!

Once Francesca and I knew who Bowed Joseph really was we decided to get to know more about him. We learned that his unusually twisted skeleton had been preserved in some manner by The Edinburgh College of Surgeons and so I wrote to Professor Dorothy Crawford who was the current keeper of anatomical specimens, asking if Francesca and I could view the exhibit within the medical college. *(In actual fact ALL exhibits in that section had been freely on display to the citizens of Edinburgh until recently for it was the citizens of Edinburgh who had donated them to the College.)* Quite apart from seeing the degree of contortion of the man's skeleton we had hoped that Francesca could communicate with his spirit-self in a more direct way. For a start we were wanting to know what Joseph, himself, thought of his skeleton being displayed in such a public manner!

Regretfully, Professor Crawford denied us access to view the skeleton.

Later, at a lecture evening held within the White Hart Inn itself on January 28th 2004, Francesca went into trance and declared before a large audience that while the skeleton had been held within a glass case at the college it had either been moved or was about to be moved after being in situ for over a hundred years.

I wrote again to the 'keeper' of Joseph's skeleton only to be told that Francesca had talked a lot of nonsense. I was a bit downhearted by this reply for I know that Francesca does not come up with nonsense…ever! You can imagine my surprise when I later read in an Edinburgh newspaper that in order to "open up science and medicine to the masses" some prominent medical items from the anatomical collection from the College of Surgeons were to "go on tour" around Scotland as some sort of travelling exhibition. Regretfully, I was in Spain at the time when this event took place so I, myself, have still never seen the skeleton of Bowed Joseph.

While I have no shares in the White Hart Inn of the Grassmarket in Edinburgh I suggest that my readers might find a visit to that establishment well worth the bother.

Perhaps I'll see you there sometime?

****

Maybole Castle

A Bit of Lost History

While this case is really a small one I rather like it because, while there is a very sad element to it, it verifies local folklore that was dying out as well as bringing forward a story about which skeptical historians were dubious.

Like many old Scottish castles, Maybole had a chequered history since its origin in 1560 or thereabouts but by the year 2004 it could be found right in the center of a small Scottish town of the same name. There is a well-defined historial connection between the world-famous Culzean Castle which stands some miles away on the Ayrshire coast and Maybole Castle which historically-minded readers can check up upon. My American readers might wish to note also that the Second World War veteran, General Eisenhower, was given a life-long gift of the use of a suite of rooms at Culzean as a "thank-you present" for playing his full part in that world war.

Maybole, like all castles, also has a chequered history of both additions and subtractions to the size of the property. In more recent years it housed the office of the Estate Factor (estate manager) for a long, long time before being used as a dwelling house for several people of note. By 2004 it was leased by a local Community Council group entitled 'May-Tag' and the rooms were used for various training purposes but I am told that the decision of this group to vacate the castle was taken comparatively recently because of well-considered commercial, social and other valid considerations.

As a final "farewell!" to the property some of the more daring staff wanted to hold an overnight 'ghost watch' or vigil to see if they could see by night the things they sometimes felt close to them by day. As none of them had any expertise in such events and as they did not really know what was…or was not…in the castle by way of spirit people, a keen young lady asked me if I could give advice. She also asked if I would bring a medium of quality to visit and to tell her (and her alone) what might be encountered on any vigil which was to take place the following week. For that reason Francesca and I visited the castle and were shown around by Fiona on a lovely sunny Spring afternoon.

"I don't know that there's all that much in the way of leftover spirit people in that castle but I am hearing a woman screaming and lamenting somewhere high up in the building somewhere," said Francesca as we drove out of Glasgow and down the A77 road to Maybole. Such a phrase would be strange enough in itself but it was even "stranger than strange" for neither Francesca nor I had ever been in or around Maybole Castle and it was still almost thirty miles down the road ahead of us. Logic decreed that she couldn't possibly know what was in the building in any way at all…but yet she did!

Fiona and Zoe welcomed us and those two proved to be very different characters. The first was outgoing and confident and willing to meet ghosts head on if necessary (or at least that was the impression we were given) while the second was more reserved and not really too keen of meeting anything at all from the other world. We chatted and had cups of tea as building plans and web-site printouts about the castle were placed before us. We looked at these but in a quiet moment Francesca whispered to me,

"Archie, there is considerable psychic activity at the topmost point of the castle and a bit on the second floor and perhaps a bit in the basement but not much more," and indeed that proved to be the case.

"Can we start by having a look at the upper floors?" hinted Francesca to the staff and off we went up a typical winding staircase… although an unusually wide one. (Castle staircases were always kept narrow for reasons of defense. Some were twisted to the left while others turned to the right, depending on whether the family who owned the property were left-handed or right-handed. This enabled best use to be made of the sword.) This wide spiral staircase became suddenly narrower for its very last length …that is at the point where we were led up to a little room at the very top of the tower. It is important to note that just before we stepped up the last tall step and into this little gem of a room we were told by Fiona that to our right there had once been another room but that it had long since ceased to have a door or entry point and appeared to have been completely sealed off at some point in the past.

Rooms with no doors intrigue me for there is always a reason for sealing a room up. We were about to find out why quite soon! ....and while we were in the 'Countess's Room' next door that we were just about to enter. What a view of the town we got from this topmost point of the castle but what a sad atmosphere I felt in there also and I caught Francesca looking 'funny looks' at me so I knew we were in the room where something very psychic existed at that very moment. After noting that there were little bundles of ancient estate ledgers with entries dating from 1751 lying flat on the floor…which I now understand were laid out there ready to be properly archived …..Francesca stood in the middle of the room with her head bowed. I knew she was entering a trance situation and within seconds I saw her mouth move gently,

"Yes, yes. All right. Caroline? You did say, Caroline, Lady Caroline.........?"

A most dreadful story slowly started to emerge as Fiona and Zoe stood beside me listening and the reason for this talented medium "hearing" screaming and lamenting high up in this castle when we were thirty miles away was slowly to become apparent.

A spirit lady was making herself known to Francesca who had apparently been imprisoned in that part of the castle in years gone by. She had been called 'Caroline' and her tale was truly an appalling one. Even yet she was unwilling to tell it all or divulge the name of the perpetrator of her imprisonment or the lover concerned in her downfall.

(Researchers might like to know that it is not uncommon for spirit people refusing to reveal some secret that they had on earth. We might think that after death the whole business might not matter but it apparently does. We talk about "taking a secret to the grave" but I assure you that some secrets are still secrets well beyond the grave.)

Caroline, who eventually identified herself as 'Lady Caroline, Countess of Cassillis' and who occupied the castle along with her powerful husband the Earl at some point in the 1600s was imprisoned for a great deal of her married life. She, herself, told us so through Francesca.

"Before I was imprisoned in this room I was kept prisoner in the other room (she pointed to the wall above the fireplace beyond which was the sealed-up room previously mentioned) and there, in that terrible place I knew not whether it was night nor day, or what week or month it was."

(I must explain here that she spoke and pointed through Francesca who had allowed the spirit lady to temporarily take her over almost completely. I hesitate to put any figure to that statement but at that point I would judge that 95% Lady Caroline stood beside me and only 5% Francesca.)

She said that she was eventually moved into the (*present*) larger room which did have a window and, indeed, a good outlook over the whole town of Maybole but she was a prisoner in her own castle and I believe she was slowly going mad due to her confinement and the woe that led to it.

Francesca stood in trance in front of the rather massive-looking stone fire-surround and her hands were scrubbing endlessly backwards and forwards over its cold stone surface….. moving, moving, always moving aimlessly. I could see by her eyes that she was really in a rather deep trance state and had been thoroughly taken over by the persona of the incarcerated Countess!

"Oh, the cold, the cold!" she lamented, "Why cannot they give me heat?"

This whole business was being caught on video camera by Fiona.

I took Francesca's ceaselessly-moving hand and drew it towards the left end of the fireplace and placed it on a carved family emblem of some sort that obviously had meaning in terms of heraldry. It was probably the Cassillis family emblem, or at least a major part of it.

"What meaning does that carving have for you?" I said to the medium, knowing that she was, in her mind, the Countess Caroline at that moment.

Her head tossed up and she began to speak with great pride and suppressed anger,

"It once had great meaning for me but now it means **nothing**! **Nothing!**" She almost spat out those final words and all the listeners in that room felt the venom in them. Little wonder if her husband had imprisoned her in her own castle!

Before we had begun on our rounds of the castle we had been told (very briefly indeed) that there had once been a rumour that some woman called 'Jean' had been imprisoned there for running off with a gypsy but that such a rumour had now been dispelled by historians. This now came back into my mind.

"Could this be the very woman? Was it, in fact, the Countess Caroline who had run off with the gypsy? Was that why she had been locked up?" I asked myself. Now I decided to ask the spirit lady herself and did so through Francesca. Lady Caroline was keeping her secret and when I put the obvious question to her as to what caused her to be locked up in the first place the evasive answer was that,

"….the stars and the moon beguiled me!"

She had taken the conscious decision not to tell me anything. Is that not amazing after a period of 400 years!

(This illustrates, of course, many things. Firstly it shows that she knows that I am present in that room and that I have posed a certain question for her and that I would like an answer. Secondly, it illustrates that at least some spirit entities can think for themselves and are not merely 'action replay' memories of some kind. This very complex business is discussed in depth in another publication by myself for it is just too lengthy to be gone into here.)

Regretfully, there was no mention of young Johnnie Faa, the leader of the local gypsy clan encamped nearby down by the river and no mention that her husband, the Earl, had eventually hung her lover from a tree known locally as the 'Dule Tree'. (We found that out phrase from an old folk poem that is printed herein later).

Caroline told us, in a very animated and agitated way that she had attempted to bribe the key-master of the castle who was called 'Thomas' and that she thought she had been successful in her ploy,

"He will come with his ring of keys (the traditional method of keeping keys together in a castle) and *he* will free me! Thomas is to free me!"

(Francesca made a circle in the air using her two hands and so I know that the iron ring that held the castle keys was about one foot in diameter. To my mind that is a rather interesting archaeological finding!)

She sounded so hopeful and yet the folk tale never mentions that she did escape to live *unhappily* ever after. Her lover, Johnnie was hanged and she was imprisoned and that was the end of it. I have a feeling (psychically) that she eventually went mad, poor woman.

****

For your pleasure I append below an ancient poem (the origin of which I do not know) but which I have stumbled across and which puts in verse and in a typically Scottish way, the sad events of the above tale. The whole business also makes me wonder how many other folk tales have been declared as *untrue* by eminent historians when they may well have had a serious basis.

The ladye o' Cassillis sits weeping alane   *(alone)*
In her room in the auld castle high.
And thinks o' the bricht happy days that were hers   *(bright)*
But noo are for ever gane by
When she roamed through the woods and the fields sae green
That sweep roond the bonnie Doon,   *(a river)*
When maidens and vassals were a' at her beck *(servants on call)*
And the homage o' Maybole toon.   *(respect of the whole town)*

But the glamour o' wanton love casts its spell
O'er this high-born ladye.
And she left her hoose and her bairns and a'   *(children)*
Tae gang wi' a gypsy laddie.   *(go with)*
And here is the pitifu' end o' it a' –
Her lover hanged on the Dule Tree,
While she is confined in this lanesome tower,
Her life-lang weird to dree.   *(destiny to fear)*

O, easy it is tae tak' a wrang step
And hard in the richt tae abide   *(right)*
But wha shall undo the thing that is dune
When ance it has left oor side?   *(once)*
Nae use for us then tae sab and lament.   *(sob)*
We maun reap as we've sawn ….nae doot.   *(must)*
It's easy tae drap idle stanes in the well…   *(drop stones)*
But wha's to take them oot?

The quaint oriel window still looks up the street
And we fancy that sad face we see,
Lamenting for aye that ae fause step   *(always +one false)*
Which wrocht a' her misery.   *(produced)*
And this is the warning the auld story tells
To ilka ane that gangs by--   *(any one who passes)*
"The glamour o' sin blins the een o' the best (*blinds the eyes*)
And steals a' oor innocent joy!"

****

We eventually left the sad Caroline to her solitary prison (which, strangely enough was known as 'Jean's Room') and moved down two floors and into another part of the castle to a little projecting, semi-circular room. Here Francesca heard some more music…for "the whole castle is full of music", she said. And she was looking out of the window when she saw (in her mind) something outside which caused words to come out of her mouth but *over which she had no control.*

"The cleiking o' the Deil! The cleiking o' the Deil!"

This talented lady said it twice over and yet she looked embarrassed by what she had just said because the words came involuntarily through her and she had no idea as to what they meant….or indeed who it was who had spoken through her. Naturally I quizzed her upon this unexpected outburst and asked her whether this was linked to the music she was hearing but she said that it wasn't. This small incident is still a mystery but I think the answer might be as follows:-

As a "cleik" is a stick with a curved or hooked end similar to the type used by shepherds to catch sheep then the puzzling phrase really means,

"Catching the Devil" or perhaps "Fishing the Devil out of his hiding place"

What Francesca caught a glimpse of was probably part of some ancient (religious?) ritual where the local population hunted high and low around the town while armed with sticks in order to rout out the devil from their community and send him packing to where he belonged …certainly not in Maybole. Not only do I find this a fascinating snapshot of social and religious history but it ties in with a somewhat similar children's seeking game I knew of as a child called, "Hunting the gowk". That meant, "Looking for the fool, the simpleton or the village idiot".

From that floor we moved finally to the basement area of the castle where we all marvelled at the arched stone ceilings of the old medieval kitchens before settling ourselves on chairs around a large table in the *modern* kitchen used by the staff. Here Francesca felt the presence of cattle from the past that she said were housed in some way just through the thick outer wall next to us. We were then told by the staff that that was the place where there had once been cattle yards attached to the castle although our talented lady could never have known that fact. Then our medium closed her eyes for she felt the presence of a human being, and named him as "John Hamilton". She told that he had been a sort of castle-manager of his era and had been a hard man to all who met him. His spirit-being was present in the old kitchen area because he had punished too severely a teenage boy who had stolen some edible game from the larder. In fact he had not just assaulted him but he had picked him up and hung him from one of the many meat hooks that were embedded in the stone ceiling. The lad had then died as a result of this! I asked Francesca how this cruel man had disposed of the body for, even in those days in the 1600s there must have been some sort of justice, surely. She replied by pointing through the wall to the north side of the castle,

"They flung him into a sort of stream which was channelled into a stone-walled culvert of some kind and left him there."

Francesca's directions concerning this event were so precise, both as to the angle and distance that this enabled me, the following day, to get hold of a local historian and ask him if there was any chance that the watercourse mentioned could really have existed. This man said that the local stream, in those far-off days, had actually flowed through the castle grounds and it would have been merely a simple matter to drag the lad's body from the kitchens by night and dump it into the culvert and then claim that he must have fallen in while fetching water for the kitchen. I think this idea is a very plausible one.

The story on page 101 of *Volume 1, The Psychic Investigators Casebook*, explains clearly what a "drop-in communicator" is and as soon as our spirit person, John Hamilton, began talking to Francesca we got a classic example of such an unconnected secondary entity introducing herself into our 'private' conversation with the spirit world. This unexpected visitor from the other world happened to be none other than the Grandmother of Zoe, the girl who was with us on our 'rounds'. I first saw Francesca's eyes twinkle and her lips purse as she only too obviously attempted to suppress a laugh and I partly guessed at the truth. I knew that Fiona and Zoe would be wondering what on earth was going on for we were, at that point, in conversation with a rather nasty spirit man called Hamilton who was on the point of hanging a boy from the ceiling. Hardly a topic to laugh at! The truth of the matter was that at that same time Zoe's Grandmother who was called 'Nancy' was attempting like mad to edge into the psychic conversation and was trying all sorts of tricks to gain the medium's full attention. *(That is quite usual for 'drop-in communicators')* This included making funny faces and telling jokes (mentally to Francesca) as well as actually tugging at Francesca's clothing and hair. No wonder the medium was forced to suppress her laughter while she struggled to complete her communication with this villain, Hamilton. At last Francesca terminated her contact with the man and allowed herself to be more fully taken over by the spirit of Nancy which enabled her to tell Zoe the good news that her Grandmother loved her and cared for her even when she was in a world beyond ours. Poor Zoe, I know, was scared of the psychic world and did not quite know how to take this news. "Was this a good thing or a bad thing?" she pondered. I was later told that she did not sleep well that night and had also decided not to take part in the overnight vigil that was planned for a few days later.

(Perhaps she thought that her Grandmother might actually appear to her in the castle by night in a visible form and that she could not handle such a possibility. Researchers should note that such an appearance would be highly unlikely, for visual formations (ghosts) of relations and similar only usually occur after a whole series of minor 'lead-in' events of a psychic nature. They need to 'work up' to making themselves visible …it doesn't just happen as you can see if you read the Minard Castle account on page 227 of Vol. One, The Psychic Investigators Casebook.)

We waved goodbye to the castle as it glowed in a broad band of sunlight at the start of our long journey back to Edinburgh but we both realised that on Friday night at midnight those members of the vigil who were in the "Countess's Room" might not be as carefree as Francesca and I were as we got into our car.

****

Something More to Think About

If I had to give a particular title to April 2004 it might rightly be, 'The Month of Gypsies' for during that period I came across a band of (spirit) Irish gypsies in a woodland near Old Gliston *(see the chapter, 'Two Days in The Life of...' later in this book)* as well as the king of the gypsies in the 1600s called Johnnie Faa, found in the above story. I would have thought that that would have been enough gypsies for one month ...but no! The following months flung up yet other strange coincidences regarding gypsies and to such a degree that in the end one of the ladies involved actually said to me,

"How do you switch this gypsy thing off?"

All of this, of course, reminds researchers of the psychic world of the age-old question,

"How many coincidences do you have to have before you begin to wonder if any of it is coincidence?"

Within days of the Maybole Castle revelations that Francesca brought forward from the past I had a close friend from Canada come to stay with me for a bit and Maureen decided that she would like me to drive her to the town of St Andrews in order to visit a friend of hers called Irene whom I had never met before. Irene I found to be a very lively lady in her early seventies and obviously not without considerable funds and someone who not only golfed on a daily basis but who was blessed with a very agile mind as well.

Sipping coffee in this lady's lounge, the conversation turned to Maybole Castle and I began telling the story of Johnnie Faa. Because the surname was so different from most Scottish names I began to spell it out but Irene halted me to my surprise and said that she knew the spelling of 'Faa' as she was related to a Mr.Charles Faa Blythe Rutherford. This man, she declared, was one of the more recent kings of the gypsies and she then went on to tell me how she, herself, was related to gypsy stock.

While I found the above incident very interesting I did not look upon it as anything astounding but gypsy things were to start to take over Irene's life very soon after that as you will see. She travels widely all the time and the coming week saw her on a china-painting course and in good accommodation in Wakefield, Yorkshire, England. She had taken a book with her that had, *by chance*, been given to her the week before and which, surprise, surprise, dealt with gypsies living out of doors. The title, I seem to remember, of this very recent publication was 'Tales from the Tent' and written by Jess Smith a lady with a strong gypsy background herself.

Upon her return to Fife in mid-June, Irene told me excitedly of what must surely be a rather extraordinary coincidence and this I now record with you.

She had been idly flicking through the book mentioned above in her hotel lounge or similar place and had chanced to stop the pages turning to look at some photographs when a lady from London *(a member of the same china-painting course)* was passing by. The next thing that Irene heard was a sharp intake of breath from the well-built lady as she bent forward and pointed excitedly to a photo of a little girl gypsy.

Suddenly she blurted out that she thought that SHE WAS THE LITTLE GIRL IN THE PHOTOGRAPH. She went on to explain that she, like Irene, was descended from gypsy ancestors but had drifted away from that humble nomadic life to become a high-flying accountant in London and that her china-painting hobby was her method of unwinding at the end of hectic days.

Naturally Irene kept looking from the woman to the photograph and back again and she told me upon her return to Scotland that she believed that she could see a definite resemblance between the two. Initially I mentally accepted that unbelievably coincidental situation but further research proved the truth ....which was interesting enough in itself.

The long-and-the-short-of-it was that this 'ex-gypsy' lady could not have been the child in the photo for Jess Smith (the author) and I contacted each other and discussed the situation over the phone. A copy e-mail received by myself in December 2004 from the accountant lady to Irene stated quite clearly that she, herself, had great grandparents called 'Smith'. I do not know what connections (if any) exist between the two gypsy families but it strikes me that we have some sort of strange coincidental mechanisms at work here.

(I think this is a lovely story in so many ways but for we researchers the question must surely arise,

"As Irene tells me that she never at any time really gave a thought to her own gypsy background and as it suddenly seemed to arise after my being introduced to her can it be said that I, in some way, triggered a series of 'gypsy events' to take place in her life?"

Had I somehow opened a Pandora's box of gypsy things with my psychic researches and had this box of mine somehow remained open and spilled over onto others around me. I think that we should all think rather carefully about what true coincidence can be, for it is quite different from an occasional chance happening, I am sure.)

****

The Mysterious Monks

It is said that "money makes money". That's probably true but I've yet to find out firsthand. I have found out, however, that "notoriety breeds notoriety" and *that* I find very helpful in my day to day psychic work for one satisfied client passes on the word to another, which produces for me a chain of future clients who claim to have encountered the supernatural. In a similar way, I find that someone who has read one of my books on the psychic world and who likes my compassionate attitude towards 'lost souls' is prepared to ask me into their family home because of my *non-belligerent stance* towards resident entities.

The client in this account asked me in for precisely that reason. The lady in question lives on a little plot of land where she and her family have several small cottages which they are restructuring and upgrading to 21st century standards, for some of the buildings are perhaps 200 years old. The one in which Crystal Delaney herself lives had been some sort of small gatehouse or lodge house to a large estate which itself had been sold off in years gone by. This, she and her children are currently rebuilding.

Over the years Crystal and her family had been bothered by a whole host of unaccountable "happenings" in this cottage. There were apparitions seen by at least one family member and there were movements (and disappearances) witnessed of everything from ordinary small domestic objects to Christmas cards. Crystal's own father who was staying over Christmas in 2002 was so amazed to see some seasonal cards start to move of their own volition that he insisted on saying the Lord's Prayer in front of the whole family and had to be persuaded not to get up and leave the building right away. There were senses of presence too and cold breezes and all the usual hints that something psychic might be lurking on the premises. On several occasions the son, Dermot, (nineteen years old) had been so frightened by noises that appeared to sound like a game of football being played on the roof in the middle of the night that he had taken a golf club outside to batter the supposed intruder. There was nothing at all on the flat roof, of course, but he subsequently refused to sleep in that room ever again.

Over a twelve-year period Crystal had had one or two psychic persons visit the house in order to have a closer look at what lay within but, unlike Francesca and myself, those persons made a charge for their services (which is fair enough) and, as already explained, Crystal thought they had the wrong approach to the problem. Their attitude of using "forceful" methods for dispelling any psychic entities found, made Crystal have second thoughts about the whole business. Quite correctly, this lady had no wish to pressurise her ghosts or entities or whatever you like to call them, into quitting the place that they had frequented for many hundreds of years and when she read my first book, "The Psychic Investigators Casebook, Vol. 1" she realised that my method of moving them on through compassion and kindliness was what she wanted.

It was then that Ms Delaney got in touch with me and asked me to visit her home.

On June 11th 2003 Francesca and I drove out through southern Edinburgh and past the amazing ancient and famous Rosslyn Chapel till we came close to the village of Auchendinny.

Here I will pause to tell my readers that I always disguise the true names of people and places out of respect for their privacy but in this case, as you will see, the very spelling of the village near to where it all took place is of great importance. I am therefore forced to break my own rule and give its correct name and spelling …Auchendinny.

We drove down a farm track and found a cluster of dwellings close to a nearby working farm (run by a farmer with the same name as myself as coincidence would have it!). Francesca and I knew that as Ms. Delaney had to collect one of her children from a sports center she'd be a few minutes late and so we had a look around while we waited, sampling the feel of the place so-to-speak. The homeowner soon arrived and after greeting us she led us into her home through a double sliding glass door.

I had expected that we'd perhaps be shown to a lounge area of some sort and offered a cup of coffee or whatever then we'd be told the story of the property before we would start on any of the ghostly stuff. That is very often the usual format when we are invited into a family home but this time my expectations along such lines never got underway at all…….and for a surprising reason!

Crystal opened the sliding glass door and walked in followed by Francesca while I came in last. That was when I noticed Francesca acting strangely.

Let me tell you that this medium always carries a handbag and she does so with it hanging down her left side in the usual manner but all of a sudden and for no reason that I could see, she suddenly slung it over her back so that it rested on the base of her spine. Nothing too strange in that but simultaneously she suddenly developed a severe stoop and was walking forward into the room as if she was being forced to pass under a series of low and invisible tree branches.

I know this lady well and seeing her suddenly take up such a strange posture (and in a client's home) made me wonder if she was suddenly taken ill.

"Are you all right Francesca?" I asked, looking to the lady's well-being.

Still in a bent-double position she said,

"Archie, it's O.K. but I've been taken over very suddenly by the spirit of an old monk."

While I was surprised, I was not unduly alarmed as I knew that this medium's state would slowly normalize in a minute or so as she became acclimatized to the contact that they'd made with each other."

Crystal's widening eyes, however, told me that this was something very new to her so I whispered to her behind Francesca's back *(or rather 'over' it)* that things were not out of control.

"Give it a minute or two," I mouthed.

Eventually the medium returned gradually to her usual self.

"Sorry about that!" she said, "But I was taken over so suddenly I had no time to think." The lady slowly rose to her usual vertical position once more.

"Who took you over Francesca?" I said.

"It was a very old monk. He may well have been in his eighties but as he lived very long ago I suppose that he could have been a bit younger but just looked old.

Anyway, he had considerable back problems due to his age and he had a leather bag slung over his back for he had been out on a herb-collecting expedition along with the group he was responsible for."

"What group was that?" I butted in.

Francesca replied in the present tense illustrating to me that the spirit people were still with her,

"There are about ten other people along with him but most of them seem to be young men of some sort. They are dressed in clothing identical to his own but I know that they are not monks. They just look like monks. The old monk has been given the task of looking after those people but they are not showing their faces to me for some reason but are pushing and shoving each other as is the way with young men. The old monk's face is visible but not theirs. I feel that they are hiding their faces from me on purpose but I don't know why."

I suddenly had an idea because I knew that every time a spirit person hides their face there is a good reason …if only I could think of it in this case. Could it be that this was an elderly monk who had been put in charge of a group of lepers? There was no known monastery close at hand so had we made some chance discovery of some outpost of a monastic settlement ……what we today might call a hospice or hospital or leper colony? Such outlying units were known to have existed outside the periphery of medieval Edinburgh but none was known at this place.

If I was correct about this being some sort of out-unit of a monastery then I knew that the old monk must know in which direction his base monastery must lie.

"Ask the monk-proper in which direction his monastery lies, Francesca," I said and her head bent down in thought.

"He says it is over the fields there……". The lady turned and put her arm forward in the manner that the monk was obviously doing.

"It's over in that direction!" she declared emphatically.

At that point I could see that he was indicating in the general direction of Rosslyn Chapel. Now that seriously puzzled me for while the chapel had been a famous place of worship for hundreds of years I knew that there had never been a monastery discovered there. And in any case if these people were lepers then the distance of one and a quarter miles was too close for comfort as far as the real monks were concerned. No one in the middle-ages wanted a leper colony on their doorstep…that was their equivalent of us having a nuclear power station or a micro-wave mast in our own backyard.

Although I could do little research at that particular moment I vowed to myself that I would tackle the mystery at a later date and you will see the answer to this puzzle towards the end of this account.

As reasonable communication had now been established with the monk I asked Francesca if she would attempt to ask him at what period of history he lived. That is always a hard question for all entities and very often I have to get around it by asking them the name of the king or queen who is on the throne when they were alive. Either the old man was unable or unwilling to discuss the matter but he did say,

"We live in the time of the burnings."

Such a phrase supposes that that event was so well known to us that we would understand its meaning (and thus the period in history) but alas we did not….at least at that time.

The word was undoubtedly plural but what was it that was being burned in the area? Was it the time of witch burnings when poor innocent women all over Europe who knew a little about herbalism were being burned at the stake for supposed witchcraft?

This was a allied question that I would have to research once I left Crystal's home and returned to my own and this we will now return to.

(The Answer to the puzzle?

About a year after writing this account I now believe that we might know the period in history which, for persons in Southern Scotland and Northern England, could be called,

"The Time of the Burnings".

*By late 1297AD William Wallace, the Scottish patriot, had succeeded in chasing every last Englishman from his beloved territory of Scotland but by that Autumn the retreating enemy from the south had seen to it that food supplies in Scotland were at a record low. Starvation for many Scots seemed at hand and Wallace, knowing of plentiful food supplies just south of the border set off with an army to retrieve the cattle that had been stolen and to return home with them and a lot more besides. To that end he drew up a large Scottish army **at a site very close to the very place that the monks had been seen** and headed south to seek plunder! I have no doubt at all that every person for miles around would know of the huge gathering of men and the purpose of their assembly. The local population would know that "The Time of the Burnings" was about to begin for the English further south! The great army moved south on 18th October, 1297 and returned home for Christmas laden with food and booty for the people of Scotland. One of the possibilities, therefore, is that the monks who we met belonged to 1298 or thereabouts but I think that there is a better answer. This tale is not yet over for the English retaliated six years later by marching north **and at the very same site** did* *battle with the Scots in 1303. The Scots were beaten and I have no doubt that the invading English army then burned down every building for miles around. Our monks therefore probably belonged to 1303 when, as you will see later, they too were probably killed merely for being in the wrong place at the wrong time!)*

Now we were invited to move through Crystal's house to feel for ourselves any psychic energies that were there that evening. There was no doubt about it, in the main livingroom there was a definite feeling that all was not well: it was as if the three of us were not alone….almost as if we were being watched.

Francesca walked around and then stopped for a considerable time and looked up meaningfully to the lintel above the main east-facing window. Crystal noticed this and said that that was where their Christmas cards were hanging the previous year when they all began to move about eratically. She said it scared the living daylights out of everybody and almost spoilt Christmas day by causing her father to consider leaving.

The medium then walked across to the other side of the room and close to another smaller window she stopped once more and looked down at the floor. To be truthful she did not quite 'stop' in the way that you or I might but in a way that I have seen her do before. If you are watching her it appears that she wants to move her feet over the next bit of flooring (or whatever) but her feet just **will not walk forward**. *(see also Volume 1, page 111.)* It was as if something below the floor was preventing her from walking forward and I rather guessed what.

"I think you've found something down there Francesca?" I said.

She turned and looked at me,

"Yes, there are two monks buried below here!" and turning towards the window by her right shoulder she added, "And there are another three buried just outside the window …where that small tree is now growing."

I watched her side-step the floor area and stop to converse with Crystal who was looking flushed. I could see that she knew something that neither Francesca nor I did.

"What's up Crystal?" I asked.

"We'd better ask my daughter, Joan, the answer to that," she replied and called thorough the house for the daughter that we had never seen. Joan came through and we were introduced before Crystal got her to tell her story for it was she who had seen the apparitions more often than anyone else in the family.

"Tell our visitors what you saw and where you saw it in this room, Joan,"

Joan, in her early twenties, told of how she had seen at least one apparition of a monk moving in the room possibly accompanied by the shadow of a second one. When asked where in the room the apparitions appeared she pointed at once to the floor upon which Francesca was standing at that very minute. I could not help but smile quietly to myself.

About that point Crystal made it known to us that now that she knew more or less what was haunting her property, she did not want it formally driven away. It was not actually harming her family and they were not harming it, so that's how things would remain.

Time was running short and as we were saying "Goodbye" to the family in their yard Francesca suddenly said,

"Oh, I see the men in monk's clothing moving about and tending a small water-wheel," My ears pricked up again and I asked the medium to describe the wheel and its orientation to the property. (I had my reasons for this, of course.)

Francesca described a small waterwheel of about five feet diameter which was propelled by water running under the paddles (technically an 'undershot' wheel). I asked her to stand with her arms out to demonstrate the orientation of the wheel and I am pleased to say it was sitting in exactly the position that it would have to sit in order to accept the flow of water from the only possible water-source. That must have been supplied as a small stream that flowed slightly downhill to the site from the only direction possible because of the curvature of the field surface. Everything dovetailed as it should! Full marks to Francesca!

The wheel was so positioned that the water exiting from it shot outwards over a precipice and the whole thing was very close indeed to where the graves were. I must admit that the proximity of the graves to the wheel rather worried me. Why were those pseudo-monks not buried in some hallowed ground, or at least in a local graveyard? Even if we could leave aside questions about the religious aspects of their burial surely common decency would mean that they were buried in some sort of line rather than just in some random juxtaposition. Could it be that they were killed during the previously-mentioned English counter-advance into Scotland in reprisal for the awful 'burnings' of 1297? Did 'counter-burnings' take place? They may well have done for, as I have already said, the English came back to that very spot in 1303 and took revenge for what had happened six years before. This is when I wish I knew more history! Whatever the reason, these monks seemed to be buried where they fell. Were they perhaps protecting their mill from something when they were slain? I just do not know the answer but hopefully it might well be discovered through work of an archaeological nature at some point in the future.

****

I still had the puzzle of why the old monk appeared to be pointing towards Rosslyn Chapel as his base when that chapel would not have existed in his day.

When I got home that night I got out an accurate map of the area and looked at the position of the village of Auchendinny with regards to the position of Rosslyn Chapel.

There was nothing strange jumped out at me there but then I noticed something which I am sure had great meaning, for if I extended the straight line from Auchendinny **through** Rosslyn Chapel for another three and a half miles we come to a monastery! We come to Newbattle Abbey, a famous Blackfriars monastery of the middle ages which held considerable power and influence in the area south of Edinburgh and which was known to have many 'daughter' establishments. Could the site we discovered be one of those establishments that had gone undiscovered up till now? The old monk was indeed pointing in the correct direction: it was I who wrongly thought he was pointing to Rosslyn when he was truly pointing over the fields to Newbattle Abbey. If he had lived (and died) around 1303 then there would have been **no such chapel** in his time for it did not come into being for another hundred years. If these men with the monk were indeed lepers then the five miles between them and the Abbey that looked after their needs, was indeed a respectable and acceptable distance by medieval standards.

I am pleased to say that at that point in my deliberations I was able to make contact with Dr Brian Moffat, The Director of Archaeology at another medieval hospital site south of Edinburgh, who very kindly volunteered to look up the old records at Newbattle Abbey on my behalf. Hopefully those ancient Latin archives might one day link Auchendinny in some way with that famous abbey.

About a week later I got a very nice letter from Mrs. Crystal Delaney thanking Francesca and myself for our work as well as telling us surprisingly that she had found out that the place-name, "Auchendinny", was ancient Gaelic meaning "Place of the burnings"! My heart leapt with excitement as you can imagine but this was soon dashed, for in my attempt to confirm what I had been told I found that the place-name in that ancient language actually meant, " Place of the high field".

I am a persistent character, however, *(as an entity once told me several times over, The Psychic Investigators Casebook, Vol. 1, page 159)* and I somehow felt inside myself that I should look more deeply into this place-name matter. I therefore contacted a professor of the Gaelic language and found that the word "*tinny*" meant "of the burnings" in Gaelic. That in turn meant that if Auchendinny had actually been spelled Auchen*tinny* at some point in the past, which is not without possibility, then it would indeed have meant, "place of the burnings". I reckon the old monk was quite correct in what he said and that the spelling of the village name had changed phonetically down the centuries.

One month later, I am sorry to say, research was not going my way for I had taken it upon myself to attempt to gain access to those ancient Latin documents from 1351. These, I knew existed and I understood that the word Auchendinny (or Auchentinny?) was first recorded there in text. Unfortunately Dr Moffat had to inform me that records of happenings which took place during the Middle Ages and which existed for many other areas around Edinburgh just did not exist for the Roslin area.

(The very fact that the little town is called "Roslin" while its famous chapel is called "Rosslyn" shows what confusion of name spellings was also taking place there as the years passed.)

While Dr Moffat told me that the monks of Newbattle Abbey usually kept good records it would appear that documents from some outlying areas like the Roslin/Auchendinny area were not being passed back into the central keeping of the monastery in the correct manner. At that point I began to doubt if I would ever find out if there really was a monastic outpost at Auchendinny and whether the spelling of that all-important name had changed down the years. Sometimes research can prove most daunting!

****

Mr. Robert Burns

Scotland's National Poet

The art of 'psychometry' is a gift many mediums have which enables them to link themselves almost immediately with memories concerning an item merely by touching it or picking the object up. It is one of the main clues to the operating mechanisms that lie behind the functioning of the psychic world and I always enjoy seeing psychometry being put into practice by a skilful medium.

When I first met Francesca she had carried out almost no psychometric work: not that she did not have the ability, for I believe that all mediums of worth have it, but because no one had ever required such a service of her. Volume one of this book holds several interesting cases of good psychometry by gifted mediums and now I add another case which I am sure will interest the reader just as much, for it assists us in understanding still further the life of Scotland's national poet, Robert Burns.

That man, born of humble farming stock in the middle of the 18th century spent his early days as a ploughman in Ayrshire, Scotland and in his thirty seven and a half years of life produced poetry which not only flowed from his heart but echoed the sentiments of his era more than any other writer. He was a man before his time and wrote of the equality of all men and women and the worth of each within his or her place upon this earth. He had a beautiful love for his own nation and yet he had total respect for others, their past and their individuality. So world-wide were the sentiments that he expressed in his poetry that he is probably the most widely known poet on this planet of ours…. a fact proved by the international rendering of, "Auld Lang Syne" which, although existing in part in his own day, was completely restructured and popularised by him in 1788.

It was some of the cherished possessions that this man had once owned that Francesca was asked to psychometrise late in 2003.

The Burns National Heritage Park, suitable sited in Alloway and adjacent to Burn's first home, houses considerable numbers of artefacts and much knowledge about this national poet and in 2003 was run by Mr. Nat Edwards, while the curator of the Burns Museum there was Ms. Eleanor Clark. These two persons were approached by Mr. Nick Kyle, a Council member of the Scottish Society for Psychical Research, with a view to two things.

The first was to see if there was a possibility that members of the Society could hold an overnight vigil on the property of the heritage group, either in the Old (supposedly haunted) Kirk of Alloway (which is mentioned in the famous poem, "Tam O' Shanter") or in Burns' cottage itself. The second thing that Mr. Kyle wanted was to see if the Burns Museum was willing to supply several items which were indisputably known possessions of the poet during his lifetime so that those items could be psychometrised to give further insight into that great man's life.

I am pleased to say that that far-seeing center manager agreed to both requests and so Mr. Kyle arranged that the curator of the museum should bring to his home on Tuesday, October 21st, four valuable items to be placed before a suitable medium so that they could be psychometrised while under the gaze of no less than three, strategically-placed video cameras. Because the work I do with Francesca was well known to Mr. Kyle he had faith enough in that work to invite us to get together with him for the task ahead. I was asked most sincerely by Mr. Kyle not to divulge beforehand the ownership of the objects and this I found easy to reassure him upon for I never tell Francesca anything about a forthcoming case prior to our visiting a site. That is how she herself prefers it for she does not want her mind swayed by extraneous thoughts beforehand.

We arrived by 7pm at Mr. Kyle's fine Glasgow house and while Francesca was taken into one room for a cup of tea I was led into the main room with the cameras and there upon a glass-topped coffee table were five objects laid out on tissue-paper squares. I immediately asked why five objects were present when I had been told that four were to be brought along and the reply came that a fifth object of the right era had been introduced to 'throw' or 'test' the medium. It had no connection with Robert Burns whatever. While being a little dismayed by such an action, I fully understood the motive and knowing that the talents of this world-class medium could handle such a situation, I made no objection to the 'rogue' object being mixed with the real items. I will now name the objects I saw before me in the order that Francesca actually picked them up later when the psychometry session began for real.

1) A hand-held seal for embossing sealing-wax on legal documents and the like. This was about two inches tall and had a small silver chain upon it.
2) A well-worn, leather-bound book of poems and notes approximately 7 x 4 inches.
3) A silver-cased pocket watch (without a chain).
4) A gold watch chain.
5) A writing pen set from the mid 1700s consisting of various quills, a bottle of ink and a pen-knife for sharpening the quills when needed. It was all housed in a neat little leather box.

Francesca was eventually ushered into the room by Mrs. Kyle along with Ms. Clark, the curator in whose keeping the artefacts were held, and set to work immediately.

It was almost with embarrassment that this talented lady picked up the seal and smiled as she asked,

"What is it?"

She held it between her hands and almost at once she raised one hand and began circling it horizontally above her head saying,

"This person always wore a white sort of scarf wound around his or her neck. It was not in any way a fancy scarf: it was not a lacy cravat or anything of that nature. It was merely a clean white length of cloth ".

While she had not even mentioned the gender of the owner of the mystery object she had already described the most noticeable thing about all paintings of Robert Burns, his liking for wearing such a neat white neck-cloth. We noted that it was well into the psychometry session before Francesca began using the word 'he' as opposed to such words as 'the owner' or 'the person concerned' and similar. (It is also of note that not in the entire evening did this medium ever use the word 'Burns' or 'Robert Burns'.) She went on to say that the seal she had in front of her had been handed down from father to son over the years. At one point the date 1704 came up in an indistinct way and I found myself wondering if the seal had been either manufactured in 1704 or perhaps purchased by Burns' father or grandfather at that date. The owner, Francesca said, enjoyed writing things down very much and had had very humble origins although later in life he allied himself with the grandeur of Edinburgh, the capital city of his country. There the seal's owner said (through Francesca) how much he had enjoyed the high life and the good things that such a city could offer. He was unequivocal in his thoughts that such "good things" were "wine, women and song" although perhaps I have put them in a different order than the poet himself might have done…who knows?

In spite of his delight at spending time in the bright lights of the capital city he said quite clearly that he was a lover of the countryside and nature and liked to live there also. This desire for ongoing union with nature and the hills and glens of his native land is something that comes through very clearly in his poetry and in fact he carried out a 'grand tour' of Scotland once his increased wealth allowed such a luxury. Through Francesca he almost shouted aloud,

"I am a Scotsman and am proud of it!" *(I write metaphorically)*

Unfortunately his living and working in Scotland meant that he was subject to the physical ailments of that country in his own day and Francesca said several times during the pychometry session that he had been an ill man for many years and had fully acknowledged his own ill-health. The illness appeared to lie mainly in his chest and may well have been tuberculosis. Whatever it was, he fought it as best he could but in the end it was that which killed him.

The picking up of the little leather-bound book changed the medium's demeanour almost immediately for she found herself with a very sad lady on the outskirts of Edinburgh and this was very much reflected in her outlook and words. She told of a fine lady from the Crammond area (down by the seashore) who wept regularly for a man she loved and who was not able to return that love. It was never mentioned why that situation had arisen but this lady could have been Clarissa who Burns certainly knew and found it impossible to court for she was already a married lady. Francesca described her as having a long dress which had puffy tops to the short sleeves and she wore a little hat which made the medium smile as she described it for it resembled the hat that "Little Bo Peep" of nursery rhyme fame is usually seen wearing in children's books. The video tape also shows Francesca actually wiping tears away from her eyes due to the sadness of the emotional stress of the lady concerned. The book itself, appears to have been either gifted to the lady by the man at one point or lent to her for a period. She certainly cherished the book and the thoughts that accompanied it but the fact that it is currently in the Burns Museum means, of course, that it must have been returned into Burns' keeping at some time in the past. (or perhaps donated to the museum by descendants of the lady concerned?)

The watch presented the medium with immediate thoughts of a person who thought of time as a precious thing ….which is rather appropriate for a man who was ill a lot of his life and who died at 37 years. Francesca told us how she saw the man continuously toying with this time-piece, moving it from hand to hand or from pocket to pocket in a sort of agitated manner. Again the man's love of writing came to the fore although not once in the whole evening did he use the words 'poetry' or 'poet'. He was a *'writer'* in his own mind and obviously an acute observer of humanity. He did say time and time again through Francesca that he so loved the finer life in Edinburgh, the drink and the women and when he was running short of money he would write another piece and sell it and then the money came in again for the next round of drinks and the high life. We think today of Burns being a 'National Bard' of high ideals. He may well have been a man of exactly that calibre but on the evening of October 21st he came across as a very shrewd man who knew how to make money as and when he needed it. "He was no man's fool!" is how Francesca put it and I'm sure she was correct.

It was at that point that this medium handed back the watch and looked next at the gold chain that lay close to it. There was an immediate look of both puzzlement and scorn on her face: it is very clear in the video film produced that evening. It was as if the possession of her mind by Burns (which undoubtedly was taking place almost as a 'mini state of possession') was still in place for she said,

"What is that doing here?" and then, "That has nothing at all to do with this evening! Nothing!" She reached forward in an almost angry state (certainly an 'annoyed' one) and pushed the tissue paper with the chain still upon it further away from herself and then bent a second time and pushed it yet further away until it nearly fell off the far side of the table.

I have never in five years seen Francesca annoyed, far less angry, but anyone watching that video can see a fierceness in the eyes at her having been cheated by having a fake item placed before her purporting to have belonged to the great poet.

I say in all seriousness that it was not Francesca looking out of those eyes but Robert Burns himself and I'm sure it was he who certainly felt annoyed at the intrusion of that extra object on the table, put there in his name. He wanted it pushed right off that table!

I knew then that that item must be the artefact placed upon the table to trick the medium for no one had informed me, up to that point, as to which of the five objects was the fake one. Her abhorrence of it was so definite! I looked across the room to a very serious-looking and wide-eyed Mrs. Kyle who nodded gently in reply to my enquiring glance. I find it most interesting…as you must…that this fake item was so easily picked out, particularly as no one had even told Francesca that there was to be a fake item placed before her for that evening's session.

(Remember in the White Hart Inn case how easily Francesca detected a 'fake' item put before her by the film crew?)

The medium then came back to her normal self again and reaching forward took into her hands the pen set. It mystified her just as the seal had done and she asked someone to tell her what she was holding.

The man's love of Edinburgh came to the fore once more and a list of places which he had enjoyed visiting was revealed. The first was the 'Netherbow' area which interested me particularly, for while it existed in Burns' day that part of the city has been demolished and the name has been long gone now for more than one hundred years. He also apparently visited the port of Leith nearby as well as parts of the Cowgate which was always well known for being not merely the poorest part of the city but also that part of the city that had more taverns and night life than any other area.

Writing and the need for money from writing, once again came to the fore and then the (one-way) conversation moved on to the medium asking Ms. Clark if she had been researching something as part of her job. (This question was necessary for Francesca had no idea at all who Ms. Clark was or why she was present in the room). Upon the curator replying that research was indeed part of her work Francesca said that "the man" knew what she was working towards and wanted to encourage her in her task. He said that it would all work out well for her as time went by.

Then came a strange series of statements which puzzled those who knew about Robert Burns, for the medium said quite unequivocally that the man relished his secret connections with royalty. At the same time she also said that she believed that she saw 'Big Ben' (the famous clock tower of the Houses of Parliament in London) away in the background. Initially there appears to be big problems here for as far as history knows, Burns never at any time left Scottish soil and even if he did he could not have seen Big Ben for it had not been built in his day.

Those who might not know this gifted medium and the way she works would be tempted to say that she was talking nonsense but having worked with her for five years I know better. I am quite prepared to believe that she saw a clock tower and wrongfully concluded that it was in London when, in fact, it might have been a completely different, but similar, clock tower in Edinburgh or wherever, but if Francesca said that there was a secret connection with royalty then I'll stick by that phrase, whether or not it makes sense to 'the experts'. In any case I believe that the problem solved itself eventually.

About three days later I drew down a dusty and broken book from the shelves of my bookcase. It had been printed in 1850 and looked every bit its age but it held not only a complete compendium of all Burns' poems but a lengthy treatise on his life. It was in that section that I believe I found the answer to at least part of the above problem and its solution lies deep in the history of the Scotland that Burns loved.

In 1306 Robert de Brus (Robert the Bruce) was declared king of Scotland and although his dynasty was not recognised by the kings of England, Robert Burns for one still looked upon that title as legal. When incoming money allowed him to do his grand tour of Scotland so that he could know better the nation that he held dear, Burns visited Stirling and then, close by, Alloa in Clackmannanshire. It was there that a very strange event took place and which may be the 'royal event' referred to by Francesca…. for it was certainly 'royal' in the eyes of Burns!

He was invited to stay at a castle that was probably Alloa Tower and was owned by a Mrs. Brus who claimed that she was descended from King Robert the Bruce of centuries before. As an ardent Scot, Burns would take this most seriously. It was during that stay that Mrs. Brus decided to honour the poet for his services to Scotland by creating him a knight of the realm! In all solemnity and before witnesses he knelt as she raised a sword and brought it down upon his shoulders before asking "Sir Robert Burns" to rise to his feet and continue doing good for his country as he went on his way.

Could this have been the "secret link to royalty" that Francesca brought to the fore? Was there some sort of large clock-tower in the proximity of that castle that the medium had wrongly concluded to be Big Ben? Perhaps time will discover the truth.

The talk of writing finally brought the medium into a very dramatic point in this poet's life …the thoughts he had upon his deathbed. I remind you, my readers, that she said that the quill set was something that this man cherished. He loved it so much in fact that he was actually holding one of the beloved quills in his hand in his last minutes of this life. He was thinking, Francesca said, that if he had his life to live over again he would make changes in it. He 'told' her that he wished he had spent more time with his family and the humble farming people of his early years who had loved him. In hindsight he said he was regretful of spending so much time in unproductive and almost meaningless enjoyment in the city. Francesca spoke softly and slowly as the video shows and with great and sincere meaning. There was a final long pause as the medium ceased to talk any more and then we saw her head gently tilt backwards and stay still in that position with her eyes looking blankly at the ceiling.

The pause was so great that I moved closer to the medium and asked her if she was all right. She answered in the affirmative but I could see that she was still far away in her mind.

"Is that him dead, Francesca?" I asked.

"Yes," replied that talented lady, who had tears in her eyes, "He died with his quill in his hand and thinking how much he had loved Scotland."

CHAPTER 4

FAMILY AFFAIRS

The Mismatch
Big Implications?
Two Smelly Cases
The Bell on the Gate

The Mismatch

Logic seems to dictate that a house is nothing more than bricks and timber and mortar but having worked psychically with houses as well as with people over the years I know for sure that there is a lot more to it than that. Houses appear to develop a "character" of their own as the years (or *centuries* in some cases) go by and that character is not always a pleasant and happy one. Somehow, when the house has seen within its walls either a very traumatic incident or a series of unhappy incidents then that seeps into the very fabric of the building…or appears 'held' by that fabric.

*(Researchers should note that those unhappy memories are **not**, in fact, held within the bricks and mortar themselves but are accessible **through** them. It should also be noted that the unhappiness does not leech out through the masonry by itself but through some invisible sensitivities in the mind of one of the occupiers. Some families can live in houses with a strong psychic link for years and feel absolutely nothing at all while other families can settle in the very same house and within the first week they are demented by manifestations attempting to get at them in one way or another. It's **not** 'all in the mind' but the mind is an important 'modem' to the psychic world and plays an important part in the degree to which the psychic world interacts with ours.)*

The house that I am about to discuss is in a delightful small town south of Edinburgh and on the coast: just a lovely place to have a holiday! It is a robust and elegant house of stone that was erected during the wealthy period of Victorian Scotland. That does not, however, protect it from being a sick house … or *"seek hoose"* as the Scots term it. It held that indefinable 'something' and whatever it was, it had debilitated the family who currently had it in its possession to such an extent that the family unit was breaking up. Yes, I know, it is an unfortunate sign of our times that families seem to break up at the drop of a hat these days but in this case the woman of the house was clever enough (or psychically sensitive enough) to realise that there was something wrong with the property. She knew there was something "not nice" in that house with them all and that it was decidedly detrimental to family relationships!

(If you are a potential researcher then you should note that statistically when someone says they feel the presence of the supernatural then the chances are very high indeed that they are correct. They therefore should be taken seriously at least initially. My own statistics from four hundred cases show that more than 99% of people can correctly detect the presence of the psychic world but almost none of them can correctly identify what particular part of that world is interacting with them.)

The lady who phoned me, Alice Toner, reported the following after she told me that she considered that some sort of catastrophic event was descending upon her family. The health aspect of herself and her child had been such that they both had ended up in hospital with separate maladies since they had taken up residence in their Victorian house about a year before. And leaving things like burst boilers and flooding to one side (for those can happen in any house) the stress of everything had caused the male partner to move out and live in rented accommodation about thirty miles away. Things had, in fact, got so bad that they had prepared themselves to put the house on the market and move on.

Even if all those things were mere chance it does not account for other happenings like footsteps often being heard moving urgently towards the front door or coming down the main staircase or rushes of air that were "just too much" to be a normal draught.

'Things' like flashes of movement caught the eyes of various members of the family as well as those of visitors to such a degree that some mirrors had to be taken down to save alarming people. There were various spots of 'unease' like the half-way landing on the stairs and the lower hallway and a strange business that occurred when the postman came down the path to deliver the mail. Sometimes light-sounding footsteps seem to run down the stairs as if some invisible person was about to catch the letters as they fluttered through the letterbox while a second set of heavier footsteps could also be heard running towards the same letterbox at times from a different direction within the house.

Anyway, there was enough in the initial contact from Mrs. Toner to give me a desire to visit the property with Francesca to find out a bit more. Little was I to realise that we were to find out more, long before we actually reached the property!

The story is this:-

We drove south out of Edinburgh on a dark and damp evening in late November 2003 and were about half way through our journey with fifteen miles yet to go towards our destination when we swung round a roundabout as we passed out of the attractive little country village of Drem.

"Oh my goodness! Oh my goodness!" I heard Francesca say and I turned and asked her what had caused such a sudden outburst.

"This is where the very first lady owner of the house came from! She lived on a farm right here. Her father was a wealthy farmer or landowner."

I was confused.

"Are you talking about something to do with the house we are about to visit this evening?" I said in disbelief.

"Yes, yes!" came the urgent reply, "I'm so glad you decided to come by this inland road and not the coast road or we might have missed this clue."

I could scarcely believe what I was hearing but having witnessed Francesca's outstanding abilities for many years I 'rolled with it' as they say.

"O.K, Let's hear what you're getting," I said as the lady beside me relaxed back into the passenger seat and closed her eyes.

"Oh she's such a little frail young lady! Not in the least what you'd think of as a farmer's daughter. She's been ill a lot and oh dear,……" Francesca paused for reflection, "I don't think that the lady has the best of mental health."

As we were both thinking of the young woman and her health, there must have been little surprise from the medium when I asked what the lady had finally died of.

I remember we were rounding a series of bends when the answer came,

"She says she died of 'the melancholy'."

I presumed, (I think correctly), that in today's terms '*the melancholy*' might well mean a catastrophic nervous breakdown and all that that entails and I was naturally sorry to hear of such a thing for it meant that the marriage may not have been a happy or satisfactory one for either of the parties concerned. How right my guess had been for Francesca then made known the fact that the entire marriage had been one of convenience from the very start. It was a sort of 'matrimonial deal' between a landowner of medium wealth and a young man who was an up-and-coming lawyer in the larger town nearby. They both, no doubt, thought that the other party was 'a good catch'. How sadly it all turned out said Francesca although we were still miles from our destination. She told of an almost completely loveless marriage where a bad mental state was made worse both by isolation and the thoughtless behaviour of her husband. Then she told me something that dovetailed completely with what Mrs. Toner had already told me (but which was completely unknown to this medium).

"He doesn't seem to consider that she is capable of even opening her own mail for no sooner does the postman approach the house than the husband rushes to the door to collect the letters before his wife can get there. I think he might even be depriving her of some of her own personal mail."

"What a terrible pity!" I answered, "If she was truly in a highly nervous state at the best of times then she'd be in a great need of mail from relatives and the like as a supportive mechanism for they had no TV in those far off days to chase away the 'blues'. I found myself not only amazed that the medium had tuned into this postman business but as often happens with me, I found myself greatly moved by the sadness of the situation, of perhaps years of mental unhappiness. What a terrible start for a new marriage and a new and lovely Victorian house! What dire and stressful memories must have been generated within its strong stone walls! No wonder it turned into a "sick house" where owner after owner came and went, only for the house to be sold on to some other unfortunate family after a small amount of time.

We arrived on time and used a flashlight to find our way up to the rear door as we had been instructed. We were ushered in by Alice and introduced to her friend June who was there as some sort of mental support.

(Psychic investigators must remember that while they, themselves, know how genuine they are, the client who is about to receive them does not. For all the client knows, even after making phone contact with you, you might be some sort of incense-swinging weirdo about to perform strange rites in their home and someone who might do more harm than good. Your first moments of meeting your client must therefore be of such a nature that it puts them at ease and fills them with confidence. As a genuine and dedicated psychic investigator, you should be glad if the client has invited a friend into her home for that all-important meeting with you and you should not be offended in the least by the presence of a third party.)

We sat around the table and had a glass of wine and a home-baked biscuit or two before we asked if we could walk around the house with Alice and June. As we walked through the lower corridor two things came immediately to Francesca's notice, the smell of lavender (from years gone by) and the presence of the swishing of long Victorian dresses of the same period. She stopped and looked towards a door and said that it had been changed at some point in the past. It was not the original door that had had so many unhappy memories for the lady who had been deprived of her mail by her arrogant (or over-protective) husband. June chimed in that it was near that door that she had heard the footsteps running towards it as the present-day postman came up the path, while Alice said that quite often she felt a wafting of air at that part of the corridor that she felt had come from 'swishing skirts'.

As this had been a Victorian house, a skeptic might say, correctly, that at least some of the things described by the medium could have been expected in any case and just for the record, I totally agree with that.

(A psychic researcher can not record as 'evidence' anything that might have been expected as a matter of course ... even if it did come from a proven medium.)

Now we moved up one flight of stairs to the middle landing in this tall house and we stood upon that landing as Francesca bowed her head in order to sense all the better, the psychic atmosphere at that spot. She said immediately that she heard the ringing of little bells as some servant was summoned to duty in the past and Alice herself added that she too had heard such bells tinkling although all the bells from Victorian times had been dismantled long before her family had purchased the property. Now as the medium stood on the soft carpet of the landing her gaze moved to the right and in through an open door to a large room beyond.

"I know whose room that is but he's telling me that I must not enter it. I know too that that was exactly the position with his wife and that she was the nervous lady who had been the initial owner of the house. The man was a lawyer I feel who did much of his work from this very room and he does not want any of his papers disturbed by anyone at all: that's why I've to stay out of the room. He still sees the room as he did in the late 1800's and I see him only from the back and seated at a very large table. He is using a strange quill-like pen as he writes some document or other about farm accounts. He's got rolled up scrolls everywhere around and many have pink ribbon tied around them. One very long roll is of particular importance and I feel that it might be the title deeds of this very house."

"Can you talk with the man, Francesca?" I said, "If we are to understand the situation here in 2003 we must know what took place in the life of this unhappy man all those years ago."

The medium's head was bowed once again as we all stood in silence on the landing.

"Oh what an unhappy man he was!" were the next words. "Oh what an unfulfilled marriage he had to an even unhappier wife for he appeared to live in one part of the house after a time while his wife was forced to live in another part. He tells me that they did have a son though and that "he grew to manhood" and prospered here in the town and he would like this present family (i.e. Alice and her partner) to put down their roots here and prosper also."

At that point the spirit-man from the past suddenly seemed to mellow: some sort of *realisation* appeared to set in.

"He tells me that he realises that over the years the unhappiness that formed around him within these walls has been felt by every family who lived here and up till now he has not been sorry in the least about that. Now things are changing for him for he says that he feels the compassion and sorrow on his behalf from all the people present in his house tonight. He feels too that for the very first time someone has taken the trouble to make contact with him and to look at the bitterness that he lived through. He is actually making a point of telling me how pleased he is that the woman of this present family has taken steps to make contact with him and it is this that has caused him to re-think matters. He says how wrong it now seems that he has kept his bitterness purposefully lingering in this house."

It was all making perfect sense to we, the listeners, but there was more and better to come.

"The man says to you, Alice, that as a reward for your wanting to alleviate his unhappiness the lawyer will soon show himself in profile to you in the mirror you use." (I looked at Alice and saw that she was unsure whether or not this was something that she would like to happen.)

"I will now leave this house forever and I will take with me *all the others** and all the unhappy memories!"

(*We really have no idea what this phrase means but we presume that it means at least the psychic presences of himself and his wife as well as someone who had not been mentioned in detail. His son perhaps? Could he too have been part of this unhappy group?)

There the communication suddenly ended and while neither Francesca nor myself knew the "feel" of that house the other two ladies present said that there was an **immediate** change in the warmth and ambience of the place. June said that a cold air draught that had been moving at the back of her as we had stood there listening to the medium had stopped suddenly.

Some other things of note you might also like to read about:-

1) That the lawyer liked the smell of the polish used by Alice and the fact that she and her family were trying hard to bring the property up to a high standard.

2) That Francesca had initially kept hearing that someone had been talking about "Bow Bells" *(a church in central London)*. Alice said that until comparatively recently she worked in the law courts in central London and within earshot of the sound of the Bow Bells.

3) That the position of a rowan tree in the garden that had been mentioned in the title deeds would come into conversation soon.

4) That the family would find the gravestone of the lawyer and his wife in a cemetery to the east of the house and not far from it.

5) That Francesca predicted that the family would slowly start to move together again "by Christmas" but that it would all take time to come to fruition.

Let us hope for all concerned that that prediction holds true. (*Frankly, predictions of any kind worry me a bit and I deal with them in depth in another publication*.) While only time will tell, I think that Francesca and I at least helped matters that evening and no matter what action we took I can't see how we could have made them any worse.

Before going to press I have been told that the move to put the house up for sale has been halted for the time being... and hopefully for a long time to come.

****

Big Implications?

A Small Case with a Large Clue?

Apparitions are somewhat rare in the psychic world even although the false public perception is that ghosts are almost the only form of psychic phenomena around. They most certainly exist but showing themselves to us is far from being the most basic way that that world has for communicating with us. Perhaps only one paranormal incident in five hundred contains any sort of recognisable visual element to it and so I am pleased to give you a new and recent example now.

John and Judy Forsyth, a couple in their early forties, had been part owners of a large hotel and caravan complex in the south of the country but due to both business pressures and family pressures they chose to move north to Largo Bay in Fife which stretches from Leven to Elie and was well known to Robinson Crusoe (Alexander Selkirk) of desert island fame because he grew up there. There the couple put their heart and soul into further development of this seaside site and everything was paying off for them although it was taking its toll of John's health for he worked and worried by both night and day.

By the late summer of 2004 what few hours were left for sleep were spent in a splendid and modern mobile home on the site and it was there that Judy encountered several interesting phenomena which culminated in her most definitely seeing an apparition. When I was first told about it over the phone, I thought (as Judy herself did) that a ghost in a modern mobile home in a woodland site by the sea where there was no pre-history of habitation was unlikely but I knew also that it was not impossible. I realised as we talked on the phone that if this lady really had truly seen such a figure hovering above their bed and looking down on her sleeping husband then it was most likely a deceased relative moving in on John for some unknown reason. I decided to visit and so Francesca and I arrived at this delightful site on a sunny morning in mid August to be welcomed by John. He was a well-built man and did not seem, at first sight, to look like a man with health problems but that is what we learned from Judy when we moved into their kitchen and sat down to talk about the general situation surrounding the case in hand.

The first thing of interest that was made known to us was that both John and Judy had had psychic experiences in a hotel building that they had once owned so the pair of them were not new to the supernatural. That also told me that either one of them or even both of them were sensitive to the paranormal world. I realised that if the spirit world had used their minds to enter our world on a previous occasion then it was more than possible that it may have done so once again. *(Persons with even minor mediumistic abilities, whether they are conscious of them or not, almost always retain these abilities throughout their lives.)*

In this new case I was very lucky that Judy expressed herself so well in writing and I will quote freely from her notes which she made out for me at the time.

"About three weeks earlier I had woken at 1.20 am and was wondering what had wakened me when suddenly a bright star-like light moved across the bedroom in a downward arc disappearing towards the floor in the corner of the room close to the foot of my bed."

The lady felt that it might have been about the size of a tennis ball or a bit less.

This slim and petite woman then told us that she had wakened at 1am precisely on Saturday 14th August to see the top half of a male figure "floating in the air" above the foot of John's side of the bed.

"The image was looking directly at John and I was seeing it almost side-on to a degree. I could not believe how like John it was in its facial features! I kept looking from one 'John' to the other and back again. The image was staring fixedly at my husband which I found unnerving and it was black and white and gray but with some sort of fawn-colored band under its arms…almost as if it had a fawn towel wrapped around the chest and waist area. Its

arms were folded and in spite of the fact that I was slowly starting to sit up in my bed the image did not seem to notice me at all at first.

I could not take in fully the enormity of what I was seeing and I looked down at my sleeping husband to see if he was reacting in any way at all to all this. He seemed fast asleep and was in fact snoring quite loudly. In spite of this I somehow got the stupid idea into my head that perhaps this was John's 'spirit self' leaving his body and that my husband might have died in his sleep so I bent over and listened to see if his heart was still beating. It was!

After that, I turned again and looked at the image once more. At that point it seemed to turn towards me full frontal and I watched its eyes move until they alighted on me and our eyes were soon looking directly into each others. I knew that now it was acknowledging my existence for the first time. I got the definite feeling that the ghost had in some way been taken aback by my being there: it was almost as if it had never even considered that there would be anyone present other than John.

It was then that it began to disappear from the center outwards. Soon there was a dark gray mist on the outer edge with a very pale gray color in the center then the outer edge seemed to turn into millions of tiny dots before it disappeared altogether."

Judy gave an exceedingly good description of the apparition proper also,

"The image was life-size and looked exceedingly like my husband except that it appeared to be about 20 years older than John. It was also a bit broader across the shoulders and had a more rounded face. It had wavier hair than John and more hair on its chest although all the other features were in common with him. It had no clothes on to the waist apart from that fawn-colored towel. Its arms were crossed but perhaps that was to hold up the towel. There was no expression on the face and the eyes did not blink in any way. The figure appeared to be completely intent upon looking at the sleeping John.

I felt that just after the apparition noticed me it came a bit closer as if to get a better look at me and all the while John never once woke up!"

It is also very worthy of note that when Judy was telling her tale to Francesca and me after we had arrived she said that as she watched the apparition's dark hair she saw one lock that was longer than the others fall forward over the left brow of the ghost man as he moved his head.

To summarise this part of the tale, I think that brave Judy should be congratulated upon the panic-free manner in which she handled the situation, for her actions gave to science a very clear description of what a ghost can look like when studied at first hand. Well done Judy!

(Researchers may like to know that the disappearance of apparitions is as interesting as the way they appear and that the method of disappearance described above is one of the standard exiting systems employed by the spirit world. I must also point out that the reverse can also take place where apparent solidity at the outside of the shape seems to turn to a mist and starts to deplete the image as it works inwards and towards the center. There are many variations in the methods of an entity going from sight and I feel that the means by which they disappear are almost as interesting as means they use to make themselves visible in the first place. There must be a reason behind the different methods used but I have so few firsthand accounts of this that I have been unable to put together even tentative rules by which the psychic world assembles and dissembles apparitions.)

To cut a long story short, Francesca said that the male entity (who turned out to be an *(initially)* unknown Uncle of John's called 'Reg'), was worried about break-downs in family bonds. He was worried to such a degree that he had decided to attempt to draw to John's attention the fact that he really must take action to pull the family together once more before it totally disintegrated. (Readers will like to know that in a very emotional private conversation with us about half an hour later, John told us the whole truth surrounding the family break-downs to which Francesca had referred and it was indeed a very sad story.)

Our clever medium lady revealed, however, that this *(then unnamed)* man was not the only player in the room for he had come along with a dear old lady who had *not* made herself visible to Judy. The four of us stood in the room as I asked Francesca to describe the lady she saw so very clearly and *presently(!)* standing precisely where the male entity had stood staring and yet a lady whom the rest of us could not see at all. I looked towards John as a very clear description of an older lady came from Francesca. Within seconds tears welled up in the eyes of this big, well-built man and I could see that while I had no idea whom it was that Francesca was describing John knew only too well. Judy walked around to his side of the bed and hugged John as he wept openly and unashamedly for our medium went on to tell of the love that this old lady had had for him while she was on earth.

Once John had dried his tears Judy said,

"Here is why John is crying......,"

And the pair then led Francesca and I through to the lounge (where we had not yet been) and there on the sideboard was a photograph of the dear old lady ...and precisely as Francesca had described her. She was standing outside the hotel with which John and Judy had once been associated. This lady was, in fact, John's grandmother who had brought him up from the age of six and who had shrewdly guided him in the early years of his successful business career. Francesca quite rightly told the couple that the grandmother had given John her ring as a keepsake about a year before she died.

At that point the conversation turned rather strange (as sometimes does happen in this sort of investigation) for Francesca found herself telling John, on behalf of his grandmother, to check the oil and water levels in the car. While no comments were made about this strange interlude at the time, you will see later in this account, a letter sent by Judy to myself about two months later in which all is explained.

Secondary information came flooding in through Francesca now and she said that someone who had been a former colleague of John's, by the name of "Andy", was plucking up courage to write to him regarding some sort of reference. John replied at first that he had never known anyone called "Andy" or "Andrew" and then he suddenly remembered that he had but added that it was not any sort of close friendship merely and 'employer/employee' relationship. More of this later too!

I will now move back to an extremely interesting fact that I have already revealed to you. Have any of my readers who are also dedicated researchers spotted an unusually interesting fact at all? I will not blame you if you did not for it is such a little fact on the surface.....but yet it holds tremendous importance for researchers of the paranormal! As I have already written in other publications, "Clues to the psychic world are all around us …if only we have the wit to see them!"

You might wish to pause for a few minutes to re-read the mid part of this case again before you move on …just to see if you can spot this enormous clue that Judy just slipped in as a "throw away" comment.

****

Here is the clue you may have missed:-

You will remember that as Judy watched the apparition move from one position to another his hair "fell forward over his left brow" in much the same way as it might have done had he been a living person of flesh and blood. Now does that not strike you as strange? It is strange for it implies that our earthly *gravity* may have actually been interacting with the immaterial structure of this apparition. His hair fell forward presumably for the same reason as yours or mine might have done if we had bent forward over some sleeping person. We know that our hair would have moved for it must be acted upon by gravity like all things physical but I would never have guessed before this John and Judy case that the same gravity might also be acting on visitors from the psychic world!

I still find this fact difficult to equate with all the other facts I know for it has far-reaching implications. Just think of this, for example:-

Some ghosts appear to walk above our present floor surfaces for the simple reason that our floors have sunk down from the days when they walked the same floors. That is reasonably understandable …or at least seems logical. We must now look slightly differently upon such a thing if apparitions are subject to our gravity for we are forced to ask ourselves why gravity does not pull them down onto our floor level. The whole business almost implies that gravity is tightly linked to "time". The ghost from the 17th century floor is being pulled down to its floor …..in, say,1606 but the gravity of 2004 seems irrelevant to it if it floats above our floor. That, to me, illustrates that somehow gravity is linked to the time and date of its initial 'use'. John and Judy's ghost was very much in the year 2004 …proved by the fact that it interacted to a minor degree with Judy. Was that why it was susceptible to 'our' gravity? I'm sure you will agree that we could get into all sorts of mental turmoil here.

For the true thinkers amongst you, all this and more is being dealt with by myself in a forthcoming technical publication on the psychic world for it all gets too complicated to go further into in this simple book of cases.

****

Often when Francesca and I visit family homes I am never too sure by the end of the visit whether the family has believed a single word of what we told them. Francesca knows better than I do about how we have been received and while we bid our client "Goodbye" and lots of nice words are spoken, once the door is closed behind us then the truth will be spoken between husband and wife. So it was in this case! I know that because some weeks later, when I was enjoying a holiday in Spain, I took the essence of a phone call from Judy that had been relayed to me through my sister who was looking after my house in Scotland.

My mystified sister told me that someone called Judy had called and wanted to apologise profusely to both me and "my medium lady". She said that she had actually disbelieved much of what had been said to herself and her husband but now she knew that it was *all true* and so she felt so humble and apologetic. Judy said that she would write to me once I returned home so that I could read chapter and verse of precisely what amazing discoveries the couple had made since our meeting in August.

On November 12th 2004 I received the letter that I had been told to expect and I now lay it before you in a paraphrased format:-

"Dear Mr. Lawrie,

I would just like to say "Thank you!" for your time and support. The atmosphere in the bedroom is now gone and things are much quieter now that my husband has looked into all the things mentioned by the medium lady.

We now know that this lady was most accurate!

The ghost man I saw was John's Uncle Reg. My husband did not know that he had an Uncle Reg until his mother told him! He had also been a farmer for much of his life, like John, and hence what the medium said about him "poaching" on neighbouring land makes perfect sense.

Reg, we now know, looked similar to my husband and was indeed older for he was nearly retiring age when he died……which is probably why I saw someone who was similar to my husband but considerably older.

Your lady mentioned an "Andrew" or "Andy" which mystified us. Can I say that just three days after you came to our house an "Andy" rang us to ask my husband for a reference! Andy had been a young man who had worked with my husband for a number of years.

The lady medium also mentioned another spirit person in the bedroom and this was my husband's grandmother who died on Oct. 3rd 2003 at an age of 96. This dear old lady was always concerned about the oil and water levels in the car engine and even to the end we always had to check those if she was going to travel in our car.

The "Elizabeth" mentioned by the medium is my husband's brother's little girl.

I could not understand it when the medium said that John had not taken his medication in the prescribed manner lately but I asked him about that after you had gone and he confessed that he had missed two days of pills …which is **very unusual** for him. Until then I was under the impression that I **always** knew when John was skipping his medication.

The medium was 'spot-on' when it came to that business about the vet having to be called "soon", for within days the horse caught her jaw on a fence post and ripped two nasty holes in her skin. The little pony was rather unwell for a bit but has made a full recovery.

Once again, thank you,

Judy Forsyth   "

After that I don't think I need to add any sort of formal ending, do I?

****

Two Smelly Cases

Just as the psychic world can project sights and sounds on behalf of the spirit occupants of that "realm" so too can it project smells. This is not done in any sort of haphazard way and when psychic smells reach us they always have some meaning, although that is not always immediately understood by us. Sometimes the smell is meant to 'say' something like, "I love you and remember you" or "Please know that I am at peace" while much of the time it is a general attention-seeking mechanism as a precursor to a heightening bond between someone in our world and someone in the next. Such smells, as you will soon see in the two following accounts, seem to act totally differently to our usual day-to-day smells for psychic smells are 'trapped' in a very limited and definite area. Psychic smells do not (and cannot) waft about. They have a very precise locus and they stick to that unless it is in their interest to move to another locus for some reason. Strange though it may seem, no amount of open windows or draughts will shift a psychic smell …….until, that is, it wants to move of its own volition! *(See also volume 1, page 31)*

(Researchers should know that almost all contact between the psychic world and our own starts through some attention-seeking process of some sort. These are many and very, very varied and come in a whole multitude of ways to all our senses. They can come to us as a soft and loving touch to our cheek as we sleep in the night or as a dramatic and monstrous visual fabrication of a seven foot tall half-man/half goat in one of our rooms. It can come as the smell of a rose around the favorite chair of a departed loved-one or it can even come, believe it or not as an incoming phone call which has not come in through the usual telephone exchange mechanism. These are all examples of psychic projections that I have actually encountered. (see also 'The Psychic Investigators Casebook, Vol. One')

This chapter that you now read is about to cover several different smells that the author has encountered recently, all of which are attention-seekers saying, "I am here. Please know of my existence and my story and recognise my presence."

Naturally, I give accounts of the circumstances surrounding the initial bonding between the spirit person and the human beings involved.

****

The Dead Fish-lady

My own house was built in 1843. It was built next to a church because it was the home for all the clergymen who preached in that church for nearly 130 years before that house was finally sold to me because the church authorities had let it get into such a sad state of disrepair. As an account of "Psychometry at Kingskettle" shows (Vol.1 of the above-mentioned book), it has its entities hanging around in the same way as almost all buildings of that age have. From the first year of my occupancy I realised that in the second week of July (and occasionally in the first week of December also) a strange happening was taking place which I now know is psychic in origin. My family noticed it in some years but not in all years and it was as follows:-

In late afternoon the smell of an old-fashioned type of sweet-smelling pipe tobacco could be smelled around an armchair which was positioned to the left of the fireplace in the main drawingroom. This smell could be walked into and walked out of but it could not be wafted away or moved around the room by flapping at it. It was centered purely around the left hand side of the fireplace and even in the early days we rather suspected that it was psychic in origin especially as we found that if we hurried into the kitchen at that precise time, that room stank of a Scottish fish delicacy called 'Finnan Haddie'. That in itself was a sort of give-away as to the psychic nature of the smell for while the distinctive smoked fish Finnan Haddie was a well-known dish in past years it is really quite a rarity now in an era of pizzas and fried chicken. The two smells being concurrent and short-lived also seems to point to the unusual nature of the event.

Either it did not occur in July, 2003 or if it did, I was not in the house when it took place. There did occur, however, a similar sort of event and I am pleased to tell you that as I was the second person to come across it on that day, it could not have been some fabrication of my own fertile mind. My daughter, Fiona, came across it seconds before me and the story is this:-

Monday July 21st was a lovely warm and sunny afternoon and my daughter and grandson, Barrie, decided that after lunching with me they would stroll in the garden and so moved out through the front door with myself walking close behind. At the very moment of passing through the doorway Fiona stopped suddenly and sniffed and looked around in puzzlement but without saying a word. I was by her side in a split second and I too sniffed. We looked at each other and said almost simultaneously, "Fish!" but then after a few more sniffs we changed our minds slightly for we then said to each other, "Its not really fish: its more like the smell on a beach with saltwater and old seaweed lying around with a fishy smell mixed in". And that was the final definition that we put upon the thing.

That was at 2.15pm and for the next 25 minutes, until it disappeared we tried all sorts of experimentation with the mysterious smell for it did not move away from that initial spot on the front door step.. We wandered out from the doorway into the middle of the lawn to see if it was somehow being blown in from the sea which was twelve miles away but there was no trace of it at all in the open. The moment either of us moved forward away from the left hand side of the front door *(i.e. as we looked outwards)* it just was not there! And the moment we moved as little as a single pace into the house we could no longer smell it so it was not sort of wafting into the house from outdoors. We also tried standing at the right hand door pillar but it was not there at all. It only occurred on the left of the door as one was going out.

The strength of the smell could never be described as "strong" or "overpowering" but neither was it weak. It somehow came and went in little bursts of some sort and did so for a full 25 minutes for at 2.40pm we could smell it no longer and moved away to roam around the garden.

We noted that it did not appear to be detectable by young Barrie who was merely four feet tall at that point in his life and we wondered whether he was just not susceptible to it or whether it was only manifesting itself at a height above his head and therefore could not be smelled by him. We eventually found that by lifting Barrie up until his feet were about two feet from the ground his head appeared to be at a height where he too could smell the smell.

My readers might suspect that, as a dedicated psychical researcher, I am perpetually looking for "spooky" explanations for things where there are none. That is not correct and although the smell did puzzle me I could not believe at that point that it had any psychic element to it at all: it had been merely a funny smell that we had encountered at the front door.

Now coincidence took a hand in matters for about five days later I got a phone call from a family near Edinburgh because a serious urine/ammonia smell that had been infesting a house for a long, long time suddenly and without any warning became grossly worse. In fact it so overwhelmed them that they had taken to fleeing the house and driving around in the countryside until the stench disappeared….which could be as much as two hours after it started.

When you encounter a smell of that intensity which comes and goes suddenly then you can count on it being of psychic origin and so I agreed to visit along with my medium friend as soon as possible.

On July 29th therefore, I found myself in the car with my medium friend and heading into East Central Scotland towards Mr. and Mrs. Wadkins and their unenviable problem.

*(Dedicated researchers might like to be reminded that the smell of urine is the most common of all smells emanating from the psychic world, followed by tobacco, followed probably by lavender. Perhaps here too I should remind you that while I have used the word "coincidence" I now know, as a researcher into all things psychic, that there really is no such thing as coincidence. In almost all cases, things that **appear** linked **are** in fact linked but not in the way that most of us imagine. Events in the psychic world respond to laws that we, on Earth, can hardly conceive of …and one of these is that events which have taken place **later***

than *primary events can actually effect or even trigger those first events. Try working that one out sometime when you feel in a mood for mental puzzles! "Not possible!" you say. I understand your feelings entirely but I must beg to differ for as I always tell people, "The psychic world is much, much wilder than your most wild imaginings!")*

But back to our main theme:-

Francesca and I ground slowly out of the city of Edinburgh during the evening rush-hour traffic …..a situation forced upon us by having two completely different cases to attend to in a single evening (Mr. and Mrs. Wadkins case as well as another one). Naturally enough we chatted about smells as Francesca sat in the passenger seat and I told her a bit about the one my daughter had detected outside my own front door. She seemed interested but she knew that, as usual, I was purposefully withholding details so that her mind would not be unduly influenced by what she was hearing.

"Francesa," I said to this clever lady, "Could it be remotely possible that we had something paranormal around us a few days ago or was it just puffs of sea breezes blowing in from the water all those miles away?"

We edged slowly forwards through yet more traffic as she shut her eyes and moved into a world that few of us have ventured into.

I must now point out, for reasons that will soon become clear, that while Francesca and I work together at least once a week we do not frequent each others homes. I have never been inside her house and she has only once been in mine and that visit was made, if I remember correctly, on a dark winter evening. She therefore would find it impossible to visualise the details of the outside of my home …and yet she knew something about it that she could not have known by the usual means.

"I can see a very old-looking lady standing just outside your front door. She looks too old to be doing the job that she is doing for she is going from house to house selling fish. She is almost eighty years old and is dressed in the traditional costume of the Scottish 'fish-wives' of that period. That is, she is wearing a white and blue stripped dress and a white pinefore tied around her waist and she has a wickerwork basket hanging over her shoulder which is full of fish for sale."

While what Francesca was saying was interesting, it signified absolutely nothing for there were such women going around all the time in the towns and cities of Scotland right up till about 1950…. and even yet little travelling fish vans still do that job.

Then we moved onto something much more interesting,

"She tells me that she liked coming to your house because there was a man there who understood about the sea and had been well-travelled upon it and so she could not only sell fish with regularity there but could also have a good conversation with the occupant of your house on matters of the sea at the same time."

(Regretfully, at that point, I had no idea at all about the identity of the man concerned. The only possible candidate that I could think of was the entity who sits in an invisible chair in my drawingroom and smokes away at his pipe on the second week of July sometimes. I mentioned him at the start of this chapter and he seems to be associated with a simultaneous fish smell in the kitchen as I have already told you.)

While I was trying hard to think of who this sea-loving gentleman might be, Francesca in the passenger seat next to me then began discussing something that I did know a lot about and that was the structure of my house.

"Archie, do you have stone pinnacles upon the top of your house somewhere…on a turret or somewhere like that?" She then indicated by putting one of her hands near her waist and the second near her chin that the items she had in mind were about 17 or 18 inches tall.

The question quite took me aback, for in 1843 when the place was built of lovely sandstone there had indeed been four nicely carved pinnacles placed upon the four highest points on the building: two at the front and two at the rear. In 1905 they were still securely in place for I have an old sepia photograph in the form of a postcard postmarked in that year showing them clearly on the highest points of the building. However by the time that I bought the house in the 1960s three of the four had gone completely. Two of those I have found no trace of but when digging in the soil in 1970 I found that one of them had been buried there about 5 yards from the front door. It was all weather-worn and I could see by the corroded state of the base that it had possibly crumbled at some point and had fallen from the building to the ground. I had always assumed that this probably took place during one of the winter storms at some time between 1905 and 1970. What Francesca then told me cast quite a different light upon matters!

"Yes, Francesca," I replied, "There were indeed pinnacles built upon this house when it was new." I purposely did not go on to tell her the details of their demise but I did tell her that I believed them to be bigger than she had indicated. I said I thought them to be around 25 or 26 inches tall. You will soon see why I wish I had kept my big mouth shut on that aspect!

"Well then," she said, "You must have one missing now for I am being permitted by the old fish-seller woman to look out through her eyes and I am looking upwards and I see a great stone pinnacle hurtling down upon me and know that because of my age and infirmity I cannot get out of its way in time!"

What a truly astounding sentence in many different ways is it not!

I was instantaneously both shocked and amazed at what I was hearing.

"The woman tells me that she died shortly after the dreadful event!"

After my gasps of amazement I pulled myself together enough to ask,

"Did she die in hospital or in her home?"

"No, Archie," replied the medium, "She died there on your doorstep! It was in mid July."

I was truly flabbergasted: I had no idea that such a tragedy had ever taken place there.

The whole thing was amazing, truly amazing! And it was just as well that I was inching the car forward at a crawl through the heavy traffic for, frankly, my knees were shaking with emotion at what I have just heard.

Before sitting down to write this account on the following day, I remembered that I still had the pinnacle I had dug up for I had placed it on a pile of spare rock at the far end of the garden and so, taking out a tape measure, I found it and measured it, looking at it with a sort of new reverence since it may well have been the cause of someone's death. From top to bottom it measured exactly 17 inches.

Francesca had been right about the size and I had been wrong!

More than that, I looked up at the apex from which the stone had fallen and came to the conclusion that if it had toppled towards the north then its trajectory would have no option but to make it slide down a broad stone coping to fall to earth exactly at that fatal spot outside my front door. It would slither down the coping and then hurtle through the air directly above the left hand side of the front door!

I now had a double problem for not only did I have a 'ghost man' sitting (contemplatively?) smoking sweet Victorian tobacco in my drawingroom in mid July but now I had a fish-selling lady who was killed apparently outside my front door in mid July also. Could those dates be coincidental? Was there some sort of link between those two events?

Did the man in the chair know the fish-selling woman? Was he the man who loved the sea? Was he totally traumatised by the sudden death of the visitor to his front door …particularly as she and he had something in common? And did the thought that he could have prevented the catastrophe by seeing to the proper maintenance of the building worry him to his dying day?

Tragic deaths on doorsteps are not occurrences that take place every day and thus the one mentioned by Francesca must surely have been recorded in a local newspaper of some sort …or so I initially thought…even although it could have been as far back as 1895 *(allowing for the above-mentioned postcard with that 1905 postmark having been printed ten years earlier.)*

I decided that I really must make time to look into this matter more deeply.

Firstly I contacted the office of the local newspaper, The Fife Herald, which I knew had covered the news in this area for many, many years. Surely, I thought, they must have back copies going back till goodness knows when. I phoned them to ask the obvious questions and while they were very helpful they said that they no longer kept back copies on the premises if they were earlier than 1900. They said that they had surrendered their older editions to the Archives Department of St Andrews University.

My next stop was therefore at the university for I live merely twenty minutes drive from that lovely town. After giving over my credentials and becoming a member of the library under 'Visitor' status I was advised that the newspaper that would be most use to me would be the Fife News because it had dealt with the news under 'village-by-village' headings since 1846. Some of these were on microfiche while later editions were there as bound editions. Each bound edition covered two years of events and news. I elected to start at the years 1900 and 1901 and move 'upwards' towards modern times in my search for news of the above tragic accident, the name of the woman involved and the name of the clergyman who lived in my house at that time.

I did not have to spend much time looking through these ancient pages to get to grips with the person who lived in my house at that period in time for it was the Reverend Mr. Arthur Simmons M.A. It was only after reading through several hundred editions of the Fife News, however, that I realised that this very man might well have been the actual person who was so admired by the lady who was struck down by the falling stonework. Francesca said very clearly that the man whom the fish-seller enjoyed holding conversation with was a man who had travelled widely and who could talk with her on "things of the sea and travel". Our Mr. Simmons could most certainly do that and more! The man appeared to be called upon to give lectures all over the place upon his travels in France, Italy, Sicily, North Africa, Egypt, and the Holy Land. Not many clergymen, even today, could give such a good world-wide account of themselves! And how had he gained such knowledge? Had he read up well on such places? Was he merely regurgitating knowledge that he had learned elsewhere?

No! Not a bit of it! He had been to those countries and had travelled widely in them. Perhaps as early as 1880 as a young man he had taken a sailing boat across the English Channel to France then had proceeded over the Alps to Italy and had travelled down its length then gone to Sicily by boat and thence to North Africa. He had 'boat-hopped' along the North African coast to Egypt and stayed there for a bit looking at the archaeology of that country before moving on to the Holy Land.

(The case mentioned on page 222 of volume 1 tells of a medium who visited the house mentioned above and who then declared that there was a spirit man present who had been most keen on Egyptology during his lifetime. Could this have been the same Mr. Simmons?)

Even after reaching Palestine he was not content merely to visit Jerusalem but travelled the length and breadth of the country, picking up real information from real inhabitants as he went.

I would be very surprised if this man was not the one mentioned by Francesca. I can't think of anyone more qualified as a man who could converse upon "things of the sea and travel". What I had to find now was a formal record of the doorstep death at the time when Mr. Simmons was resident in the house that is now mine.

My path to that was blocked in one direction with my reading the November 1909 edition of the newspaper, for at that date the man left his own church in Kingskettle forever to preach at Low Fell church near Newcastle in England. Regretfully that meant that I had seen no mention of a tragedy during the last nine years of his ministry at Kingskettle United Free Church. I was therefore forced to turn my attentions to the period *prior to* 1900: the period that I had not yet researched. It was most fortuitous that the very last mention the newspaper made of Mr. Simmons was that, by 1909, *"he has been as many years in harness in Kingskettle after 1900 as he had been before"*. I took out of that that he therefore started his career in my village in 1891 and I determined to continue my search but now in a *downwards manner* from 1900 to 1891.

I had initially chosen to *move up the years* from 1900 because that old postcard (postmarked 1905) shows all four stone pinnacles still in place. I had considered, perhaps wrongly, that it may well have been a photograph taken around the years 1901 or 1902 but on reconsideration it was probably taken even earlier and merely reprinted at the turn of the century. Back to the university archives!

After turning and reading literally thousands of ancient and yellowing pages something horrible began to dawn on me. I realised that each village had a sort of 'local literary agent' who had the responsibility of sending the village news forward each week to the newspaper office and that the representative from the my own village had been none other than Mr. Simmons himself!

I discussed the situation with several academics who understood, better than I, the workings of the Victorian mind and the attitudes of those far off days. These people were adamant that it was very unlikely indeed that the local church minister would record the death of a fish-selling lady who had been struck down on his own front doorstep. They all told me that the likelihood was that the man would quietly let the matter drop so that as few people as possible knew of it. That would have been particularly true if he had been remorseful over the fact that he had not taken adequate steps to see to the repair and maintenance of the property...which I am sure was the case.

I had known for thirty years that the spirit-being of some man was lingering in an invisible armchair in my drawingroom and contemplatively smoking his pipe...and all in the second week in July. Could it be coincidence that this was exactly the same week of the year that the fish-lady had been killed? Is Mr. Simmons my ghost man who sits in my drawingroom ? Could it be that he sat there day in and day out, shattered and contemplating the fact that his lack of maintenance had probably caused someone's death?

I don't suppose I'll ever know for sure.

****

The Cause of the Pinnacle Collapse

I am forced by the above situation to consider the mechanism by which three of the four pinnacles, which were erected on the house in 1843, managed to be dislodged by the time I bought it in 1972.

There are several possibilities although they probably interacted in some way too complex to calculate.

Firstly...I note that the stone pinnacles were mounted in position not only with cement but with rods of mild iron which were embedded in the base-stone and went up about four inches into the pinnacle itself. This told me that the masons realised that these stone items needed to be made secure. Unfortunately they had not appreciated that such mild iron metal pins would rust and corrode quite rapidly over the years. This certainly, along with the natural weathering of the sandstone itself, could well have been the basic cause of the toppling stones.

Secondly…the main north/south railway line for eastern Scotland runs very close to the house and the vibration is certainly felt from the heavier modern trains. Whether the lighter trains of earlier years would be heavy enough to vibrate the property to such an extent that that might topple the stonework I doubt, but it may have exacerbated a worsening situation as each year passed.

A further interesting thing is that when I asked Francesca at a later date if she would sit quietly one day and attempt to hear any noise associated with the death of the poor fishwife she came up with …. "I hear a couple of sharp reports as of a rifle or gun being discharged". (I thought she might say that she could hear the passing of a railway train but she did not.)

It is difficult to bring this into context. One single crack might have been the final snapping of the stonework before it hurtled downwards but two rifle shots seems to point to something quite different. Could it be that some village idiot had got his hands on a rifle and was having a pot-shot not only at passing pigeons but at things like local church towers and the upper pinnacles of any tall local house in the area?

Perhaps I am being fanciful here but I'd like to know more about the source of that double rifle-shot type noise just before the poor lady was struck down but I don't suppose I'll ever get the answer to that either.

The Mysterious Smell of Honey

May I now remind my readers that women who used to travel from house to house selling fish also took with them at times other 'home-grown' produce like vegetables or honey. That may be relevant in the above case.

As chance would have it, in the second or third week of July 1980 we had staying in the house an adult Romanian exchange student guest. On a particular afternoon I remember the whole family found ourselves hunting around the front door in search of honey for the Romanian guest had smelled it first and then we had all joined in the hunt for the source. It was certainly there hanging in the air just outside the left-hand side of the front door (as seen from the inside) and I have never had any doubt about that. We all looked for cracks in the stonework where bees could enter and leave but the stonework was in an excellent state of repair and in any case not one of us had ever seen bees hovering there, waiting their turn to get back into their nest. Such a thing was sure to be noticed by family and visitors alike for that doorway was the main entrance to the building.

At no time did any of us think that the psychic world was playing games with us and so the whole thing remained a mystery ….. that is until December 2003 when things began to make more sense, for by then I knew about the lady who had been killed at my front door and I also had an evening visitor as you will soon see.

What I have not told you yet is that, quite apart from spooky happenings taking place in the third week in July there were occasional but very minor happenings in mid-December some years. These were of a psychic intensity so low that we said to each other, "Did that happen or are we just imagining things?" and we almost instantly dismissed matters as overactive imagination. Now I am not so sure. There may have been some date in December that was important both to the Reverend Mr. Arthur Simmons and to the fishwife lady that none of us know about.

Anyway, in December 2003, at about 8pm on a dark and windy winter's night the front door bell rang and a member of the Curling Club to which I belonged stood outside ready to give me his annual subscription for I was the club treasurer. I took his money, he spoke a few words about the foulness of the weather and then he said something strange,

"Have you been boiling up honey or something in the house for as soon as I moved forward to press your doorbell I smelled an overwhelming smell of honey."

As I had not been dealing with honey in any way at all we moved out into the night together and sure enough there it was, hanging around the front door in spite of a howling gale that would have whipped any normal smell away to oblivion.

I was not in the mood to enlighten my visitor as to the possible reason for what he smelled but I was very glad that he had both smelled the honey and told me about it. I somehow think that this smell may well manifest itself to other people in the years to come.

****

The Unintended Curse of the Cattleman

While it is nice to get well-documented records from someone who calls me in because they think they might have something psychic and mysterious on their premises, that is the exception. The keeping of excellent records, however, was always the norm for Mrs. Wadkins and when her husband first phoned to say they had a recurrent and abhorrent smell in their home he told me that his wife had kept a record of 53 occurrences since it started on Tuesday 5th June 2001 at 11.30pm. For the most part the smell was centered on Mr. Wadkins himself and his own bedroom.

While I do not have space to list all of those occurrences, I will list those for this current year only which will show you that there was neither rhyme nor reason for their timing … or at least none that I could detect.

2003

Sat.	4th Jan.	11pm
Sat.	1st Feb.	4.30pm
Mon.	10th Mar.	5.00pm
Tue.	11th Mar.	11.00pm
Tue	18th Mar.	8.30pm
Sun.	27th Apr.	9.00pm
Sat.	3rd May	12.00pm

Thur.	22nd May	9.45pm	
Sun.	1st Jun.	10.40pm	
Wed.	18th Jun.	10.15pm	(both bedrooms)
Fri.	18th Jul.	12.30am	(both bedrooms)

The smell was described as, "like urine with ammonia mixed in and at times overwhelmingly strong" and before contacting me the family had had ample opportunity to look at all sorts of other possibilities, which they had done. At that early point in investigations I was a little perplexed why their dog did not react to either the smell or the psychic entity to which the odour seemed attached (if indeed such an entity ever existed) but I realised that there was always the possibility that, if it was a true psychic smell then it might manifest itself only at head-height. That would be in order to make an impact upon the human(s) it wanted to attract.

Anyway, I told Mr. Wadkins that Francesca and I would visit them as we were going to be in their general area on Tuesday 29th July to visit a second client. It was at that point that Mrs. Wadkins sent me a detailed breakdown of the times when the smell started up in their home.

Having fought our way through that evening traffic chaos, which I mentioned a few pages back, we arrived more than half an hour late and full of apologies. However, Mr. and Mrs. Wadkins were both happy and chatty people who were only too pleased to see us and to serve us home-baked scones and cakes covered with home-made raspberry jam until we were truly over-full. With such lovely food in the present house it seemed ironical that the second case we were due to attend to that evening was in a large and elegant family home on a country estate where we had been invited to a late dinner!

So as we finished eating and with one eye on the clock, Francesca and I asked to be shown Mr. Wadkins's bedroom where the majority of the smell had been recorded.

There was certainly no smell whatever anywhere in the house and that bedroom was no exception. The house was spotless, exceptionally tidy and excellently well maintained and I found it difficult to come to grips with the fact that some sort of regular foul smell could exist there. It struck me that this all pointed to the possibility that there was indeed a psychic smell which might have been coming and going of its own volition.

"Francesca," I said as the four of us stood around waiting for something to happen, "Can you move mentally into the spirit world and attempt to see who, if anyone, is making their presence felt here."

The medium shut her eyes then addressed the dear gentleman householder who was in his mid 70s.

"Mr. Wadkins, you lived in this area as a young man." That sentence came as a statement and not as a question but he replied anyway,

"I did."

"And you had friends who were poachers: three of them?" This was presented as more of a question I noted.

The man turned and looked at his wife questioningly before turning to the medium again. I believe he was thinking that his wife had somehow told this fact to Francesca behind his back.

"Yes, I had friends who would go out and catch small animals by night, like rabbits and sell them to butchers and the like to make a little cash on the side."

"You sometimes went out with them for a bit of fun."

"I used to but they are all dead now."

"Yes, I know but they are still hanging around here for they care for you still: you must have been good friends with them all." The man nodded almost sadly.

There was a pause then,

"What had you to do with large animals?"

"Oh, we never poached large animals at all, just rabbits and pheasants and the like," the man said speedily to exonerate himself.

"But I'm getting 'large animals', 'smelly large animals' connected with you. I'm being told by the spirit world that the smell is the smell of large beasts of some kind."

Let me now say that both Mr. and Mrs. Wadkins were somewhat talkative and somehow between them their arguments and counter-arguments completely swamped what Francesca was saying and thinking and so the topic of "cattle" once again seemed to turn to "poachers" and then went on to the many types of jobs that Mr. Wadkins had taken part in over the years.

"Hold on folks!" I had to say in the end to get sense back into the room again, "Let's get away from the jobs you once had and from catching game by night and onto the cause of the smell you say you have."

I felt (and I know that the medium felt) that the three old boyhood friends of Mr. Wadkins were some sort of false 'red-herring' that was distracting us from the main purpose of our being there that evening. By this time I was also looking at the clock and thinking that we were going to be very late for the next case which we had to drive to that evening. Things were just not 'gelling' in this house and good manners dictated that at least I should phone the next client to tell them that things were running about three quarters of an hour late. Mrs. Wadkins showed me the phone and I made to call while she moved into her own bedroom to look for some documents and maps of the area for us.

Once off the phone I returned upstairs and joined Francesca and Mr. Wadkins in this man's own bedroom to find the pair of them locked into endless and pointless discussion. My heart sank and I was just beginning to think that all was lost here when I heard a loud yelp from the lady's bedroom across the landing.

"It's here! It's here! The smell is back!"

I looked at my watch as we shot through. It was 7.30 p.m. spot on and there was indeed a smell, a truly awful smell right in the centre of the room and under the central light. We were all looking at each other and sniffing. I wandered around in a circle pushing my face into and back from the smell: I ducked down and found that it did not exist lower than about five feet from floor level. It was definitely in the form of a large and somewhat flattened ball of smell about four feet in diameter and perhaps two feet tall. It was there all right and it was a mixture of ammonia and urine and of medium strength. In this instance it was not overwhelmingly strong. The urine, I felt, was not of a type connected with humans and I remembered where I had smelled it last…at a farm up the road from my house. It was truly cattle urine!

(What a thing a psychic researcher has to be an expert in … 'urine smells'!)

Now we were back where both Francesca and I wanted to be for she had earlier insisted that Mr. Wadkins had been in the proximity of "large animals" but he had said that he knew nothing about such creatures. Now we had urine smells from "large animals" and we both knew that things were beginning to make sense once more.

"Mr. Wadkins, what connection had you with farms and the like as a young man?" I almost yelled at the man.

"Not much really, I used to help out ...."

The sentence was interrupted by Francesca who was getting an immediate and very strong contact from the world beyond ours,

"Toddy Rufflet, Toddy Rufflet " she repeated, "Did you ever know a Toddy Rufflet?"

I listened intently and looked at Mr. Wadkins who stood by my side, for the name was not a common one. Would he know it?

The man's eyes were widening,

"My God! Toddy Rufflet!" he repeated in amazement, "Uncle Toddy! Yes, he was a farmer all right and I helped him out for a year or so."

The whole forgotten story came tumbling out. Mr. Wadkins had known a man who he had called "Uncle" but who, technically, had not been such a relation but had been a very loving and caring pseudo relation. That man had had a dairy farm but he was irked that he had been compelled by law to start selling the milk produced solely to the new Milk Marketing Board and he chose to give up dairy farming and move to the production of beef cattle. He bought a much larger farm and in the process had bitten off more than he could chew, so to speak, for there were upon his new farm many more cattle than he had previously handled. He therefore approached the young Mr. Wadkins and greatly welcomed his help in the running of this new farm undertaking.

At last I felt we were beginning to understand the smell. It was purposefully generated by Uncle Toddy Rufflet who had decided that he wanted Mr. Wadkins to know that he was still around him in spirit. He thought (I think with justification) that if he regenerated the smell of cattle urine that would jerk Mr. Wadkins's mind back again to those happy far-off days on the farm. It didn't have the desired effect for a long time for he started generating the smell in June 2001 and it wasn't until July 2003 that he got results. I'll give him full marks for persistence though!

I often wonder if the passing of time in the spirit world is similar to time in ours. Could those two years of making smells to get noticed merely have been 'the twinkling of an eye' in spirit world terms? Who knows?

Mr. Wadkins was not only amazed at what had taken place and its explanation but was also quite emotionally overcome that someone from the past could still care for him to such a degree that he had tried so hard to make contact. If tears were not in the man's eyes they were very close.

Perhaps Francesca and I might have stayed longer with the Wadkins' to rejoice with them at the return of Toddy Rufflet but we were needed in another house about 12 miles away to solve another problem. So, grasping the two jars of freshly made raspberry jam that Mrs. Wadkins gave us as a personal 'thank you!' we got into my car and shot off to a delayed meeting with the owners of a lovely Georgian house on a country estate.

So it was, " 'Goodbye smells' for that evening and, at the next address.........'Hello, deceased first wife!'"

****

The Bell on the Gate

On 8th June 2003 I was handed an unusual item which had been found by the Gordon family who stay close by me in the village of Kingskettle. It was said to have been found in their garden and was so different an object to anything I had seen previously that I asked if I could take it to my medium friend, Francesca, so that she might psychometrise it to gain knowledge from it as to what its function was and where it was from.

Perhaps you might enjoy the fun of guessing, at this point, what the object might be so I'll give you a description of it and you can pretend that I have just found it and handed it over to you for examination.

(or you can look at it on the website, "psychic-info.com")

It is metal (probably cast brass) and about eight inches long and varies from two inches wide at the base to about half an inch wide towards the top. It does, however, get wider and thinner at points up its length and has a half-inch diameter fixing ring at the top so that whatever it is, it obviously is of a pendulous nature and hung down from something or other. In fact its overall appearance resembles a sort of gigantic earring.

On the evening of Tuesday 10th June I was sitting in the car with Francesca in Edinburgh as we were about to set out on a case to rid a house of several unwanted entities when I had the opportunity to hand over the mystery item to this lady.

She sat still in the evening sunlight and had her eyes closed as she moved into the psychic world which held memories of the item.

The conversation then went something like this:-

" Are you getting anything at all from it, Francesca?"

"Oh Yes! It was a handle of a bell-pull system....."

"It's rather large," I interjected, "It's eight inches long so it must have been attached to a reasonably large bell."

"Yes, it was and by a thick iron chain! The bell was bolted onto one of two extremely large and ornate cast iron gates.... actually the right hand one as you enter the property. These were each about seven feet broad and nearly eight feet tall at their centre point and looked very fine and expensive gates. Their highest point was where they shut in the middle and they sort of swept downwards to left and right where they met their supporting pillars. These, in turn, were two large gray stone pillars at the entrance to a driveway up to a church and close by a little house that had something to do with both the gates and the church.

The people in the house were responsible in some way for the opening and closing of the gates and the maintenance of the church. It was they who decided who should come and go and the bell on the gate was rung for permission to enter."

Francesca, of course, had no idea at all concerning which part of the country this item had been found, far less details of the village or street concerned. Her pronouncements are, therefore, all the more amazing for the object was found in the garden of a house which, up till 1960 used to be the house of the local church officer, the very person responsible for the upkeep of the church which lay up a short driveway past the house.

The dwelling itself is merely eight yards from the nearest of the two stone gate pillars, which are indeed "gray" as stated by Francesca. The gates themselves were cut down and melted into scrap iron in 1940 to make tanks and guns to defend the UK from the German aggressors and the archor-bolts which supported the massive gates can still be seen embedded in the stonework to this very day. If there was a bell mounted on the gate then it would indeed be heard by the persons in the house so that the gates could be opened up to the would-be visitor. Francesca was also correct regarding the fact that the bell would be mounted on the right-hand gate because that one was closest to the cottage. The site of the church and its associated dwellings are still surrounded by the very sturdy original stone wall so any access to the area would have to have been via those main gates: there is no other route into that property.

"I'm being told lots more about the house and the people in it," Francesca went on and I listened intently as she continued,

"The house was always very damp and people in it became ill and even died because of that dampness although I'm being told that of late it has been extensively modernised by several consecutive families and is now a good quality dwelling."

(I know that that was very true. In the 1960s the soil level around the house was about three feet higher than the floor of the house which kept the whole place exceedingly damp.)

"When the bell was on the gate at some point in the past, the church warden was a Mr. William Burgess and he had a wife, Margaret and a child."

Francesca then turned to modern times,

"The bell-pull was found by a man who was laying tiles.... big, square tiles." Then she adjusted her statement,

"Oh I see him laying those tiles outside his house! He's in his garden. He's laying big square tiles in his garden and that had something to do with the bell-pull. I do believe that he found it in his garden."

I then told Francesca that that was precisely where the object had been found and when Mr. Gordon was laying square paving slabs.

Our conversation went back to Mr. and Mrs. Burgess and Francesca said that while the spirit of the husband had no real interest in remaining in and around the house during our times, the spirit of his wife Margaret definitely did.

"Margaret probably died of a pulmonary illness and moves around 'her' house quite a bit. At times she moves within her house along with her child and the pair of them have been seen quite a number of times by two of the children who currently live in the house. In fact there is a rather strong bond between Margaret and one of the children who sees her quite regularly.... especially when she brings her own child along."

As Mr. and Mrs. Gordon seemed a little shy of discussing this paranormal aspect with their children I really don't know if any of the younger members of the family did ever see the apparition of Margaret or her child but this story must surely show the benefits of psychometry to the community in general .... and the Gordon family in particular. Perhaps when the younger family members grow up, one of them will confide in me that they 'had a ghost in the house but they dared not tell mother and father for fear it would frighten them'.

CHAPTER 5

SAD LEFTOVERS

Child Ghosts
No One's Friend
The Hungry Man

Child Ghosts

Children Dying in Cellars

This is a truly unhappy section of this book and I will quite understand if you wish to leave the reading of it to another time. However, as I said to one of the property-owners concerned who felt terribly badly about having such a past trauma upon her property,

"The things I tell of were past and gone long before you or I came onto this earth and so I cannot see how we can in any way feel ourselves responsible for them. We can only grieve in hindsight and extend compassion to the little victims involved and even to the perpetrators of any crime involved…for such malefactors must now have come face-to-face with the wickedness of their ways."

To find, in my researches, that one child had died in a sub-basement wine cellar is bad enough but to find two separate such incidents within three months almost beggars belief.

A Sad Little Tale

There is nothing more distressing than a child ghost. The thought of a little creature lost in time is almost too much to bear and yet Francesca and I stumbled on one when we were called in by a T.V. cameraman to a rather large Victorian house standing in its own grounds in Central Glasgow. The man himself was not alarmed about anything but one or two of his friends and visitors said that they felt "some presence" in the building and as he was about to be re-married he asked us to see if we could identify any presence …pleasant or otherwise. The man obviously wanted matters 'tidied up' before his new wife arrived.

Even as we were walking up the driveway to the house in the drizzling rain Francesca asked,

"Is there a cellar area to this house, do you think?"

I have known this medium long enough to realise that if she says something like that it is not merely idle conversation to wile away the time but a question arising in her mind because she has already linked with the psychic world and **knows** that there is something in a cellar area that is 'reaching out to her'.

The long and short of it was that we started by meeting the owner and telling him to his amazement that he had been dealing with the title deeds of the house when we had no idea that he'd been discussing them with his lawyer merely two hours before. Then Francesca told him that the house had once belonged to a Mr. Charles Johnson (or Johnstone) whose wealth came from his involvement in the tobacco trade for which Glasgow was once famous. The days of horses and carriages were sensed very strongly and this was especially true when we went up to the main bedroom and found that an elderly Victorian lady of a nervous disposition had died there and still 'hung around' but in a rather minor way.

(This lady should probably not have been able to be detected for she really was not a ghost in her own right but as you will see she was strongly connected mentally with something else I am about to mention so that her memory had probably been 'pulled back' to this world by having a direct link with the child entity who I am about to tell you about. Facts seem to point to the conclusion that this elderly lady was not a relation but she still might have been deeply effected by the child's death.)

The house must also have been used as a doctor's surgery at one point (obviously after it had passed out of the keeping of the rich tobacco baron) for Francesca felt droves of people with medical complaints moving into and out of the main front door and then moving into a small room close by and sitting in some sort of waiting-room area.

It was only after our walk through the house that the word "cellar" came up again and that was because the medium asked the owner point-blank if there was such a thing. Obviously whatever it was that was linking into Francesca's mind was not going to let her out of that house before she explored the cellar areas. Perhaps with a bit of reluctance on behalf of the owner we were led down a very narrow stair and to a twin sub-basement area: one tiny room to the left and one to the right.

"This is the way I have to go!" said the lady and opening a low, wide door turned right into a small, cold and dank room where there were some thick stone storage shelves. This kind of place was common in Victorian houses and such a place was used for long-term storage of foodstuffs in a time before refrigeration.

Virtually instantaneously the medium went into a trance state and began talking in a voice that was half-way between Francesca's own voice and that of a young female child.

"I'm Elizabeth and I'm eight years old but I'm called 'Lizzie'".

(It might interest my readers to know that I initially typed the word "LizzY" here in my manuscript but I was immediately 'told' by someone from the psychic world that that was wrong and that I should be typing the word 'LizzIE' and so I have now changed the wrong spelling to the one that Lizzie wants.

*Perhaps my readers will be interested to know that this is not the first time that I have come across a spirit-child making a 'correction' from the other world. Some years ago and during a public demonstration of mediumship by the famous Scottish medium Mr. Gordon Smith, my deceased granddaughter, Fern, communicated through this medium and said something that made him laugh aloud greatly. She had said (correctly) that after her death she had stood behind her father and I in her new spirit state and had seen us '**pen**' (sic) an important letter to someone on her behalf. As she died before she was even four years old, Gordon commented to the little spirit-girl in front of the audience, "That's a difficult way for a little girl to use the word 'pen'!" whereupon Fern replied to him,*

*"I said '**pen**' and I mean '**pen**'!" There was laughter from the*

entire audience.)

I talked with Lizzie in the same way as I would talk to you, my reader, if you were here with me now. I felt so privileged to hold a conversation (through this talented medium) with a little girl who had died more than a hundred years ago and to get a tale from her that was so sad in many ways but yet considered quite acceptable for the times in which she lived I suppose.

She told me that this was not "her real home" and that she did not know her own father and mother but she lived in this house. She got her food and board for nothing but in return she had to do work around the house all day. At eight years old she was therefore, for all practical purposes, both an orphan and an unpaid employee! But an employee without rights or true freedom and when we first come across her she had contracted typhoid and in order to isolate her from the household she had been put for her period of illness in this cold and damp cellar …as far away from the rest of the household as possible. Perhaps the cold and dampness was actually meant to reduce her fever as well? I don't really know. No matter what the motivation, it was in those terrible dark and dank circumstances that the poor wee soul died of her fever, lonely no doubt and perhaps even forgotten about to a degree. No wonder her little ghost is still there!

Some interesting points arose through Francesca at that point in the afternoon. One was that it was at the instigation of the lady who had later died in the upstairs bedroom that the child had been incarcerated in the downstairs cellar. That lady had blamed the child for bringing typhoid into the household in the first place. We have no way of knowing, of course, whether it was the child who infected the lady or the lady who had brought the infection into the house and infected the child. I am reasonably sure in my own mind that it is this interconnection between these two that keeps the lady's spirit-being locked onto that upstairs bedroom.

I have always maintained that when a medium links to the psychic world what actually takes place is that she places herself in a situation of 'voluntary possession'. This was borne out once again with this case for as Fracesca was taken over by Lizzie she broke out into the most terrible fever herself: not only had she become instantaneously flushed but sweat had actually started to break out on the skin of her brow and face and I could see that she was becoming flustered because of her rising temperature. It was at that point that I thought it wise to move her forward again in time and so I slowly talked with her and brought her back to 2004 and the fact that she was an adult lady called Francesca and not an ill little girl called Lizzie.

She took quite a time to cool down physically and even after walking to the car through the drizzle …..which took about eight minutes…she sat there in the passenger seat trying to cool off and get her breath back again.

Wickedness Beyond belief

About three months later and almost a hundred miles to the east, after an initial phone conversation, I was called into view a large and somewhat neglected country house which was just on the point of being totally refurbished at great expense. As the house was built around 1780 and as quite a number of guests in recent years had at times reported screams by night in two very different parts of the building, the owners considered that there might well be something "unpleasant" in the building which needed "looking at". I never tell the client over the phone that they have any particular form of ongoing psychic activity for that would be too presumptuous without a visit and an examination of the case but I have been at this business long enough to know from their explanation what the **likely** cause of their problem might be. Obviously, the fact that there were screams coming from two very distinct parts of this very large house means that it is likely that we had on our hands at least two distinct (and unrelated?) happenings. This in fact proved to be the case as you will see.

I collected Francesca from the rail station and on the way to the country estate that we were heading for, I drove once around the lovely little town of Falkland to show her the hotel of another client who had asked us to visit him in the next few weeks. He had got fed up with guests in one particular bedroom either waking him up so that they could clock out of his hotel at 3am or suddenly curtailing their stay and leaving rapidly after breakfast with lame excuses.

The driveway up to the country mansion was alive with wildlife…… fleeing squirrels, pheasants, wild mallard ducks and even four cockerel friends out for a 'lads' morning stroll together. All had to be carefully avoided for I didn't feel that leaving a trail of dead game-birds in our wake would do our reputation any good. So much young and vibrant life all around us and yet we were soon to see that we'd be finding the desperately sad death of a child within the house itself.

The lady of the house, Clarissa, greeted us and we began our customary initial chat in the large Georgian kitchen. She was wise enough, after our earlier phone conversation, not to accidentally reveal to Francesca that the source of the family's worries stemmed from midnight screaming. In fact that mattered not at all, although Clarissa wouldn't know that, for soon after leaving the rail station which was about fifteen miles away Francesca had already turned around to me in the car and said,

"Archie, I'm hearing screaming. Is this case about screaming do you think?"

I gave in and acknowledged that screams had, in fact been heard. There was little point in denying it as it was the medium herself who had initiated this conversation.

Anyway, Clarissa and I agreed that the best thing was for us all to begin a walk around the house and so we left the kitchen area and began strolling along the wide ground-floor corridor. Our intentions were to work our way upwards through the house and then as a final act we were to visit the basement areas but our medium had other ideas. I remind you now that Francesca is almost physically as well as psychically drawn towards a source of paranormal activity in some little-understood way. *(I wish that those two important words were not so similar in spelling!)*

"Can we visit the basement first? She asked and then she quickly followed this up with, "I feel there is a stairway down to it near here." Her hand made a spiralling movement.

This was in itself a rather strange statement to make because there was a main staircase glaringly obvious behind us but Francesca made no reference to it at all. The spiralling movement of the hand too was indicating to me that she had already sensed that there was indeed a spiral staircase nearby. Clarissa merely turned to her left, put out her hand to the nearest closed door and opened it; behind it was the spiral staircase that led down to the basement. I could see that Francesca was so keen to get down those cold and narrow servants' stairs and while she did not lead the way she moved quickly along the narrower basement corridor once we were down there. While it was a basement and had the usual cold, gray flagstoned floor, it was neither damp nor poorly lit and we made our way initially into an entire basement apartment area which had been used both by au-pairs and guests from time to time and which now served as an office for Clarissa's husband Paul.

Here our medium picked up upon her first entity. He was a tall military gentleman in a red uniform who positively radiated sternness, discipline and a general lack of caring about the feelings of others. He was, of course, a very senior officer of some sort and in fact Paul identified the regiment to which he belonged from the description that Francesca gave of his uniform. He was, apparently, one of two military bachelor brothers who inhabited the house in the late 1700s and who had been renowned for their uncaring attitude to their employees and their strictness in the way they ran their household. Rumours of their drunken ways were put to us by Paul who seemed to know a bit about them. They had a sister who lived with them on the premises but it is thought that she too was brought up in the same manner as her brothers so that she might not have even been overtly aware of their uncaring attitudes for not one of them cared for people as people. They thought of other humans, Francesca said, as being there to serve them and to do as they were told. It is also believed that the men were in some way involved in the business of slave trading…which was not all that unusual in those far-off days. They also had connections with well known persons of nobility in the West Highlands of Scotland …..all of which will have meaning for you soon!

Our medium did not linger too long in that basement apartment area but withdrew and led us along the corridor to an L bend in the labyrinth. Here she stopped and touched an old door with a large keyhole.

"I'm being led to here," she said. "There is a child in here and I'm hearing screaming coming from here."

She turned to Clarissa who was standing behind me in a quiet but apprehensive state.

"What is beyond this door? I feel I want to go downwards into the earth," she added.

Clarissa thought that the door might be unlocked but this proved incorrect and so she asked the housekeeper to see if she could find a key. This in turn proved a fruitless venture but eventually Paul himself turned up with a key and the mystery door was unlocked. We could see a flight of stone steps twisting sharply at right angles and going down steeply to the left into a very dark-looking area of nothingness.

We all looked at each other as Paul said,

"It goes down to the old wine cellars. We don't use them ourselves."

"Is there a light down there?" I asked him but he replied in the negative and then asked the housekeeper to bring a good flashlight from somewhere. When that arrived it was handed to me and I led the way down the very dark stairs carefully shining the light on each step behind me to allow Francesca to place her feet safely on each one. We two stood on the flagstones in the dimness and looked around. The stone wine-storage shelves were appearing dimly to the right of us and the floor below them was soaking with wetness which glistened in my flashlight. Francesca spoke,

"Archie, can I get past you? I want to be nearer to that little child in the corner."

There was a short period when we stood with the flashlight pointing down to the damp floor as I discussed with our medium whether this spirit child was, in fact, a boy or a girl. Eventually it was decided that it was a boy and that he appeared to be about eleven years old or thereabouts.

"His face is so difficult to see in the darkness that surrounds him". *(That is ...in the time when he was down there for real ...for Francesca was **now back in time**!)*

By now the natural inhibitions of Clarissa, Paul and even the housekeeper had been overcome by curiosity and I heard their footsteps coming down the stone stair behind us so that soon there were five of us down there along with the little ghost boy who was the source of the screaming that had been heard in that part of the house.

The medium described the boy as best she could for his features were unclear either due to the darkness of his own time or even due to his wanting psychically to conceal his features for some reason.

(Dedicated researchers will want to know that it is not uncommon for spirit entities to want to hide their faces for various reasons. We people who attempt to evaluate the psychic world often find it difficult to work out the reason for such actions and are just forced to accept the fact that sometimes spirit people don't want to show themselves clearly.)

What Francesca did say, however was that the young lad was not clad in proper clothing and had upon his body but the merest of rags. He had been, of course, endlessly bitterly cold and had been in that terrible hole in the ground for a long time. I, myself, was getting the impression of many, many months of misery. There was total silence from the three people behind Francesca and I and they heard me ask the medium the two main questions that filled the mind of each one us,

"Why was the child down there in the first place and how did he eventually die?"

The story was truly appalling and appeared to be this:-

The lad had been some sort of 'fetch and carry' boy who had worked around the house and who might have been even of dark-skinned slave origin for you will remember that the lad's face could not be seen readily in the darkness. Was that because his skin tone was brown or black? I don't know but I can surmise. Anyway, whatever the colour of his skin, he had dropped some article of other during the course of his duties 'upstairs' when carrying something on behalf of the sister of the military men. When the item was dropped and broken one of the two military men completely lost his temper and had first dragged the boy along the corridor, then down the first flights of steps to the basement and then had hurled him down the second set of steps into that dungeon of a wine cellar. There, in that miserable place of captivity, he was visited from time to time by one (or both?) of the military men and subjected to repeated physical abuse. He was also deprived of food to such a degree that Francesca declared that he had eventually died of starvation and being beaten. (She also told me later as we travelled back to the rail station in the car that she also knew that the child had been systematically sexually abused by those high ranking military officers but that she did not want to mention that to the family for what they now knew was unpleasant enough.)

I know that Francesca has come across a lot of unpleasant and terribly sad things during our cases together but I have rarely seen her so angry and upset at what she was finding in that dreadful cellar. How she loathed those wicked and disgusting men for what they had done! How could they appear so proud and grand in their fine uniforms, she said, and yet think so little of those for whom they had a duty of care?

It is a sad reflection of those 'good old days' that we were about to come to grips with yet another entity in that house who had also suffered badly at the hands of the previous owners of that property.

After the five of us stood in silent and in darkness for a bit out of respect for the dead child, one of us vocalised a sort of spontaneous prayer and the hope that he could now move on to where he really should be …and not haunting a cellar in a country mansion. Then we slowly moved up the stone steps again and the door was locked behind us.

It was with a heavy heart that I said to Clarissa,

"Well, perhaps you can show us up to the top floor of the house; to the place where the second lot of screams are coming from?"

The lady of the house led the way. The room that Francesca was drawn to was the very furthest possible from the main rooms of the house. It was exactly the room one might use in which to place a problem of some sort for that problem would then be both out of sight and out of mind. We were shortly to find 'the problem' although the owners of the property had never heard of her ….the problem was 'Janet Campbell'. She was a "thirteen or fourteen-year-old child" who had been "sent down" to this large country house from the extreme west of Scotland: probably from the castle of Inverary! I cannot think that it is mere chance that the two military brothers who owned the house initially were the most senior officers in a regiment that was headed by the very

Lord who lived in Inverary Castle. There was certainly ongoing intermittent contact between those three and it struck me that there was at least a possibility that the transference of this young girl from a castle in the west of Scotland to a mansion in the east was some sort of planned move .....especially when I learned through Francesca that the girl was pregnant at the time of her having been transferred from one site to the other! It seemed to me to be a distinct move to get her out of the way for the duration of that pregnancy. She was being treated as some sort of burden that needed removing and these two bachelor brothers seem to have been given the job of looking after her. A strange choice of 'minders' is it not? .....especially now that you, my readers, know that they were capable of beating and starving that other child to death.

Thus it was that this poor girl was put into the farthest attic room and left to get on with her pregnancy. There, in front of a fireplace that is no longer in the room at all *(its removal was confirmed by Paul)* an abortion took place Francesca tells us but still the girl was left alone in that part of the house for the most part …. "she just had to get on with things as best she could". It was, of course, Janet's screams of pain from the psychic world that some of the family had heard on that fourth floor. We were also told that Janet actually survived the trauma, loneliness and pain of those desperate months so we know that she must have been one tough little girl! She went on to join the domestic staff in that large mansion and indeed she worked till she died of natural causes many decades later. I watched Francesca's face and hands during the time she was in light trance and saw that she appeared to be heaping (invisible) things on top of each other. I asked her what she was doing and, speaking as young Janet, she said that she was stacking linen and carrying it to the shelves where the linen was stored. As both Paul and Clarissa were standing nearby when this statement was made the former took the trouble to tell us that the tradition linen store for the great house had been the room next to the room where Janet had spent her years. She had probably started out her career there as the 'linen girl' and our medium said that she felt that Janet was "busy, busy, running hither and thither here and there: running, running, always running at someone's beck and call."

That was all we found out about Janet because Francesca and I had to leave to move onto other things but at least we knew that the girl had had a roof over her head for the rest of her life and had enough food to eat so I suppose we should be thankful to some degree for the small mercies that life bestowed upon her in those dark days of the 18th century.

****

No One's Friend

This is just a very short account of a rather mundane haunting but as it was unfolding at the end of November 2003 I felt alarm bells ringing in my head. I was being told by my subconscious mind that there was some clue of importance that had been revealed to me but that I had failed to notice it.

I'll put down this account on paper for you and let you puzzle over what the important principle was that I initially missed. It took me two days of thinking until it came to me suddenly at 5am one morning. How could I have missed it?

There are also one or two other points of interest suitable for the serious researcher.

A nurse in her forties phoned me up and confided in me that she felt very uneasy about the stories she was getting from her daughter who had recently moved into a ground floor apartment of a brand new building in the Newhaven port area of Edinburgh. This area is down close to the water side and at one point in the past it was at the very edge of the sea for it was a fishing village in its own right with its own harbour. Boats would come and go daily and the fish caught would, primarily, be sold in the city of Edinburgh that was merely a couple of miles away. Much of the fish-selling was done in a door-to-door way by the wives and daughters of fishermen and those persons were always called '*fishwives*'. This case concerns the interrelationship between one of those fishwives (deceased) and the young couple.

Laura's mother was basically worried for her daughter because she was heavily pregnant and due to give birth in about four weeks time and she did not wish her to be upset by strange things that were taking place around her. She also added, perhaps with a tiny bit of justification, that she understood that the point of birth of a human being was one of several salient times in the life cycle where a possible possessing entity finds it easiest to lock onto a human personality.

My response to her was firstly that I would not want her daughter to be worried by anything at all at that point in her pregnancy, psychic or non-psychic and secondly, the chance of a case of possession taking place with the newly born child, while possible, was virtually zero.

I specifically advised the lady not to mention such things to her daughter as at that time in her first pregnancy she would have enough worries about all sorts of things as it was. For peace of mind, however, I said I would collect the girl's mother in the car in 48 hours and then after picking up Francesca we'd head for her daughter's home to see if any psychic thing was lurking there.

We reached the building at about 8pm and even in the darkness we could see that it had a very prominent view towards the sea although that was now a mile away for the land had been built up systematically over the years. What a lovely property it would have been if the water had still been lapping close by as it had done all those years in the past!

Laura and her partner Sam welcomed Francesca and I along with her mother and without delay I asked Laura to tell us what was happening to her which had spooked her out to such a degree that she and Sam had considered leaving the house altogether …at least until after the baby was born.

She told us about a continuous 'sense of presence' that she had felt from their first day in the house and then she went on to tell us that at all times of the day and night she kept catching sight of something moving to her left or right as she glanced out of the sides of her eyes. This 'thing', whatever it was, never at any time kept stationary enough to be truly seen in the normal manner but Laura was sure that it was there.

(I meet this business of seeing things out of the corner of the eye quite a lot: just a flash and it's gone. I now consider that this is some sort of spirit-to-human communication that is often closely associated with a sense-of-presence.)

Then she told about drawers in her kitchen opening by themselves. This particularly happened during the night when Laura got up to get a drink of water from the kitchen area. The sensible young couple had, apparently, tested the running of the drawers and they said that if anything, the drawers tended to *close* when given a minor tap as opposed to opening when touched lightly. This I decided to test for myself and so we moved into the kitchen and I did precisely that. Laura and Sam had been correct for I found that while a light touch sent the drawer shooting into the fully closed position, a reasonable tug was needed to open the drawer again.

The conversation moved forward to discussing what changes had been taking place with the *contents* of the same set of drawers. Laura told us that she looked upon herself as being a fastidiously tidy person and swore that certain things in those drawers had changed places, often in a matter of minutes after she had placed them in certain positions. She gave us a prime example by looking into a drawer and seeing something there that she knew should have been in another position. She said that she felt that someone was looking at and handling certain of her kitchen utensils.

I had to remind her that as she was getting towards the end of her pregnancy, life must seem somewhat strained for her at times but I stopped short of saying that she was imagining things: she came across as reliable and honest. Now that we knew a little bit about the case I thought that Francesca should take her turn 'on stage' and so I asked her if she could feel anything around us in the apartment . She relaxed her mind and closed her eyes.

"Do you smell unusual things at times?" she asked.

"We do actually!" replied Sam and Laura together. "Sometimes fish and sometimes a scent-like sort of smell and sometimes an unpleasant smell and perhaps even tobacco although neither of us smoke." I considered so many smells in a brand new house (which was not on a main street) a little puzzling and urged our medium to continue with her exploration into this facet of the unknown.

"Are you feeling someone around us, Francesca?" I asked.

The lady nodded and replied,

"Yes, she's here with us at this moment in the kitchen."

I quickly took steps to reassure Laura in particular that nothing bad was about to happen and that whatever lady was being discussed was not about to make herself visible to us.

"What lady are we talking about, Francesca?" I asked and the answer came back.

"And old fishwife woman called "Biddy". She's telling me that she'd been a fish seller all her days but had had a rather lonely life. For that reason perhaps she had sought solace at the local inn where she had regularly taken a good drink and had come home and fallen into bed. 'Bed' was merely a mattress lying on the floor at one corner of the second room in her humble and poor house. She came across as a sad and lonely person who had been worn down by much work and perhaps more than a little alcohol. She had died on that self-same bed and then she added that her body had not been discovered for quite a number of days. Truly a sad ending to a sad life!

Francesca pointed to the spot on the floor where the bed would have been laid if only the floor of 2003 had been the floor of 1890 and we all stood in a little circle and looked down and felt a great sadness.

At that point, especially after our mental compassion towards the departed entity, the spirit-lady might have just drifted off to her allotted place in the spirit world for expression of compassion often initiates such a happening. This time, however, that did not take place for I noted Francesca sort of twisting about in an effort to see something which she obviously believed to be behind the kitchen door which was then in the fully open position.

"What are you looking for?" I asked in puzzlement.

Our medium was smiling,

"I'm being told by Biddy that she doesn't like the basket nor does she understand what's in it but I can't see any basket although she's making me turn in this direction to see it."

Laura stepped into the conversation,

"We've a big basket all right but it is through the wall from where you are looking: it's here in the other room," and she led us through to the main room once again.

There in a bay window was a large woven-cane basket, perhaps four feet long by three feet broad and two feet tall. It had a metal hasp upon it to keep it closed.

"We just keep videos and CDs in it," said Sam as he raised the lid to show us.

"Well, Biddy says that she doesn't like the basket although she doesn't tell me why. Perhaps it's so different to the basket in which she always carried her fish. I can see why she doesn't understand what's in it though," Francesca chimed in.

(We see in this statement, do we not, several interesting facts about people in the spirit world. Firstly that they can see us and the things around us, as and when they wish to. Secondly that people from the other world do not really advance from the technical point of view after their death. I find the religious saying that "All will be revealed after death" completely incorrect. You'd think that if spirit entities could see us then they'd learn about modern technical marvels like TV and mobile phones. If you read about the famous Scole Experiments in another book by this same author you will see that even technically specialised people like the famous Edison do not seem to have picked up on even minor scientific principles discovered after their death. You would think that the same scientific mind that developed the basis of the telephone system while here on earth would take a great interest in its development from his vantage point in the afterlife.

While I have seen no evidence of this, I must admit that I do meet entities who use our science to their own ends…. E.g. they even phone people up! These two situations are difficult to reconcile surely and must remain for now as another psychic mystery.)

The final outcome of the evening was that we agreed with Biddy that, as it displeased her, we would hide the wickerwork basket away in a corner at the far end of the house (which may well have been outwith the original confines of Biddy's 1890s home) if she, in turn, agreed not to make herself known to the family or the little baby when it finally took up residence in the house with its mother and father. To date I have heard nothing further from this family so I presume that all went well in the finality of things. Spirit people usually keep their promises!

Getting back to the first paragraph of this case…….. have you spotted the point of interest that I initially missed?

It is this:-

Many skeptics (as well as genuine researchers) consider that memories held in the human mind can somehow be handed down genetically so that information is passed from generation to generation. I have never subscribed to this 'generation idea' for many reasons but those of you who do must now explain to me how such information about Biddy's corpse lying unattended for many days before being found was known to her spirit-self. Her mind died with her body and so could hand on **nothing** regarding that fact to the next generation. Surely Biddy could only have known that she lay undiscovered for many days because of one of two possible reasons,
Either,

1) She was able to 'look down' upon her 'ex-body' lying unburied upon her mattress or
2) She had, after death, access to some sort of memory system which held that information. By my way of thinking, the salient fact that the body lay unburied was automatically logged (as all facts are) in the Great Universal Memory System and it was from that source that Biddy re-gained knowledge about her former self.

(As a completely side issue, researchers might care to note that if Biddy was able to say that her body "had lain undiscovered for several days" then we have evidence there that spirit people have an understanding of the passing of time in a manner reminiscent of our own. Our general unit of time is One Day because we live under the influence of the Sun. I wonder what unit of time is understood by deceased entities who once inhabited our planet. Certainly I note that 'Repetitive Memory Hauntings'(e.g. 'Christmas Eve ghosts') do indeed pop up at annual intervals which would imply that a year (in our terms) is still a meaningful unit of time to spirit entities. All very interesting is it not!)

****

The Hungry Man

I'm going to begin this case with a 'mental health warning' for, at time of publication, it has not come to any sort of meaningful end and that aspect of it will probably drive you mad! The things keep happening ….there is no shortage of 'happenings'…but nothing seems to come to any sort of fruition. From the reader's point of view as well as the author's that means that an unsatisfactory state currently exists. If things in this account get too boring skip to the next chapter where things get decidedly scary!

Sometimes when a family is overwhelmed by some sort of psychic happening taking place within their home they jump speedily to all sorts of conclusions and, indeed, very often come to the wrong conclusions.

The Briggs family was different for they had weighed up the situation carefully and while it did not make much sense to them, they were pretty much on track when I was called in to look more closely at the strange things that were taking place in their somewhat difficult-to-get-to rural home.

I was given an address as well as a clear and descriptive story over the phone from Major Briggs but when I offered to come out to visit he swiftly said,

"Oh, in that case I'll collect you from the nearest village. You park your car and phone me when you get there then I'll come down the hill to collect you!"

I thought that final remark rather strange for while my present car is not a four-wheel drive vehicle I always considered that if I took things slowly and carefully I could get up most country tracks where a family home was concerned. I took the man at his word, however, and having collected two trainee investigators on the way I drove Michael and his wife Mary to our appointed rendezvous spot just outside the village of Fiddochhead. I then phoned Major Briggs in the agreed manner and we waited for his arrival in the beautiful Spring sunshine, all the while watching seagulls diving for fish in the nearby sea-loch which extended far to left and right of us with the craggy highland hills beyond.

155

We heard a car engine coming in our general direction but looked at each other in puzzlement for we could see no vehicle at all then suddenly the bushes and small trees about twenty five yards away flicked apart and there appeared a maroon coloured four-wheel drive Toyota with our client at the wheel. The fact that not one of us had realised that there was a track leading through the nearby bushes up to a couple of houses shows just how narrow that track was.

We left aside the obvious question of just why a retired army Major who now served as a senior director of a retirement home for old soldiers should wish to live in such an isolated place and we clung tightly to our seats as we all bumped and bounced up the track. We swayed this way and that and held on to each other for support as the wheels hit pot-holes or moved over missing planks on little bridges over streams where, through the hole, you could see the rushing water many feet below.

As a psychic investigator I had to, of course, take all things into consideration and my first thought as we bumped along the narrow and tortuous track had to be,

"If this family has lived a long time in this unusual place was there a possibility that somehow its very remoteness had turned their minds in some manner. Could it be that things which had a perfectly ordinary explanation for most of us might have taken on a fanciful nature for this family?"

(Dedicated psychic investigators should note that any investigation into a possible event should start long before the business of sitting around a table listening to stories told by the clients. Initially the geographical area of the event should be considered: is it, for example, in a place where the local population might be easily swayed by folk-lore tales of the past? Likewise, the buildings themselves should be taken into account. Are they ancient or modern and are they well maintained or in urgent need of repair? If your client lives in a new house which has recently been built on a field in the countryside and that field has been precisely that for the past several hundred years then the purported ghost of a dear old lady in Victorian clothing has to be looked at in a different light than that of a phantom which has been seen in a Victorian house in the centre of old Edinburgh. One is an unlikely possibility while the other is most definitely

a probability. If it is eventually proven that that new country dwelling has the ghost of a Victorian lady then it is probable that she may have entered the dwelling by 'latching onto' either the householder or a family antique brought into the building. As you are approaching someone's house it is worth noting whether the garden is well-kept or used as a dumping ground for all sorts of things from old cars to discarded bed-ends. While these things are themselves of minimal value in getting to the truth, they do indicate the mindset of the people you are about to deal with. A householder who keeps a neat and tidy garden is more likely to be accurate with the truth than one who carelessly surrounds his property with all sorts of thrown away junk. A careful person in one thing is usually a careful person in most things and if there is anything we need from a client it is a series of clear and intelligent descriptions of just what is taking place in their home as far as supposed psychic events are concerned.)

Jean, Major Briggs's wife, came out to meet us and ushered us into the cottage where some coffee and biscuits were offered to us. It all seemed very pleasant and it was almost with reluctance that I finally had to say,

"Right then folks, let's get down to business! Let's hear what it is that is bothering you so much."

We were told by the Major that just about thirty miles down the road and close to the nearest large city there is a large retirement home for old soldiers that had cared for all their needs for about a century. That is Bonston House. Major Briggs had been responsible for the running of that establishment for the last eight years and while he and his family had initially been living on the country estate where the retirement home was sited, he had since purchased this more convenient cottage in the countryside and had chosen to stay there while still working at Bonston.

The house in which they had initially lived in the grounds of the retirement home had previously housed a Major David Boyle and that man had 'died in harness' so to speak in 1984. He was quite a tall man and an undoubted character who, in his later years, kept fit by running up and down his stairs until one day it was all too much for him and he was found dead on these self-same stairs. He had also spent more than four years between 1940 and 1945 being held prisoner in a Japanese prisoner of war camp on the infamous Burmese Railway. There he had faced death on many occasions along with his men, sometimes from sheer starvation and sometimes from the unbounded brutality for which the Japanese army was well known. It is to his credit that he came through such horror and played his full part in the organisation of the home for old and injured service people of both sexes. It was probably his steadfast dedication to this cause that kept him mentally and physically fit into his latter years.

When Major Briggs moved into his new post and replaced his predecessor both in the office and in the tied Manager's House at Bonston his family had never expected to find any "leftovers" from the previous David Boyle era in that house. However, they soon found that at least three separate things were taking place that could only really be accounted for by reason of them being connected with the previous tenant Mr. Boyle.

Firstly there were many times both during the day and at night when someone's phantom footsteps would run up and down the stairs in their new house. The house stood in its own grounds and so there was no question of footsteps reverberating through some intercommunicating wall.

Then there was the needless and mysterious pulling out of telephone and computer jackplugs from their sockets. This too would happen at all hours of the day or night.

And lastly (but most annoyingly for Mrs. Briggs) the family would find empty (or sometimes 'half-empty') food containers around the place that none of the family had removed from the cupboards. These would often be hidden in some way, like behind larger domestic articles stored at the back of some little-used cupboard. The old cupboard which lay under the stairs was always a favorite for some reason: there, all sorts of packages 'stolen' from the 'fridge and food-cupboards could be found! Sometimes such packs were completely empty but occasionally they held the remains of partially eaten food still in place and it was the awful smell that usually gave their hiding place away. Sometimes, amazingly, (to those who do not understand the abilities of the psychic world) the Briggs would find a 'stolen' package where the food had been completely removed and yet the seals on the package had not been either tampered with or removed! Somehow the family, consisting of mother, father and several children took all this in their stride until they finally moved away to their new home in that country cottage. While it did not worry any of them, father thought for the sake of this deceased fellow soldier, Mr. Boyle, that he would ask that a local Church of Scotland minister should come along and put a blessing on the Bonston Manager's House just as they left. This was done but to what degree it stopped the psychic activity is unknown. Very little I guess.

Anyway, the Briggs family started to enjoy life in their new and truly rural home. The children grew up and (except for young Robin who was still seventeen) they went off to university and the like. By 2003, however, some strange things had begun to take place in the cottage that reminded them all once more of their stay in the Manager's House in the grounds of the Bonston House. Once again empty or half-empty food packages were being found in all sorts of odd places and at odd times. Father and mother were perhaps a bit suspicious of their own boy initially for the youth must have had a goodly appetite like all lads of his age but the obviousness with which some of the empty packs were flung down...like in the middle of the kitchen floor at 7am... was such that there was a feeling in the air that those packs were sometimes being left exposed on purpose in order to draw attention to something or other.

This attention-seeking simultaneously appeared to take on other forms, one of which was repeated over and over again as it had been years before at Bonston House. That was the purposeful pulling out of the phone jackplugs so that the domestic phones and computers would suddenly go dead. Once the family realised the nature of this latter problem they would merely push the plugs back into their sockets again, curse the family ghost and get on with life.

(As you will see later, when we made a second visit to the property, it was discovered by the medium employed on that occasion that the entity was also attempting to gain attention by turning up and down the volume of the music centre. Unfortunately none of the family seemed to realise any of this.)

The disappearance of items varied in format every now and again and while the disappearance of a tub or two of ice-cream or a pack of sausages might have gone unnoticed, when two cooking pots went missing Mrs. Briggs thought that enough was enough and told her husband that perhaps now was a good time to get someone along to the house who knew more about such strange goings-on than they themselves did.

At that point I was brought into the whole business.

****

While I often go out to private' cases with other associates, on this occasion Michael, Mary and I represented the Scottish Society for Psychical Research for it was through that Society that the case had come to me.

For almost two and a half hours we listened and questioned the Briggs family as well as their son, Robin. At that point in the investigation it was the fact that the young lad was living perpetually in the house that was the sticking point in any theories as to who or what was apparently causing psychic activity within the property.....if indeed such activity existed.

If we left Robin out of the equation then certainly, the Briggs seemed to have worked out at least some of the situation for themselves. Namely that the spirit of David Boyle had somehow moved with them from Bonston to their cottage and was moving food through time and space (as entities can) for a reason best known to himself.

A whole host of unanswered questions obviously arose. Was the entity's obsession with food something that was a leftover from the years when Major Boyle was a prisoner of war and being slowly starved towards the point of death? If so then what was the point of his keeping pulling out the phone jackplugs? And why on earth would he want to take away kitchen pots?

At that point I felt that we were actually dealing with a range of attention-seeking devices but why on earth the late David Boyle should want to contact a family that he had never met in life was most certainly something of a mystery.

(I pointed out such points and paradoxes to the trainee investigators I had brought along with me and I am sure they enjoyed taking part in all the arguments and counter-arguments. I also drew the attention of the trainees to the fact that we had no idea at all (at that point) as to where the missing food was

going. The psychic world can switch off our laws of physics as and when it wants if it is to its advantage, so I had no difficulty in accepting that the missing food had gone in the form of 'apports'. For readers who have not encountered that word before it covers such items that travel through time and space by methods that no one understands. Apports are not all that uncommon when dealing with the paranormal but the actual consumption of food to provide nourishment is completely unnecessary in the spirit world and so the question must arise..... "Having taken away the food from the packaging where had it been put for it most certainly had not been eaten?" Had it, for instance, been transferred to someone else's 'fridge? Apports are sometimes 'hidden' for a period by an entity and then returned to their original (or some other) situation but I began to consider that there might be a problem with a decomposable substance like food. We know almost nothing of the mechanisms used by the psychic world to move or store our physical items: I rather think that food, like other material substances, may well be reduced to a mere binary code sort of situation until it is necessary to reproduce it and show it to us once again. That is, there is no 'real' storage of anything at all required. Perhaps food would not decompose 'in absentia' from our 3-D physical world but my guess was that it was being removed from the packages in the house and being put somewhere. Little did I know that our follow-up visit would shed further light on that matter!)

As the current rules of the Scottish Society for Psychical Research forbid the presence of a medium on an initial visit to a case I was unable to take along the very talented medium, Francesca, with whom I often work. This rule seems to stem from a genuine desire not to 'contaminate' a situation under examination and was brought into being by people of a scientific mind who were used to dealing with science as we know it on our own planet. What they had failed to understand is that the psychic world not only does not work to our laws of physics but can overrule them as and when it thinks necessary. Under those circumstances the only way we can get a reasonably strong toehold into that other world is by using people who have unusual capacities concerning that world...in other words we must use proven *mediums*. By the end of that initial visit that was indeed proving to be the case for while we all had ideas, those were not blending together particularly well: we still lacked a unified theory as to what was taking place in the cottage and why. This case was proving yet again that a good medium was required to move the knowledge forward and telling Major and Mrs. Briggs precisely that, we said "Goodbye" and promised to return.

****

At midday on Sunday, April 27th, 2003 I set off on my 240 mile round journey, initially to pick up the medium, Francesca, from Edinburgh and then to meet with Michael and Mary in Glasgow before we all headed for the Briggs household once again.

Unusually, because of the distance involved, I had to tell Francesca beforehand where roughly we were heading for the sake of her family who would be waiting at home for her return. I usually tell her very little before we set off to a case.

It was she who began the conversation with me on details of the case before we had even left the Edinburgh city limits and still had nearly a hundred miles still to drive,

"Archie, I felt this morning in my house that we are dealing with a case where something or some things are being flung away into undergrowth near a cottage. I feel that there is water there and lots of red flowers. Could they be poppies?"

I was truly thunderstruck once more by this woman's talents. How could she possible know that I would be asking her at some point if she could identify the disposal place of the missing food? I decided to 'play it cool' and said very little.

I think that she felt my purposeful silence and nothing much was said for the next few miles then she came out with several things that bore no meaning for me at all ...although if Francesca said it, I knew that it might well form part of the psychic jigsaw that we had not yet uncovered,

"I am also getting impressions of a long roll of something like parchment or similar. It's all rolled up and quite old and I see a man unrolling it. It's long and it is important!"

That meant absolutely nothing to me for what I imagined her describing was some sort of ancient title deed to an old property

162

and seeing that I did not seem to relate to what she was telling me, Francesca moved on to yet another topic,

" I feel there is also some sort of slender connection between the place we are going to visit and a large institutional type of building of some kind."

Now my ears really did prick up: could Fancesca be feeling the link with Bonston House that could undoubtedly be thought of as an 'institution' of some sort?

"Develop your thoughts along that line, Francesca. What kind of 'institution' can you feel?"

I watched as the lady sank into deeper thought and probably a mini trance.

"It's an orphanage!" she finally said triumphantly, "It's a children's orphanage!"

Bang went any thoughts I might have had that she had locked onto the Bonston House home for old soldiers....unless that premises had once been an orphanage, which I was pretty sure was not the case.

From many years of experience with her I knew that Francesca is rarely wrong but what she was saying at that moment was making no sense in the context of what we had already been told on the first visit to the Briggs cottage: there might, however, be a lot more to this story than we already knew.

I decided not to continue matters along such lines as we drove so the conversation was dropped and we soon began talking about almost everything under the sun to cut the boredom of the many miles that lay ahead of us.

We picked up Michael and Mary in Glasgow as before and a further hour's run found us waiting to be picked up by Major Briggs at the appointed rendezvous point. The bushes parted and the estate car poked through to take us bumpily up to the cottage once more.

After the last gulp of hospitality coffee I turned to Francesca,

"Ask the Major about that roll of parchment, or whatever, that you spoke of in the car," I said and she did. As Frances seemed to be quite excited about this item during our car journey I watched the man's face anxiously to see if his expression would light up with some sort of recognition when the word "scroll" was mentioned. It didn't! He had no idea at all what the medium was talking about and said so robustly. Mary, who was doing all our note-taking, felt let down I'm sure but I've been through that scenario a thousand times in people's homes and seances so I was not unduly surprised. I wish I had a dollar for every time I've had someone deny the existence of some piece of information only to come to me (or Francesca) later and admit sheepishly that "Of course I know about XXX! I can't think how it escaped my memory!" I've come to the conclusion that many people put things so far to the back of their minds that some sort of blockage takes place at times like this.

Anyway, I told everyone that we'd leave that discussion of the scroll till later and we'd move on to talking about the missing food once again.

"Mrs. Briggs," I said, "You were going to keep records for me* over the past month as well as any empty packs of any food that went missing......" I did not finish my intended sentence before I saw an embarrassed look in her eye.

"I'm so sorry! Here are my two pages of typed up notes for you but someone (she looked meaningfully at her husband) accidentally threw out all the packages that I'd kept for you, with all the trash. But I do have one emptied pack of chocolate biscuits, the contents of which were stolen from us yesterday." The lady smiled and handed me the packet which had one corner crudely torn open showing that all the contents had been removed. I thanked Mrs. Briggs and quickly glanced down the list of the month's happenings that she'd kindly prepared for us. Yes, all the usual ....plugs pulled out and food going missing. I passed the list into Mary's keeping and went on,

"Let's get back to this food thing. Francesca, can you now tell us all about that business that you mentioned in the car .... about something being found beside water and red flowers and the like."

The medium began telling what she had felt about something that always seemed to go missing from the house and where it could be found. (Remember that Francesca had not been with me on the initial visit and so did not know anything about the disappearing food before the conversations of that very afternoon.)

"I just feel that something is being taken from the house and flung away into the bushes and grass near here. It is beside water, running water, and I feel that there are red flowers in that area." The Briggs were looking meaningfully at each other and soon smiling.

"You've just described an area outside our garden which leads onto the bleak hill moorland behind the house. There's a rushing stream there and in the Spring of the year the rhododendron bushes are splendidly in flower at that part." Their smiles grew larger.... "Do you know what?" said Mrs. Briggs, "The dogs were always snuffling around there and we always wondered what they were paying so much attention to but perhaps it was a continual supply of food from our own freezer they were enjoying!" Interesting!

I kept the conversation centred on the disappearing food, especially where the empty packages had been recovered of late.

An increasing number of them were now being left where they would have been easily noticed and from experience I knew that any psychically-originated happenings that are so public are usually a mechanism for drawing attention to the presence of an entity. This blended well with the most recent spate of plug-removals as well as telephones actually being lifted out of their cradles. Both of those things had so recently been bothering the family more and more.

(For a diary of the events of one month please see later in this account)

"Why would David Boyle want to bond with you, Major Briggs?" I asked. "Why does he appear to want you to know that he is here with you?" I had not got an answer to those things before Francesca slipped into an altered state again and began acting as a half-way-house between Major Briggs and Major Boyle, deceased.

"David Boyle says he wants to help you with the problem that you are struggling with. He says that both he and you are on the same side and want the same thing for Bonston House. He says you both know "The Fighting Spirit" so let's apply it to good ends and we'll win through together!"

(Unbeknown to at least some of us in the room at that moment there was a pun being given to us by Mr. Boyle, deceased, for

"*The Fighting Spirit*", we discovered an hour later, was an oil painting which hung in a corridor of the Briggs's cottage depicting a military battle scene where men of a Scottish regiment were overcoming an overwhelming enemy force through grim determination.)

As Francesca spoke further it was becoming abundantly clear that not only was David Boyle a constant but invisible companion of Bobby Briggs but that he was with him not only in the family home but also in his office at Bonston House.

"What's this problem that David Boyle keeps mentioning?" I asked and then began a whole saga that we had heard nothing about previously and which may have been the crux of the entire affair.

Bonston House was originally a large and fine country house built in the last century which lay close to a major city and which was eventually turned into a hospital and retirement home for old and wounded soldiers from the 1st World War. By the year 2000, when funding for the establishment was not as good as it once had been, eyes were turned upon the great area of valuable estate land that lay around the majestic house. Greedy (or sensible?) people decided that they could raise funds by selling off this asset for either a golf course or for new housing. Leaving aside totally the rights or wrongs of the respective cases, it was clear that both Mr. Boyle and Major Briggs truly loved Bonston House and all that it stood for and neither wished to see its lovely and tranquil grounds turned into either housing or a golf course. The problem, however, was not on the plate of Mr. Boyle, deceased, but on that of Major Briggs. Perhaps the first man wished the second to know that he had his full backing and that he would be behind him (in more than one way) when superiors had to be stood up to and home truths put forward even at the expense of losing one's job.

It was then that IT happened!

In order to explain a point about the Bonston House estate and grounds, Mrs. Briggs went behind the door of the very room we were in and brought forward a tall cardboard box which measured about 3 feet by 4 inches by 4 inches and drew from it a rolled up architects' chart of the area. I looked at Francesca and it was she who blurted out,

"That's it! That's the long and important scroll that my mind saw you holding as we were driving here!"

Major Briggs unrolled all seven feet of it and it was indeed a "long scroll" and of a parchment colour although actually it was of very thick and yellowed paper.

"Game, set and match to Francesca!" I said under my breath.

Through this medium Mr. Boyle expressed the thought that the future would see more normal times ahead for Bonston House and that "someone of great importance would reverse decisions that appear to have already been taken but this news will not come to you (Major Briggs) either by word of mouth or by telephone but by a simply worded letter." It will also interest readers to know that Francesca said at that point that Mr. Boyle was waving a long dagger-like letter-opening knife at her to illustrate the means by which the final pleasing information was to arrive at Bonston House office.

****

There were still several loose ends to tie up in this case and for your enlightenment and information I'll now put them to you.

Firstly, I have to remind you that as we were travelling towards the Briggs home Francesca picked up upon "an orphanage". She was most definite about it.

We discovered, before we left the Briggs home that day that there was also the entity of a teenage ghost girl in the cottage and here I must point out that it is not uncommon to have several entities within a single building.

(Whether she and Mr. Boyle knew of each other's presence we do not know for sure but there were certain similarities in their actions that might lead one to believe that there was interaction at least to a minor degree.)

This girl probably belonged to the Victorian period and was dressed in the most utter rags. I do not mean merely 'poor clothing' I really do mean 'utter rags'. Francesca felt her presence in the cottage in a very weak way but as we walked through the rooms that entity's energy was far, far stronger in the western rooms and Mrs. Briggs explained to us that most of their cottage was built in the 1970's. That made it probably a hundred years later than the girl's time but there had been an old cowshed at the western end of the plot of land that had been incorporated into the structure of the new house. It was there that the girl had spent considerable time obviously ...no doubt milking the cows. (Or even sleeping each night in the hay?)

A very old stone cottage to which the cowshed had initially belonged is very close to the west side of the Briggs's cottage and is still inhabited. I rather imagine one of two things...... either the young girl lived in that cottage in her early years and when her parents died **she ended up in the orphanage which is merely two miles away or she was a resident in the orphanage and was put out to work on behalf of that establishment in order to bring in some sort of income**. I think perhaps that the former account might be more true for I cannot see a large and 'official' orphanage sending out their children to work in the ragged condition that Francesca described to us. Anyway ....an orphanage most certainly did come into matters exactly as Francesca had predicted.

Francesca is always very keen to point out to me that the spirit world, while quite willing to help to unscramble the many cases that we come across, likes in each situation to let family members involved know that their parents, grandparents or whoever, are really there and watching over them. While I was leaving the Briggs front door at the end of our day there, I noted Francesca purposefully lingering behind to talk with Mrs. Briggs. She told that lady that her mother was there in the room with her and I heard her being very precisely described. Mrs. Briggs was agreeing to that description and once the chat was finished that lady opened the drawer behind her and took out a wedding photograph and put it before Francesca.

"There," said the medium, pointing to a lady mingling with others at the wedding, "That's the lady who says she is your mother." It was!

****

Diary of Unexplained Household Events
(March 31st to April 27th 2003)
Kept by Mrs. Briggs

Mon. 31 Mar.

midnight: Clock radio alarm went off-checked/reset for 6am

2am   Clock radio alarm went off- checked/reset for 6am

3am   Clock radio alarm went off- checked/reset for 6am

Tue. 1st Apr.

Phone plugs pulled out - when returned from shopping

Wed. 2nd Apr.

New carton of ice-cream missing from freezer bought Apr.1st

Thur. 3rd Apr.

Carton of new custard creams missing from kitchen cupboard

Fri. 4th Apr.

Discovered toilet roll in small drawer in shower- room

Mon. 7th Apr.

Empty potato-salad container found crammed in a bookshelf in the study: dated "Feb. 03"

Tue. 8th Apr.

Phone plugs pulled out in morning

Discovered 2 cans of "Fanta" in wrapper in TV room last seen in drinks cupboard in drawingroom

Wed. 9 Apr.

        Phone wires pulled out in morning

        Custard creams re-appeared in TV room - half eaten

        2 beefburgers (raw) disappear from 'fridge - no sign anywhere of them

        Strange brown glutinous substance appeared on door of hall cupboard

Fri. 11th Apr.

        Half carton of wafer-thin chicken disappears from 'fridge

        Empty biscuit carton found in TV room

Sat. 12th Apr.

        Small stainless steel saucepan disappears (part of a set of three) The largest of the set had already disappeared in a like manner at my previous house!

Sun. 13th Apr.

        Replacement ice-cream carton disappears from freezer

Mon14th Apr.

        Phone wires pulled out in morning

        Empty packet of oatmeal biscuits found in TV cupboard

Wed16th Apr.

        Clock alarm radio turned off in the night

Thur 17th Apr

        Phone plugs pulled out

        Pack of biscuits disappeared from kitchen cupboard

Tue 22nd Apr

    Discovered ice-cream carton with mouldy ice cream and part eaten packet of chocolate biscuits under chair in TV room

Wed 23rd Apr.

    Phone wires pulled out twice: once morning , once afternoon

    Empty ice-cream carton appears in diningroom: not sure when it went missing.

Thur 24th Apr

    4 sausages in broken wrapper appeared in 'fridge: complete packet of 8 had been in the freezer

    Bag containing many wrappers etc which I had collected for further examination by Mr. Lawrie was inadvertently put in the trash can for disposal: I will look after the next lot better! *(she did)*

Fri 25th Apr.

    Packet of chocolate fingers (only 3 fingers left) discovered under sofa in TV room

Sun 27th Apr.

    Packet of 8 croissants disappeared from freezer (bought last week)

(signed)Mrs. J. Briggs, Sun. 27th April 2003

****

At that point the case was not really resolving itself in the manner that I would have liked: some sort of false end had been arrived at. There were just so many loose ends and remaining probabilities that I knew intuitively that there was more to happen here yet. By June, I knew that the next phase had been embarked upon for Major Briggs phoned and said that not only had the food started going mysteriously again but that money had started disappearing for the first time.

The missing food problem was definitely increasing in strangeness for the pattern was not making any sort of gastronomic sense. For example in a single night the top half of no less that three bottles of tomato sauce which were stored in the 'fridge would go. Common sense dictates that if any human was stealing food from the 'fridge then surely they would use up one bottle of sauce fully before starting on a second or a third to say nothing of the vexed question of why anyone should use up the equivalent of one and a half bottles of sauce in a single night.

The money situation was far more worrying, for both coins and paper money were disappearing and from places which were reasonably secure within a family setting …like pockets of trousers on a chair by the bedside, from a locked briefcase and from a locked cupboard.

When hard cash begins going then I must be careful that things are not more truly linked to human beings rather than to entities and this I said to Major Briggs. In the nicest way possible I reminded him that he had a boy in his late teenage years living at home and that at that time in life youths tended to be unpredictable and to do unpredictable things. I was quite pleased that this was something that he had already discussed with his wife apparently and the pair had at least taken some steps to see that Robin was not dipping his hands either in the 'till' or the freezer.

****

By then it was early July 2003 and if I had thought that that was the end of this strange story then I was to be proved very wrong, for by mid July the Briggs family were in touch again. They arranged to meet me at a festival and book exhibition that I was attending in Edinburgh and they told me some new really strange and surprising things. The food was still going missing on a weekly basis but by now their phone lines were not just being 'tampered with' …they were being physically cut! Even the method of cutting was strange in as much as the five strands of wire within the general 'phone cable were being snipped at various places along the length of the cable so as to make it more difficult to mend the line. For example the orange inner wire was snipped near where the line came into the house while the next cut occurred about a couple of yards further on and another cut went through the blue wire some yards further on still. It appeared to be a form of sabotage rather than just some sort of act of vandalism. And that, unfortunately, is as true for human activity as it is for psychic activity for at that point we could not yet rule out the possibility that one person within in the family circle was playing long term tricks on the rest of the family. The disabling of telephone lines was one thing but the removal of money was to be quite a different thing. One seemed to be a vandalistic act while the other seemed to be plain theft. And where did the disappearing food come into matters? If I had been a detective working for the police I'd be looking for a hungry thief who regularly broke into the same cottage, week in and week out, in order to steal money and eat while he was in the house. But why should he choose to then hide the food containers behind and under articles of furniture within the house? Would a normal thief not just throw down the food containers where he was standing at the time? And while a normal thief might rip the phone line out its socket to delay the family calling the police if he was disturbed in the act, this thief spent valuable time snipping the line in several places along its entire length! The money too, I heard again, was disappearing from a locked briefcase and even out of jacket pockets hanging by the bedside and even (latterly) from wallets kept under the pillows of the family.

This now definitely looked more psychically originated than the work of a human being.

Unfortunately for many reasons like holidays, family illness and distance we were unable to make a further visit to the Briggs family at that time although we dearly wanted to.

By November 2003, at long last we had an opportunity to travel the 200 miles there and back and so Francesca and I made our way towards the west but this time we thought we'd visit the Old Soldiers' Home where Major Briggs worked rather than his own house.

The whole episode turned out to be rather disappointing. Yes, Francesca did find the spirit-being of Mr. Boyle on the premises as well as sensing his presence from afar in a second building that was under total reconstruction and into which we were not allowed to go. But "No," we did not find any evidence that the money that Mr. Boyle was supposedly removing from the Briggs household was ending up in the coffers of Bonston House in order to assist the general funds of that institution.

(While the work of psychic investigation is exceedingly interesting it is also exceedingly frustrating for statements of all sorts should be checked thoroughly but for a whole host of reasons that is not always possible. Psychic investigators are NOT policemen or detectives: we have no powers to instruct or command, we have no powers of search and no powers to ask to see or examine any documents. In short we have virtually no authority at all.)

Once it was explained to us that perhaps Mr. Boyle was "collecting funds" on behalf of the institution we suggested that a check be made of the identification numbers of paper currency notes kept on the Briggs home property to see if, once they'd 'disappeared', they might be found in the office safe at Bonston House. I know of no such checks having been carried out to that end and yet such a thing would have been reasonably simple.

(Strange though my readers might find it, I have no problems with the money 'moving through time and space' from point 'A' to point 'B' for I know that psychic apports do precisely that …even if we humans don't understand the mechanism by which such a thing is undertaken.)

Communications with the Briggs family seemed to have broken down somewhat in early 2004 and by mid summer, when I had not heard anything from them for some months I e-mailed them to ask if the strange things in their lives were still active. The reply was in the affirmative and I now reprint some of the reply that I was given to show my readers the extent of the ongoing problem. I had suggested that a metal cash-box with money enclosed be sealed in the presence of witnesses and then re-opened after one month had elapsed (again in front of witnesses) to see if the money had been taken.

I realised that because we were dealing with the psychic world such a procedure might well have flaws but I thought it worth trying. If the money did disappear and then re-appeared at Bonston House then it would tell us a great deal.

I have paraphrased this incoming e-mail from Mrs. Briggs.

"Dear Archie,

We would be happy to take part in this research, but are a little concerned that, for whatever reason, the 'entity' might not take the bait – possibly sheer bloody-mindedness, because he/she/it has heard us discussing it!

(comment by the author …I feel that while "bloodymindedness" is possible from the spirit world, it is unlikely.)

My husband has carried out one or two experiments of a similar nature e.g. leaving money in his locked briefcase and not telling anyone in the house. The money has always disappeared.

The level of food 'theft' is still quite high – probably on average something every day or every two days. One of the latest wheezes was to put a bowl of rice krispies and milk with a spoon sticking in it into one of the favoured hiding places – the bottom of the leather armchair in the TV room. We have had to pull the material away from the bottom of the chair to retrieve the many items which end up there- usually mouldy empty ice cream cartons, tins, and dinner plates – which is curious for we check it most days, so the time for things to go mouldy must be limited.

We are not at all worried about the confidentiality thing and do not mind our identities being known* we really just wish to get this resolved and to stop the 'thefts'. We will let you know as soon as we have set up the experiment and the whole thing is underway.

Regards etc., etc."

(* I had commented in a previous e-mail that I would supply independent witnesses if the Briggs family felt that they did not wish to bring neighbors or friends into their psychic problems.)

By late November 2004 I had heard nothing from the family about how the above experiment had gone and so e-mailed them to find out. I got a long e-mail in return on December 6th giving me details of further mysterious happenings before the family told me that, in the presence of witnesses, they had placed cash into an old steel ammunition box, padlocked it securely and then sealed (with sealing wax) all hinges, openings and lock mechanisms.

Here are some of the other latest happenings mentioned in that e-mail:-

1) Coffee mug goes missing (yet again) and is found, complete with "decomposing liquid" in an upright manner inside(!) the bottom of the leather TV chair. Access via a small hole in the base. Very difficult to do!

2) Along with the above was an almost empty jar of sandwich filling that had disappeared many weeks before. "As is the norm, there was no smell of decomposition from the food remains." (Is there some sort of clue here?)

3) On Saturday 4th December, two packets of Scampi and Crispy prawns were bought and put in the freezer. By the morning of Dec. 6th an empty packet of prawns was discovered behind the bread bin but the Scampi was still missing. This was later found by the family cat …..unopened and in a receptacle on top of the very tall upright freezer.

And that, regretfully, is where this tale must currently end as the publishers await this text. Perhaps volume 3 will show if Major Boyle is merely 'messing about' as opposed to having a main aim of some sort that appears to involve Major Briggs.

While I feel sorry for this rather unsatisfactory ending, I am not to blame for what you read as this is no 'ghost story'…it is a true account of a chain of ongoing happenings, all of which are outwith my control.

CHAPTER 6

BODYSNATCHERS

A Grisly Business
The Secret Morgue

A Grisly Business

The part of Edinburgh called "The New Town" was built around 1800 and constructed with care and using the most beautiful sandstone and was eventually populated by persons of wealth, grandeur and some with pretensions to both.

Some of the best doctors and surgeons of their time lived in that area and while, by day they would not soil their hands with crime, by night they held liaison with the scum of the earth in order to deal in stolen bodies. This unholy alliance was not some sort of warped desire to take part in demonic practices but entirely due to the need to get hold of bodies and parts of bodies for anatomical research and tuition. In those far-off days, professors of medical science had to rely solely on the corpses of hanged murders and the like when it came to getting specimens for their dissection lectures and, to put it crudely, there were just not enough of those corpses going around. The end result was that the law of 'supply and demand' took over: the medical people doing the demanding and the local rogues doing the supplying. The whole process brought together the most unlikely bedfellows!

Little did I think that I'd have a brush with bodysnatchers when I set out one sunny Spring evening with Francesca to help a lady, Mrs. Danskin, who had just taken up residence in that affluent part of town and who could not settle at all in her new apartment. No matter how she placed the furniture it seemed all wrong she said, and she felt it had nothing at all to do with the shape of the room, its lovely large size or its fifteen feet high ceilings. It had everything to do with 'the feel of the room'. The room felt plain "wrong" she said, almost as if it resented her being there at all.

With this merest hint of psychic activity Francesca and I entered the house and the very minute we stepped in through the front door my medium detected a dark entity darting out of the entrance hall and hurtling surreptitiously up the main staircase.

"Someone sure wants to get out of the way quickly!" she whispered to me as we were invited into the main room.

Mrs. Danskin gave us coffee and scones and over these she related how the entire house had originally belonged to a prominent doctor a couple of hundred years ago but had since been split up into several luxury apartments.

We listened to the tale the lady had to tell us both about the house itself and the feelings within it but I noticed that Francesca did not seem to be getting down to business in the usual manner at all. Instead of making comments which would allow me to make counter-comments and thus open up the whole situation, she was merely listening quietly and looking every few minutes past the householder and out into the hall and towards that staircase that we first saw.

This was not the Francesca that I had come to know and it soon dawned on me that she could see something and sense something that we could not (which was not surprising) but more than that, she had chosen to make no comment at all upon it... which I knew was a purposeful omission.

"Why was she not telling us what she was feeling and seeing", I asked myself and I knew the answer must lie in the fact that it might be considered too upsetting by Mrs. Danskin. It is our joint aim to assist people to come to terms with their homes and what is in them but not to scare them out of their wits.

Then, completely out of the blue, Francesca said,

"And who lives in the basement apartment below where we now are?"

I could not, for the life of me, think why she had started on what was or what was not taking place in the apartment below when we had scarcely started on what lay within the apartment that we were currently in.

"Oh," said Mrs. Danskin, "They are a little bit of a strange old couple. He's a very tall gangly man who walks awkwardly and who always seems to dress in a black suit while she looks like a bit of a witch but other than that they seem a harmless old pair who keep themselves to themselves.

Francesca was beginning to look a little bit upset and although our stay in that house had been very short, things seemed to be drawing to a close for Mrs. Danskin had said that, even before we had visited, she had decided to move out of that apartment for another as things seemed so wrong for her there.

(While it has nothing to do with this actual account, I thought readers might like to know that when I met Mrs. Danskin by chance some months later, she told me that even her very last minutes at that apartment had been marred with controversy for apparently some attempt was made to seize her keys and keep her there against her will. That whole episode in her life must have left her with lasting and unhappy memories.)

The whole evening had, from my point of view, been a sort of 'non event': almost a waste of time.

We said our 'goodbyes' and walked out into the evening sun once more but after we had rounded the first corner on our way back to the car this medium put her hand to my arm and stopped me in my tracks to talk.

"Oh, Archie, what dreadful things were in that apartment and those above and below it!"

We stood in the evening sun of that empty city street and I listened with awe as she said that she now knew that that property had indeed housed a doctor of note in its early days but that he played a major part in the resurrectionist schemes of body-snatching throughout Edinburgh. She said that she knew that while the man himself was happily ensconced with his lovely family enjoying themselves in their upstairs sitting rooms the basement was being used for something very different. It was a body store! But more than that: it was a dissecting room! The medium said that she mentally saw rows of severed arms and legs as well as other body parts all laid out ready for despatch to medical colleges and the like within the city. While the teaching and researching of medical knowledge was a fine thing in its day and a credit to the academic life of Scotland, the means by which it had to be achieved was something quite different.

I could see that Francesca was quite shaken by the surprise finding of this unofficial mortuary in the basement to say nothing of seeing phantom messengers running upstairs to the doctor to seek advice as to what body parts should be sent out to what clients.

"Who are the main players in this, I wonder?" I said to her as we stood at the corner of the street.

" I've no names coming forward but the chief man in the basement with the bodies is a very strange looking character!"

Francesca went on to describe a tall thin man of unfortunate appearance who had a definite twist to his body, a twist to his face and an arm that did not seem to function in the usual way. She also said that he seemed to have one leg considerably shorter than the other and the result was that as she watched him walk across the floor between the bodies on the tables he dragged one foot all the time. He walked by resting one leg and sort of dragging the other past it before he repeated the process. Francesca also said that she felt that he had a speech impediment although she had not actually seen or heard him talk to anyone.

I took the medium back to her house and headed for my own home which was an hour's drive away, thinking all the time of that basement and what it had once contained. By the time I arrived home I knew what I was going to do and picking up the phone I phoned an author friend of mine who lives about one hundred miles north of me. Norman Adams (real name) knows more than most about bodysnatchers of that period and has written a book upon them,

"Scottish Bodysnatchers", ISBN 1 899874 40 2

He knows the kind of work I undertake and after telling him that I had had a brush with some people who might well be bodysnatchers I asked,

"Norman, if I were to give you a description of a rather strange male entity who appears connected with the events of this evening could you try to link that description to a name? The fact that he seems to be in league with a well-known doctor in the city leads me to believe that he just might be a key player in this resurrectionist business."

I passed on Francesca's description to Norman and I actually heard him gasp at the other end of the line,

"Archie, you've just given a very good description of Andrew Merrilees!" he blurted out. "He was indeed a main player in this bodysnatching game and he was linked to some very influential people."

Norman went on to tell me that Merrilees was well known to the infamous pair, Burke and Hare* who were tried for their crimes in Edinburgh on Christmas Eve 1828. Burke was executed while Hare was banished. Andrew Merrilees himself might well have been charged and hanged but for the fact that he was too valuable a prosecution witness and I rather think too that he had friends in high places in Edinburgh….a prominent surgeon perhaps?

While the visit to that house in the better part of Edinburgh that Spring evening was of minor consequence in itself, the addendum of the bodysnatchers I did find fascinating as I hope you do now. That was the third house I had, in fact, been called out to in that street. I wonder what else lurks behind the doors that I have not yet been invited to enter?

(* See also, Chap. 3. The White Hart Inn)

****

The Secret Morgue

Because of the very nature of this business of 'dipping into the psychic memory system' the medium and I often stumble across things that we never expect to find. Here now is another classic example of that.

Prior to October 29th 2003 Francesca and I had been asked to take part in a 'psychic sweep' of a large shop in central Edinburgh as part of a greater enterprise and we proceeded with the task at 7pm that evening after the shop had been shut to the public. It was about to be a Halloween we would never forget!

I had already had vague discussions earlier with the senior staff as to what past changes had taken place in the life of the building for if it had been a shop ever since the erection of the property around 1780 then the likelihood of strong psychic memories were small for no one usually gets murdered or emotionally traumatised in a shop. On the other hand if the property was built as a domestic dwelling and later converted to a shop, as is often the case in a city, then anything goes: domestic stress always, love and hate and even brutality or murders. When I heard that the shop now covered an area that had once spanned the width of two streets as well as the gardens that had once lain between the two blocks I realised that the chances were high that we would stumble across something of interest. What an underestimate that turned out to be!

Fortunately, Francesca and I were supplied with a pretty and sensible young lady called Wanda to escort us around the large shop. I use the word 'sensible' with meaning for what we were about to discover might have 'freeked out' some silly skittish girl. The last thing we wanted was to end up with some overawed and highly emotional young woman running loose around a shop at that time of night, screaming and with her hair standing on end.

Wanda led us in a downwards direction for my medium had felt that a good starting point to our investigations lay at the original ground floor level of the building. Francesca led us through the warren of basement rooms until we moved through a door and found ourselves looking at the base of a circular round tower which had obviously once been the outside of some building although it was now very much within the confines of the modern shop.

"You are obviously following some innermost feeling Francesca," I said and she replied that she was attracted to that spot by the spirit 'leftovers' of an older man with a pipe who had been one of the original owners of the building. It had been his house and home for much of his life. The pipe, she noticed, had been of an older type that matched its owner and had one of those very long curved stems that led from the man's lips to the bowl of the pipe. He was a happy and contented man, the medium said, and was merely having an evening stroll in his garden. He would be seeing his surroundings as a garden but to us in the 21st century we were standing in the middle of a well known shop.

(I would like to think that as my readers work their way through this book they will gradually start to accept the attitude that a whole host of things are always around us but that we only see things that are pertinent to our own age and time. We must rid ourselves of the selfish thought that only we are present in the room at this moment. We are not!)

We moved back and forth through several rooms for a bit which had covered the area of that original garden to allow Francesca to mentally walk in the garden along with the man. She chose not to take up the mental attitude of actually making psychic contact with the gentleman but it was interesting to note the place and extent of his garden.

Wanda and I were then beckoned by Francesca to follow her for she said that she was being mentally pulled very strongly towards a very powerful entity who she felt hid himself away in a very obscure part of the building. I can read Francesca's mind and expressions after working with her for many years and I could see some sort of agitation rising within her. Her steps, which are usually calm and steady, were somewhat hurried and jerky and her words with Wanda were bordering on being flustered,

"Let's see. Is it this way or that?" She'd turn and look and then move quickly in a certain direction. There was no doubt about it she was being drawn or pulled towards something but what was it? We went through quite a number of rooms and doors in the lower basement until we finally found ourselves standing outside a door marked, 'Office'.

"I feel I want to move through there for some reason," the medium said and switching off the alarm system and punching in the numbers on the digital lock, Wanda showed us into that office.

What we saw was an office like any other but at the far left-hand side there was another door with a humorous notice on it. I thought that it might merely have been an office store cupboard but the notice and the obviously unused bolts on the door gave the game away.

"STAFF SWIMMING POOL"

I knew at once that whatever lay beyond it was not a swimming pool: the notice was obviously some sort of joke. Then Wanda explained that that part of the building was so low that in certain weather it flooded badly and had always done so. It was therefore used for nothing at all and was in the original condition as it had been when the building had been put up in 1750. This was soon to become only too apparent to us for Francesca asked, "Do you think that we can get in there? I feel I've got to make contact with some entity who is in there."

I felt the hairs rise on the back of my neck.

Wanda checked that the door did not carry an alarm system and then together she and the medium worked away at the little-used bolts until the door could be pulled open creakily to reveal a dark void.

"Can you find a flashlight ?" I asked our guide as the eyes of our medium and myself were growing accustomed to the gloomy vault in front of us. Soon we were able to see that we were facing into the original 18th century basement stonework and a large stone arch curved in front of us with a further vault beyond.

"I feel there's been another smaller arch here somewhere that has concealed something terrible!" said Francesca softly, as if that was an ordinary everyday statement that she was making. Wanda arrived with a battery-powered light that was more like a table lamp than a flashlight and while it gave off a poor illumination it was better than nothing at all. With it held in front of me I moved forward a little in front of the medium and shone it against the opposite wall.

The light reflected off a puddle of water on the floor and showed at the far side of the chamber what we thought, at that point, was merely a wall of well-cut stone. However, for some inexplicable reason, both the eyes of Francesca and myself centred on a particular section of this stone wall.

(Here I must explain that somehow, when we are together investigating, the medium's abilities 'rub off' on me to a degree in some strange way: it is as if we are almost one person engaged in a single task)

"Look closely!" I whispered in the darkness. "Look there and you'll see that there has once been a second and much smaller archway leading to somewhere under the street outside but it has been very cleverly blocked up!"

The more we looked the more obvious it all was. There had initially been a smaller stone archway about three feet tall and two feet broad leading to some third chamber under the city street above but at some point, stone of exactly the same type and color had been used to build in and block up the aperture. This had been done in such a skilful way that almost none of the original curvature of the arch remained visible: it almost looked as if there had never been an arch there in the first place! I did not know at that point where our investigations were leading either psychically or physically and the question that immediately arose in my mind was,

"Why on earth should someone in the 18th century spend considerable money and time hiring a skilful stonemason to block up an opening in a damp and flooding basement so thoroughly that no one would ever realise that it had existed in the first place? Why had some old rubble not been thrown into the hole and cemented into place just to block it off? After all it was merely a damp and dismal cellar under a public street. Why had identical stone been used and chisel marks been put upon that stone to make it look identical to the original surrounding stone?"

At that point it all seemed meaningless until Francesca said.

"Oh dear, oh dear, oh dear! We have something very, very nasty here!"

Somehow I knew at once what she meant and my mouth opened in amazement, as I suppose Wanda's must have done if I had turned to see her.

"You don't mean bodysnatchers* again?" I exclaimed, for we had discovered a similar cache in the basement of an 18th century surgeon's house two streets away in 2002.

"I'm afraid so," the medium almost wailed.

"And is there an entity present at the moment?"

"I'm afraid so," Francesca repeated.

I couldn't help myself,

"My God," I said, "Don't tell me it's the same man as we found at the other place in Humberland Street?"

Francesca didn't answer that question but started a thread of her own,

"He's one very angry man! He's telling us to back off sharpish! He wants us to get out of here NOW! NOW!"

I turned to an amazed-looking and wide-eyed Wanda and reassured her that nothing of a Hollywood type was going to leap out at us and grab us by the throat although I did ask her to move back further into the office area behind us….which she was already doing in any case. Francesca by now had ceased to mouth words to the entity and was backing both physically and mentally out of the unenviable situation. Her hands were being held over her ears and her head was bowed and shaking from side to side as she edged backwards out of the chamber along with myself. "All right, all right!" she was saying to the unseen entity before us.

The two of us stood in the office-to-vault doorway now and paused.

"I'm dizzy and disorientated," said the medium, "And he's on the point of attempting to go for me physically. He's been mentally hammering away at what I call my 'third eye' and I've been made to feel very afraid by him.

(An entity can envelope a human being with any emotion he wants, when he wants: this can be love or hate or fear or happiness.)

"The last time that happened to me was in the Cornsheaf pub almost three years ago," Francesca continued.

(I remembered the incident Francesca was alluding to very well: she had to duck and dive in an attempt to get away from the clutches of an entity who was not going to let her go down a flight of stairs to safety. See Vol. One, page 125.)

*(For those of you who do not know of the term "Bodysnatchers", it is a common word to cover people who assisted in the removal, theft and sale to the medical profession of freshly buried corpses. Lecturers on medical topics in universities, surgeons under training and the like purchased those in the early 1800s because insufficient human anatomical specimens were available. While it was a grisly trade, such resurrectionist exploits enabled medical science to move forward.)

All three of us moved back and the door was bolted shut once again. We walked slowly and somewhat carefully out of the office and into a basement sales storage area and then into the shop proper where we stood at the bottom of the stairs to get our breath back so to speak. I applauded Wanda for keeping a cool head in a situation that must have seemed very strange to her while Francesca's mind was returning to a more normal state. After a little rest Francesca spoke first,

"There is a person on the staff who has already met that entity in some form or other.....at least she knows he's there. The girl is a slim girl with red hair and in her early forties."

I turned to Wanda and gave her a questioning look. She, in turn, told me what I had expected, namely that a girl of that very description was the bookkeeper in the office that we had just left and she has always refused to work late in the shop by herself.

At that point Francesca started what appeared to me to be a completely different conversation and asked if some company promotion had been talked about recently. Wanda looked puzzled and said she knew nothing of any promotion pending in the shop. As that topic had nothing at all to do with a "ghost hunt" both Wanda and I wondered why the medium had brought up such a topic. I must now tell you that within 24 hours it was made known to me privately that the slim, red-haired girl bookkeeper had been notified that she had received promotion!

*(We see in that little side episode a good example of the workings of the psychic world and how it is completely linked with everyday things. What took place there was that meeting the entity had 'opened the box' so-to-speak on the red-haired girl and once that 'box' of information had been opened Francesca was able to move into and out of the information therein. In other words she was able to gain access to the girl's mind and her business. The whole thing is a knock-on domino effect that would then enable Francesca to move through that girl's mind to things that she was connected with. She could, for example, have moved into the girl's boss's mind and from there to the state of his professional relationship with the girl etc, etc. This form of psychic linking and communication is not only awesome but its speed is **instantaneous!***)

After this pause at the base of the main stairs our medium decided that she would move upwards to the highest point in the building. Neither of us asked her why but Wanda led the way to the main gallery until we were looking down upon the main part of the shop from the highest possible vantage point.

The first thing that we all noticed was the coldness of that area. While I am very sceptical about so-called 'cold-spots' that amateur psychic investigators find all over the place (and usually without a thermometer in sight) the temperature at the apex of the main shop should have been the warmest place of all and yet it was almost beyond 'cool': it was almost 'cold'.

Leaving that aspect aside, Francesca said virtually immediately that that part of the building had been almost totally restructured at some point in the past but Wanda was unable to confirm or deny that thought as she had no knowledge about it at all. That type of conversation might have moved forward a bit more except that both Wanda and I noticed that the medium had not only become very red but had also visibly started to perspire. This, of course, took us very much by surprise particularly in the light of the conversation we'd just had on the coolness of that area. Francesca stood there for a minute or so tugging at the top of her jersey and looking ever more hot and I'm sure Wanda thought that the poor lady was about to become dreadfully ill. I knew otherwise because of my ongoing work with this talented medium and I was not surprised when she said,

"There's been a dreadful fire here in the past!"

Understanding how Francesca's body takes upon itself the effects of various happenings *(that is, she is partially 'possessed' by the entity with whom she is connecting)* I knew that I had to get her out of the heat.

"Come on, Francesca," I said, "Let's move into the next room," and I took one of her arms and the three of us moved towards the next room. Half way to the room just mentioned the medium rested on a stair-head landing, sweating and gasping with her right shoulder leaning heavily against a shelf of books. At that point I was looking closely at the condition of Francesca with a view to reassessing the situation when I noticed the title of the book right behind her head. I couldn't believe what I was seeing for it read,

"GET OUT OF THE HEAT"

If only I had had a camera! I didn't but I did have a split second to draw Wanda's attention to the book as a witness to something that I feel was more than coincidence.

*(As the reader becomes more knowledgeable about the workings of the psychic world he or she will come to realise that whatever 'coincidence' is …it is **not** coincidence! This is not merely my idea*

but a philosophy generally held by persons with close contact with the world of supernature)

Francesca was still sweating profusely and looked very uncomfortable so I realised that mentally she was still very much in the middle of that raging fire. Whatever fire this was, it had obviously covered a much larger floor area than I had anticipated and therefore I had to move the medium still further back out of the psychic flames and smoke. I knew even at that point that there was a considerable quantity of smoke involved for Francesca was spluttering and finding her breathing becoming more difficult. I therefore once again took her arm and with Wanda we moved down a short flight of steps and through into another very large room in the shop. It was just as well that the premises was closed to all customers that evening! Here we found a long table and chairs and I led Francesca to the end of this table furthest from what I considered to be the heart of the fire which, by that time, must have been fifty or more feet away from us. The smoke she was still seeing and feeling all around herself was now much more meaningful than the heat of the flames which I believe I had successfully moved her out of.

I must now tell you that even before we were ever up in the gallery area, even before she had mentioned any fire, I knew that this medium had been advised psychically by some past spirit memory that she should move to that part of the building for there was a story to be listened to there.

*(You should know that a medium's place within mediumship is that she places herself mentally at the disposal of the psychic world and allows cognitive memory systems within that world to **work through her.** She comes to a subconscious mental arrangement with them that (in this case) she is moved to a certain part of a building so that powerful memories of what took place there can be both given to her and relayed through her to others in her presence. So strongly is this memory passed through a good medium that she takes upon herself the feelings of the place involved in the memory and, as you will see soon, the memory of any human being on the site during that particular event. As a witness to many such situations I must tell you that what I see is very close indeed to the unpleasant happening which we know as 'possession'. It is as if the medium has come to a*

mental arrangement that, with her permission, her body can (to a degree) become possessed by some psychic agent.)

As Francesca sat in the chair she was agitated, still breathing with difficulty and looking around herself. Maybe I was wrong but I felt that she was somehow looking for a way out of this room and I was just about to take that topic up with her when she suddenly said,

"There should be a wall there!"

She was pointing to a space about twelve or so feet wide that lay between one department of the shop and another where a very thick wall did extend to left and right.

It was at that point that I got some sort of ......what can only be described as 'a mental jolt'! I suddenly KNEW what Francesca must have known for the last ten minutes but had never mentioned: I knew that there was a fatality in that dreadful fire and that that fatality had been a little girl! I knew that she had suffered facial burns and had finally been overcome by smoke inhalation and had slumped down against the wall. Somehow, inside my head, I could see the child dressed in a pale-coloured smock quietly slide down the wall and lie still. Somehow too that whole realisation had lasted a mere fraction of a second and so I now turned to Francesca again and said,

"Is that gap in the present wall where the original wall stood and where the little girl died of smoke inhalation?"

"Yes," replied Francesca sadly, "It was."

Please note that not once up till this point had this medium actually mentioned a fire victim, far less a child victim.

I had no heart to continue this conversation further for my mind was totally filled with the sadness of seeing the little girl slump down the wall. Where there is such a sad catastrophe uncovered I somehow immediately lose all desire to question Francesca further and just want to let matters rest: perhaps the psychic world arranges that for me, I just don't know but that was most certainly the case that evening.

We walked quietly away from that Children's Department because, ironically, that is where the child perished and then we moved slowly through the brightly lit part of the main shop until we stood at the bottom of a second staircase. There our medium looked upwards.

"What's up there?" she asked and was told that there was the restaurant area but that it was closed and the alarm had been set so that we could not go in.

Just as Francesca had been advised by the spirit of the dead child to move into the gallery area in order to hear her dreadful account of the fire so next was that medium being asked to move upstairs towards a restaurant area by the memory system of some other spirit person. We moved up the staircase and stood on a broad landing outside the double doors of that locked area.

"There is a lady making herself known to us," Francesca said. "She is telling me she had so very, very happy times with three friends here. She is disappointed that they are not here now with her and somehow she is attempting to get out through this entrance but cannot." The medium then turned to both Wanda and myself and asked if we could see bits of her pushing through the present doors but we both replied in the negative.

(If this lady was indeed 'trapped' in this restaurant then it was most certainly not by doors either past nor present. As any child will tell you, ghosts can walk through walls! If there was indeed anything keeping that good lady where she was it was her own mind. Perhaps each time she left that restaurant in her own day she moved from friendship and pleasure to loneliness and hardship which must have made that place a sort of haven from which she would rather not move. While that may be merely my speculation, that is the type of reason why a spirit person might be mentally trapped in a certain place.)

When I finally asked Francesca which era the lady had belonged to she described a slim and elegant lady wearing the 'pencil' skirt of the 'New Look' period of the early 1950s which is precisely the era that the medium told us that she had frequented that restaurant.

It was a very different Wanda who finally locked up the shop that evening and then walked out with us into the sparkling city lights. While this young woman was merely a few hours older I'm sure she was a lot, lot wiser.

(I am pleased to tell you that just before this account went to the publishers Wanda was promoted and sent to look after a larger branch of the shop.)

CHAPTER 7

TWO DAYS IN THE LIFE OF …

Three Cases

****

The Movie Star Who Wasn't

People sometimes ask me to describe an average day in the life of a psychic researcher like myself. While there really is no such thing as an *average day* because each day is so very different, here is an account of two days where I delved into several very different types of cases along with Francesca .

Firstly, to demonstrate that a psychic investigator's life is not all 'doom and gloom' I will now explain that in the early days of February 2004 I received a short but puzzling e-mail. It came from someone I'd never heard of called 'Judy' in New York and while it was short and virtually meaningless to me, it did mention a family member by name so I replied to it and asked for further enlightenment. The next day I found a faint message on my answering machine that said that Judy had called and would phone again later. "That," I thought, "will solve the puzzle of who Judy is and what she really wants of me."

Well, the phone did ring some hours later and the voice at the far end said,

"Hello, I'm Judy. I'm Judy Garland."

And as there was a 'Judy Garland' film on TV that evening I thought this was some sort of 'wind-up' by some female with a warped sense of humor.

I should have paused and thought a little longer about matters upon hearing the name of a past and famous movie actress but I couldn't help myself from being a smart-ass so I said straight off,

"Oh yeah and I'm Gregory Peck so how are ya doin' these days, honey?"

Yes, it was my big mistake! Suddenly I realised that the lady at the other end had a local Scots accent and while she had a world-famous name she was not a world-famous person …just a housewife who was worried by something spooky lurking in the bedroom of her four-year old son.

Having dealt with many hundreds of cases I now know that if someone claims to have something "spooky" in their house the chances are statistically more than 99% certain that they really do have something present ….even although they are often wildly incorrect as to what it actually is. *(You will see an example of precisely this at the end of the chapter.)* I acted upon this statistic alone for what a four year old child does or does not see in his bedroom at night is anyone's guess. I will admit, however, that the mother's claim that the boy saw the same "burglar man" *nearly every night* made me prick my ears up.

"Yes," I said, "I'll come and visit as soon as I get a second case in your area."

(I am really forced not to venture out to a one-off far-flung case unless it is particularly urgent for Francesca and I charge no fees for our services and thus both travelling time and travelling expenses have to be considered. We wait until there are two cases in the same area and then go out to both at the same time.)

That time came on February 16th for a lady from a very rural community asked for help to identify the root cause of what can best be described as 'gross energy drainage' from herself and her family and her cottage. At the end of *her* phone call I got the distinct impression of a 'seek hoose' once again. Such sick house situations are usually reasonably easy to identify early on in an investigation and the source or cause of the depressing feelings (and often ill-health and malaise) can likewise be worked away at until the mystery is teased out of the mass of information that comes forth. The part of the business that causes most difficulty is the actual dispelling or dissipating of the psychic leftovers that are the usual sources of all the depression and the negativity.

Now that I had two probable cases in more or less the same geographical area I was now in the happy position to tell this second lady that I would indeed visit her also on the appointed day.

(Because we seem to be heading towards a 'sick house' situation once again I will pause here to bring in the topic of Geomancy. That is the so-called 'science' upheld by dowsers where they claim that lines of 'energy' that they call Ley Lines run through and under properties giving those properties and the people who live in them certain energy levels: some of those being of a negative or depressing nature. A subject linked to this dowsing business may be the Chinese 'science' of Feng Shui although usually that deals with interiors and furnishings of buildings as much as anything else but as I do not know much about that art I will not criticise it.

What I do know is that I have been called in by literally dozens of disappointed householders who have been under the impression that they can be helped with a particular problem by dowsers or geomancers. Such dowsers often claim to discover (with justification) ley lines running this way and that, under and around the house. Some of these lines they claim have 'bad' or negative influences on the house and these they then claim to counter by an assortment of measures like driving copper stakes into the ground around the house or placing magnets here and there as their art dictates. In virtually all of these cases either their work appears not to have made a bit of difference or, at best, to have made a betterment of the situation lasting merely a few weeks before the 'tiredness' sets in once again. That is often the very reason why Francesca and I are often called out to an already-dowsed property in the first place.

While many of these people pay considerable fees for their services, the work of these dowsers cannot be deemed to be fraudulent because most of them truly believe in their art. It is a great pity, however, that these well-meaning people cannot get themselves sorted out scientifically for as soon as they mention the word "energy" they should be challenged to say exactly what the energy is in terms of its electrical frequency and voltage and the like. All the energies currently known to physical science can be measured and really very easily! Dowsers should also be challenged to give both an explanation as to the energy source ... for all energy has to be generated and given a directional force....

and to say by what mechanism it is effecting the people within the property. I have no doubt that ley lines exist and that they are absolutely everywhere. Such lines are natural phenomena stemming from the earth's magnetic field and there are neither more nor fewer lines of geopathic stress under your house than under your office or factory where you work or the roadways upon which you walk or drive. If you really want to worry about matters concerning geo-magnetic stress then find out about the piezzo-electric effect of granite-type subterranean rocks grinding slowly against each other. Such pressure between those rock masses causes electrical disturbance under our feet in various parts of the country but its power and effect is completely measurable although how it reacts with humans is not clear… if indeed it does.

As we are discussing strange energies here I must include the surplus electromagnetic field energies which spew out in every direction from overhead power lines. These are quite unbelievably large and should be avoided at all costs. The effects upon health from such overhead grids are well documented and have no connection whatever with psychic forces.

*The whole point of this part of the chapter is to get across to you that if a house is a 'sick house' then the answer lies in the fact that there is probably within it, **residual psychic memories** that are the leftovers from previous inhabitants or from inhabitants of a property that once existed on that site and which has been demolished at some time in the past.*

I have nothing at all against dowsers and while I, myself, once had considerable ability in that practice I have seen no proof whatever that an unhappy house has anything to do with the chance co-ordination of ley lines.)

But back to the tale…..!

I met Francesca as she exited from Kirkcaldy railway station around 9.30am and we drove straight to the home of the namesake of that well-known film actress, Judy Garland.

Mrs. Garland was a down-to-earth woman who now explained to us that her son kept seeing a dark shape bending over his bed each night. This took place only in the upstairs bedroom in which the child slept and that presented me with a mystery for the house had only been built a few years previously and I was told that no one had therefore died within any part of the building. The chances of an entity being present as the result of an unpleasant deathbed situation was therefore ruled out. Similarly, because there was nil psychic activity reported to have taken place on the ground floor of the property I had to conclude that we did not have some leftovers from happenings that had, for example, taken place in a cottage which had previously existed on that site. If there was a haunting in an upstairs bedroom then it looked as if that entity had been brought into this house in some way.

"Are you a collector of antiques?" I asked Mrs. Garland as I looked around. The puzzled lady wondered why I asked such a question so I had to tell her that entities can latch themselves onto antiques and thus get transferred at times from place to place by accident. She reassured me that the family did not really have any antiques in the house and certainly not in her son's upstairs bedroom. I still thought that an entity had been accidentally introduced into the house and so kept plugging away at that prospect. Francesca, at that point, gave me a silent and knowing look that told me that she had picked up something but wanted me to continue down the mental track that I was already taking. Suddenly I knew what I was looking for.

"You don't dabble in psychic things do you?" I asked straight out.

"Well I did," the woman confessed, "Until quite recently I used to go to spiritualist meetings in a little community hall in Dysart which is nearby."

I looked at Francesca again and mentally invited her to take over where I had left off and she obliged on cue.

"Well, I've got to tell you that you accidentally brought a spirit man back home with you on some occasion."

"I thought that that might have been the way of things," moaned the embarrassed lady.

"I've got to tell you, however," went on Francesca, "That the man in question did not latch on to you within the hall you visited or during any part of the meeting. He latched onto you as you were walking down the street after the meeting."

My ears definitely pricked up here at the unusual nature of this 'spirit attachment' as it is called.

(Spirits can attach themselves to humans under a whole range of circumstances that are too lengthy to go into in this publication but it is rare (although not unknown) for one to move into the mind of a mere passer-by.)

I wanted to know more and so turned to Francesca again while I glanced back and forth to Mrs. Garland.

"Could it have been that Mrs. Garland had psychically opened up her mind during some part of the seance or whatever she had been attending and had not closed it down properly at the end of the meeting?" I asked.

"That's exactly it !" replied the medium who then turned to the householder.

"Is the hall you attended up a little lane of some sort?"

"Yes," came the answer.

"And is there a sort of cross roads at the bottom of the lane… just a little way down it?"

"Yes there is," the lady said.

"Well, it was at that precise spot where the man decided that he would enter your mind and move home with you. He tells me that he wishes you and your family no harm. He merely wanted a home. He tells me that he didn't have a real home before he died and missed family surroundings so much."

At that point I believed that the poor man might have been the victim of a tragic traffic accident that had taken place at the road junction that had just been mentioned but you will see soon that I was wrong in that belief.

"He wishes you no harm," the medium stressed for a second time that day.

"Can you ask him to turn off his ability to make himself known to any of the family please, Francesca," I said. That is a little bit different from 'evicting' the spirit gentleman from a house and home he was finding so important and nice and is a much kinder thing to do I feel. This 'switching off business' is something I have found works admirably and pleases many clients. A benign entity can be where it wants to be and yet the family are in no way aware of the presence of it. In this particular case the child would not normally continue to see 'the burglar man' lurking in his bedroom from then on unless the mother, who has some uncontrolled psychic ability herself, dwells mentally on the topic. In that case, her excess mental energy might enable him to manifest himself once again, although I didn't feel any true desire in the man to do such a thing. I think he just wants to exist quietly and invisible in a family home.

Sometimes something makes me smile when we go out on our little trips to people's homes like this and that day proved no exception.

"Have you been clearing out your deep freeze, Mrs. Garland?" Francesca said.

"I have been actually ……and re-organising it! But how did you know that?"

"The spirit man told me that he had been watching you doing what you had to and he tells me he kept saying to himself,

"What a lot of frozen food! My! What a lot of frozen food!""

****

The name "Jack" came to the fore a few times during all these deliberations and at first I thought that Jack was the name of the male entity visitor that we'd been discussing but no!

"Did a lady drop down dead outside this house and was her name Mrs. Menzies?" Francesca asked straight out as she looked at Mrs. Garland.

"Yes!" answered the amazed lady and pointing out of the window to the monoblock paved area she went on, "She and her husband were the original owners of this house and she did drop dead out there one morning I'm told. Her husband was called Jack"

"Well, she's telling me that she'd like Jack to know that she is all right where she is and is thinking of him."

Mrs. Garland said that she thought that Jack was still alive (which tallied with Francesca getting the message of course) and added that if her own husband met up with him he would pass on the message. (Apparently they knew where Jack worked.)

With that we bade the householder goodbye and drove away from the house.

****

Now we were driving out of the town of Kirkcaldy and towards our second objective that lay well into the countrified hinterland of Fife. As chance would have it we almost immediately found ourselves passing the area which Mrs. Garland had spoken of …..the small suburb of Dysart which, coincidentally, is famous as the birthplace of Stuart McDowall, the first man to cross Australia from south to north.

"Why don't we take a little diversion and have a look at the hall that Mrs. Garland left that evening before the spirit man latched on to her? We'll see the road junction at the end of the little lane where the man was killed too." I added, still thinking of the man as a traffic accident victim.

So I diverted our car into a delightful little village that had obviously been a fishing village that had grown up in the Middle Ages of Scottish history. What a lovely sunny winter's day it was for such an expedition and after asking a few local people as to the whereabouts of the local hall that had been used for spiritualist meetings we soon found it and we sat in the car at the bottom of the lane just thinking of past events. The whole area was on quite a slope for it all banked up steeply from the shore and the sea that lay to the south of us.

Francesca was looking around in a sort of worried way and this I noticed.

"Don't tell me that this isn't the place!" I said with a little alarm.

"Oh no! This is the place all right but how it has changed. Some buildings have been torn down allowing more light into the area and the old cobble stones have either been lifted or at least covered in tarmac. It looks so different now." And then this clever medium threw new and unexpected light on the manner of the man's death.

"I see the cobbles stones of the sloping road all wet and shiny," said Francesca, "And I see the man's heels flying in the air above the greasy stones and I see the back of his head striking the hard roadway. Oh dear he's dead I feel!"

Thus the truth of the matter came out. The man had not been a traffic accident victim as I had all too hastily imagined but the victim of a sloping lane of wet or perhaps icy cobbles.

We sat in the car for a few more minutes and each in our own way silently expressed our compassion towards the unfortunate victim and his sudden and untimely death before I drove off into the delightful countryside and to the next case.

****

Ill-health and Mental Exhaustion

We were heading for Old Gliston that was a strung-out rural hamlet of about a dozen homesteads and some twenty miles away.

Now I must tell you that if you want to grade the amount of 'ruralness' in any part of the countryside then the gradation might well be as follows:-

There is 'rural' at the lower end of the scale. There is 'truly rural' a bit further up the scale and at the top of the scale there is 'Old Gliston' for there are not many places left in the U.K. where the hens and geese run in and out of the open doors of the cottages as if they and the humans own them jointly.

However, the psychic activity started about **twelve miles** back down the road from Old Gliston for Francesca was true to her usual form.

"Archie, I'm getting a feeling of witchcraft! Why should I be getting that?"

It was such a strange thing to say that I couldn't believe my ears and asked her to repeat what she had just said,

"I thought you said, "witchcraft" there for a minute Francesca! Please run what you said past me again."

Well, the long and the short of it was that she did, of course, repeat that she had picked up upon "witchcraft" but this story takes a rather strange twist because as this medium was using such a word she had no idea at all that we were passing very close to a certain factory. That premises had produced, some years ago, resin ornaments of witches and other figurines concerned with magic. In my continuous search for logic in all this psychic business I then said to the lady by my side,

"Oh, Francesca, I'd better tell you that we're just passing a figurines factory that once made witches and the like…….."

The lady interrupted me almost as if she already knew that fact (which she couldn't possibly) and merely said,

"That may be so but I KNOW we are going to come across a witchcraft or pagan type of situation at whatever place you are now taking me."

Well, we duly got to the little village and after getting over the initial hurdle of identifying which cottage was the one we were looking for we walked onto the property to be met by gaggles of geese. They appeared to be wondering what we were doing on 'their' territory while little groups of hens roamed this way and that around our feet as both their movements and ours were being watched from the top of a well by a rather large and self–opinionated cockerel.

Jane eventually came out to greet us and welcome us into her picturesque cottage to meet her several dogs and eight cats. A friend's tractor drove into their yard as this troubled lady started to tell us over a cup of coffee that she felt that something was sucking the energy and the very life out of their house and everything that was in it and around it. She explained that it felt perpetually cold in the cottage no matter what amount of heat they pumped into it and that no sooner had one member of the family recovered from an illness than a second member was struck down by something completely different …and so it went on. Her husband was an ill man on a long-term basis she added. The whole story was not a happy one. What she was telling us sounded pretty much par for the course as to what one might expect from a building or site suffering from the psychic 'sick house' syndrome but in spite of that I, personally, was not feeling that indefinable feeling that I get under such circumstances. I'd really wanted to say quietly to Francesca at that point,

"Are you feeling any true sense of 'sick house' here at the moment for I am not at all sure that I'm feeling that, although I *am* getting something here that I have not met before."

However, as we were all sitting there close together, I was not in a position to say anything at all in confidence to Francesca. In fact it was she who moved the situation forward…and in a totally unexpected manner for she simply raised her left arm and pushed it straight out and then swinging herself around a bit in her chair until she faced a blank and windowless wall opposite, she said,

"Is there a wood out there somewhere quite close?"

Jane simply replied, "Yes, there is."

"And is there a circle of trees in that wood at the closest point to this house?"

I saw Jane start to speak but Francesca continued her sentence,

"And there should be a large fallen tree now in the middle of that circle of trees."

Jane's mouth did open again but she gasped initially rather than talked.

"How on earth could you possibly know that? Yes, there is!"

Francesca then went on to tell Jane that that area had been traditionally used for the purposes of withcraft in the past and during those far-off years at least one of the main participants of the group had lived in this cottage where Jane now lived.

Having never been on a real witchcraft coven site and wanting, as a researcher, to see Francesca's reaction to it, I asked Jane if she could take us a little walk over to the circle of trees. The day was cold but bright and it was not too far although we were required to take a roundabout route due to land ownership problems. As we were about to enter the wood, sadly we were confronted by a deep and water-filled ditch and at that point mobility problems also came to the fore for a member of the group. The upshot of the whole business that day was that we did not manage to make it down that path and through the wood to the circle of trees where goodness-knows-what took place in past years. We knew, however, that at some future point we might try to make it to that circle once again when the weather was warmer and the land not water-logged.

Once back in the cottage, Jane let us know that she was quite well qualified in homeopathy which caused some interesting conversation to take place in the car as we drove home. Francesca and I wondered whether Jane had in fact known about the witch site and its significance and had even perhaps known that one of the coven members had once lived in her house. Was it chance that this lady lived there and took an interest in homeopathy or had that house somehow 'inspired' Jane to take up that particular healing mechanism? I wonder what she knew or cared about herbalism which was always part of witchcraft? Maybe the past does play some part in the creation of the present….who knows?

Back in the cottage Francesca did come across the spirit entity of someone she called a "Puritan lady" standing by the bed in the main bedroom which puzzled all three of us for the Puritans of Cromwellian England had no influence in the neighbouring country of Scotland and were rarely seen there. Perhaps the figure should, more correctly, be described as a "female covenanter" and thus part of another religious group that did occur locally in that part of Scotland at the end of the dreadful period of witch-burning. Just how the spirit lady came to be there must therefore be quite a story in itself. Jane said that she had felt for some time that something of a spirit nature was often lurking at that place in the bedroom. Somehow that entity lady and her possible story got 'glossed over' and we moved onto other topics before saying our goodbyes.

(Shortly before this account went to press I learned that Jane had been attending a course in homeopathy in a building that had once had very close connections with the Quaker religious movement. Whether this had anything at all to do with the mysterious Quaker entity lady of the bedroom I have no idea. Could she have come home with Jane?)

Usually when we leave a property (especially a 'sick house') I feel satisfied that we have identified the problem that has worried the householder and that we have bettered it to some degree. I usually have an inner feeling of 'satisfaction' and 'a job well done'. Somehow or other I did not feel any such emotion on this occasion and I'll even admit to feeling dissatisfied over the whole visit. I kept feeling that there was a 'complete something' that we had not discovered there but whether this 'something' was psychically-based I doubted. What I kept feeling was what I feel when gigantic overhead power lines are in the area but yet there were no such power lines there to suck energy out of the family as had initially been suggested. Yes, there was illness and coldness and perhaps bad luck but that does not mean that spirit energies are responsible for those things.

"Never mind" I thought to myself as we left, "We can't win them all!"

Perhaps we might get called back there in the future, who knows?

****

Well, the future did arrive …on a sunny April 20th morning to be precise and we were able to go back to that property to have a look at something that might have had a bearing upon matters. You will remember that we never got to the bottom of what link there was between the house and the mysterious circle in the woods that had apparently been given over to some pagan practices of some sort; now was the time to correct that omission.

Jane's husband had changed into suitable footwear for a walk through the woods and had brought out a wooden pallet once we had arrived. That was placed over the deep ditch so that we could all walk down the narrow path through the trees and so to the 'witches circle' as we had started to call the area.

Sometimes when archaeological sites in fields or woods have been spotted after many years it is difficult to make out what the original shape must have been without carrying out some sort of excavation work. That was not the case here for we immediately saw a large outer circle of more than thirty feet in diameter and an inner circle of perhaps twelve feet diameter. There was indeed an old fallen tree that Francesca had described some weeks previously. It was lying a bit to one side of the outer circle and there was the stump of an even older tree right in the middle of the inner circle. Indeed it was all just as Francesca had described without her ever having left the main room of Jane's house all those weeks previously. It is worthy of note that not one of the four of us chose to enter even the outer circle, far less the inner one. We were in no way 'frightened' or mentally overpowered by the circles but it was as if somehow we intuitively knew that we were not wanted there. As you will read, more understanding of this feeling comes later, after the end of this episode.

Before we could know whether any of this had any bearing at all upon the life of Jane and her family we had to know what the circle truly represented and who was concerned with it.

Francesca went into one of her mini-trances and told us that the main participants in the rites that had taken place here were Irish horse-dealers and traders who had lived in the village. As well as buying and selling horses these people would also hire out horses to the local farmers for ploughing and the like for this was done in much the same way as tractor leasing is done today. As the descriptions kept coming from Francesca it appeared more and more likely that these people were probably Irish gypsy stock attempting to start a new life in Scotland. They had brought some form of pagan religious practices with them which they adhered to in their newly chosen country and which the local population obviously thought were demonic in origin. I realised then too that these 'gypsy horse-hirers' probably lived in the line of cottages (or on a previous site of these) where Jan and her family now lived.

The situation changed rapidly for not only did our medium then catch a glimpse of a little spirit girl swinging (dancing?) with her arm wrapped around a thin tree that grew on the rim of the outer circle but Francesca actually had a mental communication from a tall spirit gentleman who stood at the far side of that same outer circle opposite us. That entity did two things simultaneously; he made communication and also made himself visible to Francesca as he spoke to her. He was dressed in smart, dark clothing and wore a tall brown hat and he informed her that his name was "The Reverend William Haught". He actually spelled it out to her! And she to us,

H-A-U-G-H-T !

He said he was a Presbyterian minister from the local church (he pointed across the fields to the village of Ceres) and he further told her that he had been brought in by a local population who wanted that site spiritually cleansed of all things evil that the pagan worshipers might have left in that area of land. Mr. Haught, deceased, then showed Francesca by mental processes, a large carved stone that had great meaning for him (and us?). This lady put her hands out in front of her and made them curve downwards to left and right to illustrate the curvature of the top of the stone and she added that some sort of story or similar had been carved below the ornate top of the plaque and covered a considerable area of the stone. Jane, who had been watching with great interest, said that a 'coffin road' ran past the circle site and down to the church and burial ground in the village of Ceres and that in olden times this track had been delineated by marker stones. Francesca said that the stone she had been told about by Mr. Haught was not one of those and that *his stone* could still be found closely connected to the church in Ceres.

We all walked slowly back up the woodland path, over the ditch and then back down to Jane's house. Naturally as we walked we talked and as before, both Francesca and I came to the same conclusion...... we could see no real psychic connection between this circle and any ailments or unfortunate happenings in that family home. There was no overwhelming psychic presence of any kind within the home and there were no unfortunate entities 'latched onto' any member of the family that we could detect.

One of the original Irish settlers might well have lived in the property (or a house that once stood on that site) but that did not mean that there was some sort of evil residue still there. Francesca found no evidence of such a thing and I, myself, sensed nothing of that sort.

We left Jane and her family a little sadly as we sometimes do with a family if we feel we cannot help them in a positive manner and wished them well.

****

An Interesting Experiment

As I explain in another publication, a medium makes contact with the psychic world either directly or by using various other contact methods. Some of those are weaker and some of those are stronger. I realised that standing in the open at the side of two mysterious circles with the wind blowing through her hair was not the best way for Francesca to gain information. It would have been a bit better I thought, if perhaps she had peace and tranquillity to consider such psychic matters in depth.

Because I had taken a few photographs of the circles when we were all there I thought that I would attempt to carry out an experiment with Francesca. I sent her copies of the photographs and asked her to find a quiet moment in her own home when she could relax in an easy chair and hold and concentrate on the photographs.

As her ability at psychometry is second to none, I knew that we would gain some knowledge from her and I asked her to write this down for me.

A few days later, when we were driving down the long road to Maybole Castle which was about 150 miles away she showed me the hand-written results of her quiet seat with the photos. This was quite amazing from several standpoints ...not least that I knew from the writing that Francesca had been in a state of trance as she had put pen to paper. I now enumerate those points.

1) There were three (unlinked) sketches on the paper. One of the two concentric circles complete with the central tree stump (which appeared to have a large hole cut horizontally through the trunk about one metre or so above ground level.) One was of the carved stone already mentioned by Mr. Haught and one was a sketch of the same Mr. Haught but without his hat on. His hair was almost shoulder-length and cut very straight and level above his stiff, white collar.

   *An arrow was drawn pointing to the tree along with the words, "This tree was used in some way for sacrifices. Most were animal sacrifices **but some were human.**"*

2) There are nine lines of handwriting on the paper. Of these the first three are of normal or medium-weight pressure as might occur on any page but the last six were very forcefully impressed into the paper surface and so showed up more darkly and strongly. I was informed by the medium that her hand was pressed down on the paper very firmly by some unseen force during those latter lines. You will soon see why.

3) The text in lighter ink was as follows, "The human sacrifices were not of their own (people) but stragglers or people who were in the wrong place at the wrong time."

4) The very bold text was as follows, "You cannot enter the inner circle unless you are chosen! The young girl who showed herself for a split second was a sacrifice! William Haught cleared the area (spiritually?). Many were killed and he razed the land."

5) *Now comes a very interesting point for Francesca, you will remember, had probably been taken over by a spirit person as she started writing. That is why some of the writing is of normal force while some is of great boldness. She apologised to me for misspelling the word "*__razed__*" and told me that she knew it should be spelled "*__raised__*" but I pointed out to her that the text was, in fact, correct. Mr. Haught had very probably flattened most of the elevated twin circles and flung the stones associated with them hither and thither in order to destroy the circle outlines. He had indeed* __RAZED__ *the circles!*

I deemed this experiment a success and will try this kind of thing again.

****

Latest Information on the Above

The following information will no doubt interest you as much as it fascinated me and it came to me in a phone call from the gypsy author, Jess Smith, in early December 2004 …eight months after the above events and shortly before this book was due to be published..

Jess told me about traditional Irish gypsy burial ceremonials and how they had arisen. She said that because of the thought in the Middle Ages that gypsy people carried the dreaded plague with them from place to place the monarchs of that period had hounded the gypsy population in such a fierce way that they were forced to go through life in a very covert and secretive manner. Burial ceremonies were no exception to this …particularly when a government-sponsored scheme appeared to exist to dig up and actually behead dead gypsies!

I was told that gypsy burials were of such a secret nature that they were only carried out in hidden wooded areas and anyone spying on their ceremonies might very well find himself a victim as opposed to merely an observer. Two concentric circles formed the usual gypsy cemetery where the deceased was buried with ceremony in the inner circle while their possessions were buried in the outer circle.

This was, of course, precisely the situation at Old Gliston.

Perhaps the Rev. Haught had actually been brought in by the government of the day to obliterate the circles: perhaps it was not the locals who wished the area 'cleansed'?

****

While we had a second case to go to that day the time was only 11.30am and the other visit was to take place in the town of Glenrothes at 2pm. That meant that we had time to visit the village of Ceres on the way to see what local knowledge, if any, remained of the Reverend William Haught.

To cut a long story short we did indeed find a stone plaque almost three feet wide and almost five feet tall embedded in the front retaining wall of the church property. As this retaining wall was about ten feet tall at this point the plaque was at face-height and above, and thus what had once been carved upon the stone plaque would have been clear to all who passed by. The ornate top of the stone memorial was *exactly* as Francesca had earlier described it when we had all stood in the woods together.

Unfortunately the weather had so defaced the writing on the stone that nothing at all of it had remained but I knew that as the stone was so prominently positioned, the details about it must surely be known to the church authorities. Getting further corroborating facts from those authorities is now one of my many new tasks concerning this case but a difficult one as the clergymen change as the years go past.

At the moment the only Rev. William Haught I can turn up on the Internet was a minister in the USA in 1923 and while he could have taken a boat across the Atlantic to preach in the U.K. he appears far too late in history to be the man we want to track down.

****

A Guardian Angel?

As this is a chapter about the work that I undertook over a couple of days then I must tell you that we moved on directly from the church in Ceres to a house owned by the local authority in Glenrothes and rented by a woman and her sixteen year old daughter.

What I'd like you to notice about this case is that it can be contrasted with the case mentioned above in the rural area of Old Gliston. There we had a family whose troubles concerned their health and well-being and while we found only a very slender link with the world of the paranormal (a person who took part in some witchcraft or pagan rituals had probably once lived on the site) we found no strong connection to suggest that the psychic world was making life difficult for that family. That is, in the Old Gliston case we had suspected that there might have been psychic interference of some sort within the property concerned but we eventually found little evidence of this. In the next case that I am about to describe we found the reverse. As you will see we found that there *was* psychic interference when I, at least, thought there might be none. The reasons why I thought that, I will now explain to you.

Mary appeared to be in her mid to late thirties when we first saw her and it was she who phoned me on several occasions to tell me that there was something she both felt and saw in her house. The problem, from my point of view, was that the entire town of Glenrothes differs from almost every other town that ever was in as much as *absolutely everything is new and recent.* The whole place was build from new on a 'green fields' site by town planners between about 1960 and the present day. That meant from the psychic aspect, to put it crudely, that there could be few "ghosts from the past". That is not strictly correct of course and I lay out in volume one of this book on page 73, various reasons why brand new homes can be haunted by entities. I felt that if there was anything in Mary's home then it might well have come in for one of those reasons. I had also to consider something else I knew about that area for I, myself, had once lived in that new town and not all that far from Mary's house. There had been an old farm and farm buildings quite close to that area if I remembered correctly, and while the farmhouse itself had been refurbished and used as a community centre the little cottages and farm outhouses had all been demolished. There was a tiny possibility that Mary's house could have been build upon the site of one of those. Such a re-building process might lead to a present day psychic event.

At precisely 2pm that afternoon Francesca and I drove into an area of small but tidy end-to-end local authority housing and knocked at Mary's door. We entered just as her father and a friend were leaving. Not knowing at that point whether Mary was an over-imaginative person or a young lady with real problems I was intending to take a 'softly, softly' approach initially but in the first moments in the house I noticed an indescribable 'something' flash across Francesca's eyes. I did not know what it was that she'd seen or felt but I knew it was something. I said nothing at all but put the obvious question to Mary about what she was seeing or feeling that she considered so strange. She began telling us about the apparition of an old lady that she'd seen several times; sometimes on the stairs and sometimes in the room where we were then seated. It was during this session of describing the apparition that Francesca interrupted Mary's story-telling both by ending her sentences for her and by further describing the spirit lady who had been putting in appearances from time to time.

"Yes," Francesca would say, "But not only did the lady have grey hair but you'll remember that her hair was all swept up at the front and brushed backwards over her head towards the crown area." I saw Mary's mouth open again and again as Francesca *told her* the description of who was in her house. The explanation was, of course, that the medium had seen this small, dear old lady as soon as she entered the door of the house! Now that we knew that both Francesca and Mary were aware of the same entity we knew that this woman was totally genuine in her need for help and we could thus progress forward at a rapid rate. We discovered that the ghost-lady was an Agnes Hepworth and some sort of far-off relation to Mary. Agnes had apparently died as she was coming down a flight of stairs and as she had been seen on Mary's stairs the question arose as to whether she had been a previous tenant of this very house! While that could be possible I thought such a thing unlikely and I rather think that Agnes died on her own stairs in quite another house somewhere. Anyhow, she was most certainly in Mary's house and I wanted to know why.

Then the truth of the matter began to come out for Mary had had a previous relationship with a man who himself claimed to have psychic abilities and who upon Mary's leaving him said that he would "haunt her till her dying day". Whether this man had any paranormal abilities I doubt, but the sad thing was that Mary seemed to have believed what he had told her in their last hours together and as the years passed she felt that all the bad and negative things that entered her life did so because of a sort of curse that her past partner had laid upon her. During her darkest days and in her mind she had asked for help (from any source?) to counter this negativity in her life and somehow this dear old apparitional lady called Agnes had arrived to give that help. Mary described something that sounded either like an unusually vivid dream or an out-of-body experience in which she and the grey-haired lady were together in a lovely cottage of some kind with a nicely burning fire and with everything all clean and tidy and homely. The old lady led Mary towards opening double windows that seemed to lead outside to a lovely garden we were being told when Francesca butted into the story,

"But you found that you could not go through those glass doors…..!"

"You are absolutely right!" blurted out the woman, "But how did you know that I couldn't go through those doors?"

"The gray-haired lady has just told me! She said that those doors were symbolic of passing from the human world to the world of spirit and that it was not your time to move to that other world……

(Dedicated researchers might like to know that symbolism is rife in the spirit world and widespread use is made of it. I really can't think why but it is!)

……..In fact she has just told me that that whole episode was a sort of 'projected' *(the author's word)* pleasant fantasy episode to make you feel good in a time when you felt exactly the opposite."

I then began to tell Mary the truth with the hope that it would give that young woman further confidence in herself and her domestic situation.

"Mary," I said, "You are really a very lucky person because this Agnes lady from the other world is genuinely interested in your well-being. And while I don't like the phrase 'guardian angel' I'm sure you can now think of yourself having such a thing. I suggest that you should not feel frightened of Agnes but accept her as someone who has you best wishes at heart."

Mary pointed out to me that she had never been frightened by the apparition but now that she knew why she was around she would look upon this mysterious lady in quite a different way. Then Francesca chimed in again,

"But you have a second person from the other world who looks after you too don't you?"

Mary looked sheepish!

"You mean the young man who took his own life?" she confessed. This was another spirit person who she had been aware of in her home but which she had not told us about. This entity's presence was then confirmed by Francesca although she quickly brushed aside the 'suicide' bit of the revelation and I purposely did not pursue whether the ending of the young man's life had taken place in the very property where we then sat. So it turned out that there was the very strong presence of this young man, whose name we never discovered, but we do know that he was thinking exceedingly kind thoughts towards Mary although we believe that he never knew her during his own lifetime.

(See also Volume one, page 139, where a young spirit man gently and tenderly looks after a young woman in this world that he could never have known in his own lifetime. It all makes one wonder if the impossible actually exists...could it be that we are each allocated some sort of guardian angel? If so why and by whom? And where were the guardian angels of all those poor people when they died so miserably in nazi concentration camps during the Second World War? There is an immense amount of research needed here.)

All this enabled me to re-enforce what I had said a short time before …that Mary was a lucky girl to have spirit people looking after her welfare and that she should acknowledge the thought and move positively forward in life knowing that she was not really fighting the big bad world alone!

****

We then discovered that Mary's daughter, Suzie, was also seeing spirit people in her bedroom …mostly people of a disabled nature. While psychologists would, no doubt, declare that Suzie was in some way afraid of being maimed or injured (who isn't?) and that that fact was preying upon her mind during the hours of sleep I rather think that there might have been more to it than that. I am remembering here that the ability of people to bond with the spirit world runs in families *(Yes, it does!)* and that means that if Mary was able to detect and see two different spirit entities in her house then Suzie might well have the same ability. Just why Suzie kept seeing injured or ill people in her room I am currently unable to say. My guess…for that is all it is…. must be that we may in some way be looking into this young girl's future for *time* in the other world is not as it is in this.

Francesca and I left that home, we feel, in a better and happier and more understood state than when we had entered it an hour or so earlier….and that's what Francesca and I are all about….. enabling others to understand more about the psychic world that is all around them!

CHAPTER 8

UNUSUAL SPIRIT PEOPLE

The Drunken Granny
The Man in the Attic

The characteristics of spirit-people are no more and no less than the characteristics of all the diverse forms of humanity who have ever inhabited this Earth of ours. There are wise ones and stupid ones and loving ones and nasty ones and strange ones. Here are a couple of strange spirit personalities that I have come across of late.

In the second case I'd be interested to know if you can work out for yourself, as you read the second account, just why that man spent all those years alone in that tiny attic space. He must have had a most compelling reason!

****

The Drunken Granny

As this story is somewhat strange I must initially put before you that it was neither written nor published on Aril 1st, April Fools Day.

Francesca's most famous phrase is,

"I give what I get!"

Which means that whatever messages or thoughts the psychic world allows to pass into her mind then it is those thoughts and those alone that she passes on to us …no matter how strange they may seem either to herself or those around her. It is a very brave thing she does!

Likewise, I myself give to my readers very accurate accounts of what has taken place during each of my cases although I fully realise that as each reader has his or her own understanding of the paranormal each will accept or reject what they are reading.

I am only a presenter of information: it is you, the reader, who must be the final arbiter.

In early November 2003 I was telephoned by a couple in their mid thirties who lived in central Edinburgh. They were acting very sensibly and responsibly for they had realised that for more than a year there had been 'something' living in their ground floor apartment with them…something from a world that they did not understand. Together they had discussed their situation and had come to the conclusion early on that, whatever was with them, it seemed neither wanting to attack them nor to frighten them unduly and might one day perhaps leave them alone.

"After all", they thought, "If we ignore it then perhaps it will ignore us …or even move away."

This realistic attitude worked reasonably well until half way through 2003 when their new baby girl was put to sleep in their spare bedroom. The room itself appeared to be extremely difficult to heat and had a 'feel' about it. The wise couple attempted to put that down to the structure of the house but noted that while their baby would sleep very happily in the room by day, by night she woke regularly. We 'experts' who have had several of these little creatures in our keeping know that babies wake for a thousand different reasons at all times of the day and night and so the couple were not initially too perturbed. They did feel, however, that their little girl was being wakened by something rather than merely awakening by herself. Eventually, at about eleven months, when the girl was wakening and struggling in the middle of the night and her parents were coming into comfort her and tuck her in again they noticed something strange. They noticed that when the child was picked up and cuddled, no matter which direction the parent faced, the girl would attempt to rotate her head to one particular corner of the room and point to that spot and 'talk baby-talk' to it as best as she could. As the weeks went by, this behaviour became so marked that it could no longer be ignored as mere chance and these wise parents paid particular attention to their child's reaction. It was always the same during the night hours: she would twist and turn in her parents' arms until she faced that corner and then she would "coo-coo" to it. It was also recorded by the parents that the child seemed 'agitated' at such times: she drew more tightly into her mother or father as she pointed to the unseen something in the corner.

At the same time the parents began to notice small, red marks appearing on the child's body which gave rise to the possibility that she was being prodded in some way during the night. It was an accumulation of those happenings along with many other small happenings like things disappearing only to reappear in exactly the same place a little while later that finally made the pair invite me into their home to take a closer look at the situation.

Because of the travelling involved, I always try to see two or more cases on the same day in the same area if that is at all possible. Initially that week I had a poltergeist case to look at where, amongst other things, a light bulb lying on a dressing table by a child, was supposedly lighting up by itself! As this case was geographically quite close to the one above I thought initially that Francesca and I could visit both. Unfortunately, poltergeist cases both start and stop very suddenly and this one did just that so the Grandmother involved asked me to make my call at a later date when she felt that she could better confirm a definite end to events….or at least that is what she told me.

On Wednesday November 5th with the crack and swoosh of fireworks all over the place (for it was 'Guy Fawkes Day' in the UK), Francesca got off her bus and met me outside the couple's apartment in Harrison Street. It was a solid-looking, stone building we noticed with the date of 1942 over the door and we found the ground-floor apartment with ease. The couple welcomed us and offered us tea, which we declined through pressure of time and so we launched ourselves straight into the chain of events that led us to the present situation. We sat while we had described to us all the above events plus a whole lot of other things which might/ might not have been psychically originated and by 7.15pm I had heard such information that made me consider that there might indeed be some entity within this home which was attempting to make itself known.

(Almost all entities who disturb families in their homes do so as a 'cry for help'. Their desire is first and foremost to draw attention to their presence in the building. After that there is a whole multitude of reasons for their being there.)

At that point I asked Francesca to link mentally with the spirit memory system to see what entities, if any, were then present in that couple's home and I watched as she sank back in the armchair and closed her eyes. In about thirty seconds she spoke,

"I'm getting someone called "Willie" who is here with us at this moment."

Brian, the householder, sat up next to Linsey, his partner and began to take notice for he knew more than he had said. He turned and looked meaningfully at Linsey.

"Willie was sometimes called Billy and was ill in this house for a very long time he tells me. He was very closely associated with it although he never owned it personally and he tells me that his final minutes on this earth were sudden and tragic!"

Brian was now sitting up even more and looking agitated at what Francesca had just said.

"That could be my Uncle Billy," he said. "My father owned the house and when Uncle Billy became ill he lived here and then, in the end, there was a tragic accident!" I noted that Brian had used the same word as the medium, "Tragic", but I did not ask details of the tragedy as there was no real point in raising the stress level by verbalising such unhappy memories. I considered that Uncle Billy had killed himself rather than succumb to further pain and misery.

Francesca went on knowingly,

"Willie tells me that he and your father were considered 'rough diamonds' and would go out on the town drinking and sometimes getting into fights," and that, Brian readily agreed with.

He also understood it precisely when he was told that his uncle loved nothing better than to play cards in the very room where we were then sitting.

"They used to spend days playing cards and drinking here," he added.

Then Francesca said quite clearly that not only had Willie declared that he had nothing to do with touching the child *(which illustrated very clearly to the couple that Uncle Willie was listening in to their worries!)* but this was reiterated by Francesca who went on to say that she had now made contact with an entity who *did admit* to touching the little girl in her bed at night.

"I have a lady standing by my left side here who was a very forceful lady in her day….Yes!, VERY forceful indeed!" Francesca's chin pushed forward and I could hardly believe her arm movements for they moved into the position of a boxer defending himself with one arm outstretched and the other held tightly against his body.

Both of Francesca's fists were clenched!

Wow! I thought to myself. What kind of woman is this that we had in this house?

I did not have long to wait for the answer for the medium went on to describe the dress of the woman to such an accurate degree that tears began forming in Brian's eyes.

"You've just described Granny Bruce to a "T", he said, shaking his head. That's my Grandmother without any doubt at all. She was a hard and very physical woman. If I or my brothers ever stepped out of line she hit out at us first and asked questions later. No wonder my father and Uncle Billy were always fighting in a physical way."

And then Brian went on to say that Granny Bruce actually used to join in mock fights with her sons.

Not having met a woman with such characteristics I was somewhat taken aback at what I was hearing but I could not doubt my own ears: the woman that Francesca was describing was precisely the woman that Brian was acknowledging as his Grandmother.

"She's standing here with a cigarette in her hand……", the medium began again.

"She was always smoking!" Brian chimed in. "It killed her in the end just like it killed my Dad."

"And not just smoking, was it Brian?" Francesca queried, raising her right hand to her face as if holding a drinking glass. "She liked a drink or two didn't she?"

"She was always drinking," he said as the tears flooded his eyes again. " I loved her as a Granny but she really liked the whisky!"

"Well, she's right by me now Brian and she's swaying back and forth: she's giving all the appearances of being drunk. Yes, I'm sure she's drunk!"

(While Francesca thought nothing about the above statement

and continued her description in an unabated manner my mouth opened wide for I realised the enormity of having a person from the psychic world in an inebriated state. The reader will notice too that I have not fallen into the trap of unintended puns by bringing the word "spirits" into things. More of this later.)

"Granny Bruce tells me that it is she who likes to look at the baby each night. She says that the little girl is her great-grandchild and she has a right to touch her if she wants."

The tone was undoubtedly belligerent and as aggressive as one might expect from the characteristics of that spirit lady.

There was a momentary lull in our conversation and deliberations while we all considered the possibilities that lay before us due to Granny Bruce's last sentence but at least we now knew the sources of the psychic activity in the property. Uncle Billy and Granny Bruce had both come forward and had both been acknowledged and identified by the householders.

Now it only remained for Francesca to carry out what she always considered her mediumistic duty …that is, showing the couple that the psychic world is perpetually around them and taking an interest in all family matters. The medium had started repeating to Linsey and Brian what she was being told by the spirit world regarding everything from family health to their forthcoming holiday plans ….all as a useful mechanism of demonstrating the proximity of that spirit world when all of a sudden she was almost overwhelmed by at least five other spirit entities all wanting to make contact with the couple through her! Whatever plans we initially had for the last part of the evening were now completely upset: Francesca was not able to continue with giving personal information to the couple and I could not launch myself into my usual summary and conclusion phase.

The medium paused and tilted her head a little and then said,

"Oh there is someone else here and wanting to communicate with you," and then went on to give the information she was given. Then followed an absolute torrent of information from other deceased persons who were all in some way or another connected with this family. Linsey, in desperation to keep account of the rapidly growing amount of information, grabbed a piece of paper and a pencil and began rushing down what she was hearing as fast as it was coming in through Francesca. Brian, to whom most of these people seemed to be related was mentally wrestling with all the relationships which were cropping up.

"Now if Auntie Jean was married to Billy then that would make Norma the sister-in-law to ………", was the sort of sentence that came tumbling out of Brian. Naturally, he and Linsey kept presenting each other with facts and counter-facts as they struggled with the relationships of their deceased relations until at long last the medium eventually switched off the communication. It had taken an additional twenty minutes to deal with these keen relatives who wished to make themselves known and now things really had to be drawn to a close. After all, we had found out what we had come to discover….who or what was causing the psychic unease within the property.

Now my time for the resume and conclusion was to hand,

"Right folks!" I said, "Let's get back to square one. We have discovered two entities closely associated with this house where we are now sitting and both you, Brian and you Linsey have identified Granny Bruce and Uncle Willie (or Billy) as being these two entities. We know that Uncle Willie has not been getting up to any mischief here and he, himself, has said that he has not touched the baby in any way at all and I tend to believe him. We do know, however, upon her own confession that Granny Bruce has indeed touched the baby …and might have even been disturbing her sleep on a regular nightly basis. For that reason I am going to ask Francesca to communicate with this deceased lady to ask her to back off."

Perhaps it might surprise readers to know that not only can the entities present see you and hear every word you speak but also have access to your own thoughts before you yourself can vocalise them! However, for the sake of the young couple I had to put a slight theatrical dressing upon the situation and so speaking purposefully to the air and space in the middle of the room I said aloud,

"Right Granny Bruce, you know we are here and we know that you are here also so you will understand that this nice young couple own the house that you, yourself once owned. They love it and cherish it as once you did and just as you would not have wished to have intruders, visible or invisible, in your house so too does that apply to Linsey and Brian and their children. You are bound to know that neither of the pair wish you any harm or animosity and they do not wish to drive you away from somewhere which you have once loved but they do not want to feel your presence or have you touch their baby for we humans find such things difficult to understand. Please therefore do not make your presence felt. Turn off that part of you that allows us to know of your presence. You are here and we all acknowledge that: now please go and leave this couple in the peace of their own home!"

I paused and turned to Francesca and said, really for the benefit of the couple,

"Francesca, can you please pass that message on to Granny Bruce."

I watched as the medium dipped her head but no sooner had it gone down than it shot up again with a large smile on her face.

"She's gone!" exclaimed Francesca, "I made to contact her but she's not around to contact….she's completely gone!" The medium looked to her left where the spirit lady had been but she just smiled again and moved her hands apart and shrugged her shoulders,

"Gone, all gone!"

It was a good result to an interesting evening.

****

Notes of interest concerning this particular case

Intoxicated Entities

I can see how this can cause serious credibility problems at all sorts of levels and initially I myself found this sort of thing very unsettling when I first came across it as a member of an audience in Dundee when the famous Doris Stokes was on stage. She had just told a member of the audience that her mother was present and wanting to talk with her and so a two-way dialogue was soon underway when the audience lady asked her deceased mother where her father was. "Was he by her side?" I remember her asking and then was flabbergasted by the response of the deceased, "No, Mary. He's down at the pub at this time of day."

It was all so matter-of-fact but yet it nearly blew the top off my head as a young man.

How could he be down at the pub?

They don't have pubs in Heaven surely.

What good was alcohol in the afterlife anyway?

And if they drank alcohol where did they get it?

How can there possibly be distilleries there?

These questions arise because there is so little known about the workings of the psychic world and what *is* known is often twisted into a format that many people would ***prefe***r to believe…. much of it handed down through religious traditions.

Consider these things which I grade from being what most people know to what fewer of us understand:-

1) Most (or at least many) people accept that apparitions exist.

2) I know of no naked apparition (not even Lady Godiva) so it must be generally accepted that the psychic world *appears to have* clothing.

3) On that clothing there are belts and buttons as well as swords and daggers and so *it appears* that there are people in the psychic world who weave and also manufacture metal artifacts.

4) One ghost I know appears with a cigarette in his hand. Are we therefore to believe that there are fields of tobacco in the afterlife being changed into cigarettes in order to supply the nicotine needs of the hereafter? If we go down this line of thinking then what we soon end up with is a parallel world of some kind, identical to our own but yet being completely insubstantial.

I have seen no indication whatever that such a world exists!

What I have seen is a truly awe-inspiring supernatural memory system: I meet it all the time and tap into it when I have to via the talents of Francesca.

That system is one of pure memory but with a difference, for the memories that most people believe that we hold in our heads are static and fixed memories of a person or a thing or event. The memories in the psychic memory bank are *living memories* for they can move of their own volition, communicate with others and we earthlings when they wish. And when they decide to appear to us either mentally or in the form of an apparition they can choose in what format they appear. While a particular entity lady might have been 90 when she died she may wish to make herself known to us as a girl of 25. *She can decide* and I believe the decision is usually taken with a view to being as fully accepted as possible by the viewer.

Now that takes us back to the alcohol problem again for if an entity enjoyed a bit of a drink in this life then she might very well conjure up a 'self' that is a memory of herself when inebriated. Remember that the characteristics of an entity are *exactly the characteristics of the human* in their own lifetime. That is, you don't really have a drunk ghost…..you have a projected memory that is meant to have meaning to the recipient.

Drop-in Communicators

While I still have a lot to learn about spirit-to-spirit communication I have met many of those 'chancers of the psychic world', the drop-in communicators. They break into the middle of 'private' communications time and time again and can be quite a pest to a medium who might be in the middle of a very intense session with a recently bereaved mother for example.

While I am not unused to meeting such entities, five in a series like this is something I had not encountered up to that date. See Vol. One, page 101, for an excellent example of such a drop-in communicator who proved Francesca's great ability.

****

The Man in the Attic

On Christmas Eve, 2001, I visited the house of a Mr. and Mrs. Harrison where we found that the paranormal disturbance caused to a sixteen year old girl was possibly originating from the entity of a boisterous boy of about fourteen who, through his own misplaced bravado, had been drowned during a teenage prank. *(The story occurs in full in Volume 1, page 88.)*

While I had no doubts whatever about the boy, the prank and his unfortunate drowning, I was never at all sure that we had found everything that was to be found in that house. I always had a conscience about having missed something. I felt that if we had stayed longer we might have found more but it was, after all, Christmas Eve and both my medium and I felt that we should retire and leave the family to traditional Christmas Eve family activities. Besides that we were heading out through the gently falling snow to visit a second and quite unique case that night. (See the "Three in a Bed" case recorded in Volume 1 also.)

My precise reason for having a conscience was this:-

To a minor degree symbolism is used by the psychic world and I find that in many cases where death is in some way connected to height then often footsteps (or noises) are heard overhead.

This was the case with the Harrison household and I did not find that too unusual as the child concerned had jumped to his death from a viaduct into a river...which would have possibly been all right if he had not accidentally struck his head on the branch of a tree first. My worry was that we never did find out the real connection between the lad and the property: it could have been his house (although we thought not) but it could have been his grandparents' house from where he left prior to his fatal accident. I felt that the distance from the house to the site of his death may have been too great to justify the overhead footsteps in the attic which were being heard by the occupants. In that case it could have been that the footsteps originating in the attic had some *other* significance. In 2001 we never found out.

****

Almost exactly a year later I received another call from the family saying not only that footsteps were still being heard occasionally but that when Mr. Harrison had taken on the work of making the attic area into a little study for himself he was being very frightened by something he could not see.

It appeared that as a handyman with time to spare, Mr. Harrison had opened up the whole attic area by stripping out a myriad of cross beams that gave some sort of support to the roof timbers proper. Leaving aside my worry about the weakening of the structure when I viewed the whole business for the first time, I saw that the man had made a lovely little office for himself which he was panelling with timber.

Entry and exit from this little study was by way of a hatch in the ceiling of the upper hallway that lay below, and through this a mattress had been introduced to the room. No bed to support it had yet been placed there so that mattress merely lay upon the 'study' floor for the time being.

The new room could thus be used as extra overnight accommodation for the daughter's teenage friends or whoever.

I was then told that Mr. Harrison had contracted a heavy cold at some point just prior to Christmas 2002 and due to his nose being stuffed up he went through a period of nightly restlessness and snoring. For the benefit of his working wife and to give her a good night's sleep, the man bravely volunteered to sleep for a few nights in his new study and upon the recently installed mattress until his health returned to normal.

That was the plan but as you will see he was to discover the hard way that all things in the attic were far from normal!

Mr. Harrison had forgotten all about the footsteps in the attic on that night when he first pulled the covers over himself as he lay on his mattress and attempted to get to sleep. He felt that sleep was definitely trying to elude him but he supposed that that was quite natural for, after all, he was trying to sleep in a new place and on a floor mattress. The air around him had turned strangely and suddenly cold too, almost as soon as his head struck the pillow but that, the man put down to being unused to his sleeping in that place.

Then it happened!

All of a sudden he felt a weight upon his chest which got heavier and heavier and for a moment Mr. Harrison even wondered if he was about to have some sort of heart attack but then the load spread over his whole body. Eventually (it felt like minutes but he had truly lost count of time in this panicky situation) he knew that there was an invisible 'someone' lying on top of him.

That 'person' appeared to be about the same size and weight as himself and, *horror of horrors*, not only could he now hear that person breathing but he could actually smell the invisible person's unpleasant breath! The situation could have been straight out of a horror movie! But it wasn't!

The coldness of his body had now upgraded itself to a state of 'severe coldness' and had somehow moved upwards from his feet until his entire being was chilled to the marrow.

The man had no idea at all about what had overwhelmed him but he suddenly realised that he was paralysed for he could neither shout out nor move! He realised instinctively, however, that he had now got to play a sort of mental game and WILL whatever had taken him over to move off him again.

Eventually the mental concentration paid off and normality returned although Mr. Harrison found it impossible to tell me whether that had taken ten minutes, twenty minutes or an hour: time seemed to have stopped having meaning for him during that unpleasant episode and I can quite see why.

(This business of two persons, one deceased and one alive, occupying the same body-space must seem very strange to anyone newly begun upon researching the supernatural but there are, in fact, many cases recorded of this sort of thing and I have met it on several occasions.

*It can vary greatly in both intensity and manner and must be one of the most frightening aspects of the paranormal.... although I truly believe that there is no intention at all of the entity **purposefully** frightening the human involved. The victim is frightened as a natural consequence of something very strange and rare that is taking place around him and through him and not because of any wish that the entity harbours to scare him.*

The blending of the two people can vary in completeness from merely having limbs taken over to having the whole body paralysed as in Mr. Harrison's case.

Probably the most famous case is recorded by the well-known psychic Matthew Manning where the victim not only finds himself completely taken over but 'compressed' in some way so that he is actually looking out through the mouth of the everpowering entity. In fact, halfway through the business, the victim found himself genuinely wondering why he appeared to be looking out of a pink cave where there were arcs of castellations at both the top and the bottom at the entrance to that cave. Can you imagine his horror when he realised that he was actually looking out of the mouth of the entity who had taken him over and had somehow 'compressed' him.

Very often the event is triggered by the human unwittingly taking up a position within a room or a bed or a chair that an entity used to use and had a particular attachment to.

(See the case concerning the tips of the elbows of Mrs. Watkins in the Case of the "Paraplegic Rip Van Winkle" in volume 1, page 116.))

****

Francesca and I turned up at the Harrison home at about 7pm and after a friendly re-introduction we got straight down to work.

As I use ladders at times for painting the outside woodwork of my house, I had forgotten that Francesca, who had a little of a hip problem, might find it difficult to mount the aluminium ladder that was the key to entering that attic area. However, I was so pleased to see just how well she moved up it to emerge into the well-lit study above.

I watched as she stood and looked around herself: I could see that knowing look in her eye.

"You've got a rather mysterious man up here with you," she said and then she went on, "I can't think what on earth he's doing here but he's telling me that he actually stayed up here and rarely, if ever, came down!"

The Harrisons and I all looked at each other. "How could any man have lived up here?" we were all thinking. After all, until the present owner began cutting out all the criss-cross timber supporting batons there was virtually no space at all to live up here. Even spending an hour or so here would mean that that person would have to duck and dive a dozen times merely to get from one end of the short attic to the other.

Initially I thought that the whole thing sounded not only stupid but virtually impossible but as the information came forward bit by bit I eventually realised that strange though it was, it might just be true.

Mr. Harrison, at that initial point, had not got around to showing us where his mattress had been but Francesca pointed down to a part of the floor and said that the entity was telling her that he slept at that particular spot. He said that he had put some planks of wood across the main floor beams because he would otherwise have fallen down to the room below through the plaster ceiling. We immediately turned to the householder and sure enough, Mr. Harrison confirmed that that was the very spot where he had chosen to place his mattress.

He had, after all, floored the entire attic area and so, unlike the entity, he could choose where he would lay his bed for sleeping upon. How strange, was it not, that he chose the very place where the entity had lain?

We looked at all the cross timbers that Mr. Harrison had cut away for they were still piled at one end of the little room and realised that there must have been very few possible places in that attic where the entity had enough space to lie down. There just would not have been a clear floor-space of 6 feet by 2 feet available to him in those early days! Yet strangely enough, one of those few possible bed-areas was exactly where Mr. Harrison had chosen to sleep.

All this talk made me realise what a dreadful existence Attic Man would have had up there, for any movement at all would require him to weave back and forth through a network of cross beams that were absolutely everywhere around him for the attic had never been designed as a room: it was merely a structural area of criss-cross timberwork to support a heavy roof.

Fresh from those first startling facts, Francesca turned fully about and looked into the far corner of the tiny room then said,

"There used to be a main metal water tank for the house there when it was built in the 1930s but it fell into disuse for some reason and was empty and shut off by the time that your family took over the property."

"Yes," replied the man in amazement, "I took it out and dumped it."

"What did you do with the old black kettle that you found in it and its lid?"

I saw Mr. Harrison's mouth open,

"How could you possibly know about ....?"

He and his wife were looking at each other in amazement but Francesca went on,

"And how about the brass candlestick with the short length of candle?"

"And how about ......?" Francesca named several other things that Mr. Harrison had found hidden away in the old metal tank.

The householder man then began explaining,

"The tank was an absolute pest being where it was because it was large and there was no way I could get it out in one piece. I therefore took the old kettle and the brass candlestick out of it (he could remember no lid) and cut the tank up into four quarters to get it out of this attic. We had the black kettle lying around for a bit but I cannot think of where it is now; perhaps out with the trash!"

"Well, that old kettle was a very important part of the entity's life," said Francesca. "The man used to dip it into the water in the tank as a source of water for himself and I also feel that he used to use the candlestick in some useful way too: perhaps that was his sole source of light!"

And then she added that the man's food was passed up to him on a daily basis by the family who lived as normally as possible in the house below his 'roost'.

The situation was getting more and more peculiar by the minute, I felt.

"Francesca, would you ask the man if he was up here for days or weeks or what?"

The answer was not as I had expected,

"Count the notches on the wooden beams!" came the man's reply and the medium and I looked at each other puzzled but I saw Mr. Harrison first shake his head in disbelief and then break into a smile. He obviously knew something that we did not.

We watched as he walked to the pile of timber beams that were stacked at the far end of the room and which still had use for him. He tugged at one in particular, took it out and held it up for Francesca and I to see.

Now it was the turn of our jaws to drop open with amazement.

The beam that had been selected had a series of deep cuts carved along one edge of it. The long cuts were fully four inches long while the three shorter ones which lay between the long ones were about two inches long: the whole pattern being regular and carved along the whole length of the five foot long beam. One long followed by three short cut in again and again and again.

If those were weeks and months (as the man eventually confirmed through Francesca) then he must have lived in that attic for several years for Mr. Harrison said that there were many beams with such markings although it would take time to pull them from the pile if we wanted to see them all. Other matters were pressing and so we did not halt the flow of the investigation to pull out the appropriate beams: Mr. Harrison could do that at his leisure.

As far as that matter was concerned I took a shortcut which perhaps I should not have done as a researcher but I wanted to know more of this mystery. I asked Francesca to ask our mystery man just how long he was alone in that attic and he said that he was there for more than two and a half years before he died. I then asked the reason for his death and he quite clearly said, "Consumption". That was the common terminology for "tuberculosis" in Scotland in all periods up to about 1950 when the more correct term began to be used more widely. Francesca felt that he was in his early to mid fifties when he died.

You don't need to be much of a detective to see that we have a very puzzling mystery here. Why should a man want to live alone day in and day out for years in an attic? What relationship did he have to the family who lived in a normal manner (?) below him and handed up his meals to him daily? Yes, he did have tuberculosis and that is a transmittable disease but so did a hundred thousand other Scots in those dreadful days but they didn't hide up attics.

Try as she could, Francesca could not get the man to tell us the reason for his self-imposed hermit state and that at least gave me a clue to something, for if an entity has some sort of secret that he was reluctant to reveal in life then that same reluctance is there also in death.

(See volume one, where in "Schoolhouse Inn" we meet a rural young man who has been drafted into fighting on behalf

of his superior and who, even after death refused to reveal the reason for the fight that eventually killed him.)

Once we had descended from the attic and were sat again in the warmth of the livingroom downstairs the questions we've just discussed were those that we puzzled over. I found it difficult to believe that the father of the family had volunteered to secrete himself away from the others in order to prevent the spread of infection. Could he not have been put into a bedroom by himself if he was unwilling to enter a hospital? What a cruel thing to do if he was 'requested' by his family to go up there to die: I can't believe he was. The time factor was also too long for that. Two and a half years is just too long a time 'to die'.

I felt that the answer was that the man himself **choose** to be where he was for some reason but goodness knows, we found it very difficult to think what that reason could have been.

We eventually ran out of questions and answers and bidding the family, "Goodbye" we set off for home.

It was only when we were driving away from the area once more that I suddenly had a flash of inspiration.

"What could be worse in the1940s than hiding in an attic for month after month?" and then it suddenly came to me!

The answer might have been, "Dying for one's country!" The man, I now feel sure was some sort of draft-dodger evading his duties to his country which was in the middle of a fearsome world war. Maybe this was his house but maybe it was the house of a brother or similar where the military police might not search for a deserter or draft-dodger.

Whatever the answer might be I'd like my readers to know that I am currently attempting to find lists of addresses of potential army deserters who once lived in the South Edinburgh area. We'll see what (if anything) comes from that line of research for I'd like to know just why "Attic Man" chose to be precisely that and who he really was.

There is also the unsettled question of what relationship (if any) he had to the young boy entity who we found in that property the year before.

Yes, searching for entities can often raise more problems than it solves!

CHAPTER 9

ANIMALS

The Lost Dog
Horse Sense

It is not part of the remit of this book to go into any sort of detail regarding the Great Universal Memory System that continuously monitors and stores the finest details of all atomic particles and our memory systems as well. However I must now touch upon this topic as the system it depends upon concerns minute electrical charges of a type that run continuously through our brains.

As this Universal Memory System only cares about the collection and logging of electrical charges it really does not care about the sources of those 'electrical particles': if they exist then it records them ....and that's it. The construction of the system is such that it has not the slightest desire to differentiate between, say, electrical pulses coming from the brain of a higher primate like you and me and the electrical pulses coming from the brain of a feline specimen like your cat. Human, horse, cat, dog or even the slug at the bottom of your garden are all equal in the eyes of the Great Universal Memory System for all it wants to know about are those minute electrical charges given off by the brains of those creatures and the charges showing the positions of the atoms of their bodies from micro-second to micro-second.

Because mediums can tap into this truly vast Memory System they can, in both theory and practice, pick up memories and thoughts from *both* humans and animals. I can vouch for that because I have seen it done quite a number of times and I rather imagine that the skill of 'horse whisperers' is truly a mediumistic skill where the mind of the 'whisperer' and the mind of the horse are tuning into the identical part of the Memory System.

The upshot of all that is that mediums **can indeed** communicate with animals.

****

The Lost Dog

Finding lost cats and dogs is not really something that I can afford to get caught up in …not because I don't love these furry and hairy companions that share our lives but because there is just not that much time in my day. There are probably about 50,000 lost pets reported each year to the animal shelters in Scotland alone which means that I'd have a never-ending task of organising gifted persons like Francesca in hunting them down. Meritorious though that is, it is just not practical to undertake such work on anything other than a one-off basis.

Such a 'one-off' situation took place after a week of nasty snowy weather in late January 2004 for a lady who lives quite close to me and who runs a voluntary rescue center for maltreated and abandoned Wolf Hounds and Lurcher dogs phoned me to tell me a distressing story. While I did not know Sibyl in any personal way I was overwhelmed, almost to tears, by the sadness of the situation she began explaining to me.

Quite some time ago she had taken into her care a Lurcher dog in a rather poor and distressed condition. It had been a 'one-man' dog and its master had died and the dog missed him terribly. Tenderly, carefully and lovingly she and her husband had nursed it back to full health (along with the others she cared for). By Christmas 2003 it was in a suitable physical condition to be re-housed with a new and loving family although it still probably bore the mental scars of what it had experienced in the difficult last year of its master's life. The family chosen lived in the town of Cumbernauld, which is about fifty miles to the west and they came from there on Sunday, January 25th to collect their new friend.

The family loved the dog from the start and the dog seemed to take to the family. It went joyfully into the car and all went well until they got back to their Cumbernauld home. They opened the front door to welcome the dog into its new abode after leading it out of the car and then the teenage daughter slipped off its lead saying,

"Right, 'Doggie', this is going to be your nice new home!"

The dog looked up at the girl and with a muffled grunt which, in hindsight, must have been a canine 'John Wayne' equivalent of, "The Hell it is!" the dog took one almighty leap and clearing a five foot hedge he promptly disappeared over a second, third and fourth garden until he vanished completely into the storm of swirling snow that was descending on the community at large. His long legs and strong well-fed body had assisted his flight and in thirty seconds flat he was nowhere to be seen. In fact for the next week he was nowhere to be seen as far as his new family were concerned!

In desperation and total despair the new owners did everything they could think of before finally picking up the telephone and confessing to Sybil that they had lost the dog. By the time the dog had been absent-without-leave for 48 hours there wasn't a police station, vet or animal shelter within a twenty miles radius that the new owners hadn't contacted. On hearing the desperate news Sybil, of course, was shocked and jumping immediately into her car drove west and joined in the hunt but all to no avail. She returned to Fife completely inconsolable and as an act of desperation she suddenly remembered reading in my Volume One of the *Psychic Investigators Casebook* of the marvellous abilities of Francesca. I therefore got that inevitable and very sad explanatory phone call on Thursday January 29th which was right in the middle of a week of snow blizzards. I knew that Francesca, who has a dog herself, would understand my phoning her up about this poor lost creature.

"Perhaps, you can just have a little quiet seat to yourself this afternoon," I said, "And see if any information comes to you about this unfortunate animal." The good lady said that she would do just that and within half an hour my phone rang again. I was really amazed to have Francesca back on the phone so soon. Did she want further information I initially pondered but she did not! In fact she had a bit of an answer for me although she was apologetic regarding the quality of her information.

"You'll be glad to hear that the dog is indoors, is well and in the keeping of people who are caring for it because they understand animals." *(I must admit that I thought of a farm location at that point.)* "It is currently in one of three gray-colored buildings that are close together and are connected in some way."

In fact Francesca said that she felt the dog had somehow been moved from one of those buildings to another at some point after its arrival there but said that she did not know the reason for such a movement being necessary.

"I feel that it is being moved between buildings but I don't know why", were her exact words.

"The buildings themselves", she went on, "Are low in height and identical and are not in a town but at the edge of it and on a country road of some kind because there are trees and open grass areas nearby and the buildings are set back from the road by a bit of land."

Having thanked Francesca for the information that I knew would be helpful *provided it was acted upon in the correct manner* I phoned Sibyl to pass it on to the distraught family. Then I could do nothing more than wait to see what result, if any, took place.

A few days later, on Sunday February 1st, I was in for a delightful surprise for, acting on Francesca's information, the Cumbernauld family had homed in on each and every Cat and Dog home for miles around and until they came across one that tallied with the description that Francesca gave: three related gray buildings parallel with a country road and set back from it. They discovered the Shetlington Animal Shelter!

Only when they had satisfactorily identified the structure and the situation of the premises on the phone did they dare to ask the burning question,

"You don't happen to have a Lurcher dog in your keeping by any chance?"

"**Yes we do**!" came the amazing reply. "We had one brought in this very week!" And within hours the dog and its new owners had been re-united.

On the 6th February I received both a letter of thanks from the lady who ran the local animal protection center ….St Hubert's Hound Sanctuary… and a cheque for Francesca and myself to assist in the furtherance of our psychic research work.

In the letter I noted that the dog that was lost for a week in the storm had itself been called, "Storm". Most appropriate I thought!

(For psychical researchers there are a lot of lovely clues in this story are there not? It is surely the *'connections business'* of it all that truly boggles the mind for while Francesca loved dogs that, in itself, was not nearly enough to move the situation forward from a dog being lost to that dog being found.

*I have no doubts at all that if the medium could sit opposite a dog she could communicate with it.....but that is **not** what took place here. She'd never met or even seen the creature.*

The really wild explanation is this:-

I now know from experience that if I want to lock Francesca's mind onto the mind of a second person from a distance what I must do is to first phone and talk with the person involved and later pick up the phone to Francesca and talk with her. Somehow by merely talking to that second person I have been enabled to unlock and open their entire memory system. I have not the psychic ability to actually carry that process out but the 'key' to the situation has been 'handed to me' so-to-speak.

When I later phone Francesca she then appears to 'download' from my mind not only access to my entire memory system but all the things in it......which includes, of course, the key to unlock the memory system of the third party that I had just been talking to.

*I know that all that sounds strange **but some mechanism of that type has to exist because I do truly lock Francesca onto some people by purposely talking with both parties.***

*Getting back to our lost doggie, you can see that it was not just two phone calls that were needed **but a whole series of mental communications and phone calls**.*

The thing had to start with the dog itself for two reasons,
1) The whole thing revolved around the dog
2) The present (geographical) position of the dog must already be known to the Great Universal Memory System (as all things are).

The chain of information-passing had therefore to be this:-

The Great Universal Memory System knew where the dog was for it was directly connected to the dog (as it is with all things) and the dog was already bonded mentally to the Sybil. By Sybil phoning and talking with me that coupled me into the chain and by my phoning Francesca I was lengthening the chain to include her. That is, I had enabled her to tap into the 'databank' of the dog itself (and thus its current surroundings).

*I am fully aware that this may well sound nonsense to many readers but I **know** it is correct and I challenge skeptical readers to come up with an alternative explanation for this amazing account if they do not agree with my assessment of it.)*

****

Horse Sense

We humans are not very good in admitting it but we are all animals. We try to show otherwise but now and again some of our species let us down and it is all too apparent. If you've any lingering doubts about it just look at the hair on your skin or the claws at the end of your fingers (if you haven't got the bad habit of biting them).

I am making the point with purpose I assure you and not merely reminding you about our humble origins as some sort of perverted pastime. I've always found it strange that a skeptic who I know is quite happy to accept telepathy as a reality but no other part of the psychic world. I enjoy catching him out by asking him whether he can be telepathic with his dog as well as his wife and this causes him problems for he sees his wife as something very different from his dog. Yes, of course she doesn't run around on all fours and whimper to be taken a walk every evening (at least I hope not) but genetically she is remarkably similar to her dog and as I have pointed out in the preceding case I know from years of experience that whatever mechanism is operated by the psychic world on behalf of we humans, that same science works in an identical manner when we are dealing with animals.

Lower animals (I'm not too happy about that phrase I'm afraid) feel happiness and pain and hunger like higher animals and while their cognitive abilities appear more limited, they have a mind that works as a modem in an identical manner to our own. That is, everything they see, hear, sense and think is immediately passed into the Great Universal Memory System as in our own case. I know it is, for if that was not true then how do I keep meeting spirit animals from the world of all deceased things? They are there!….and like deceased humans, seem to have the same habits and characteristics as they had when they were on Earth with the masters and mistresses who once looked after their well-being.

Francesca is a medium of world-class standards but she would be the first to tell you that she is a "doer" and not a "theorist". It is I who are the holder of the theories and so, during the first week of August 2003 I had a chat with her in the manner of the above paragraphs to show her the reasoning behind something that I knew she already realised….that mediums can communicate with animals (living or dead!) in precisely the same manner that we use to contact deceased humans. The process is identical!

I reminded her of that because I had a friend whose horse had very suddenly and dramatically 'switched off' in some strange manner. 'Jake', the horse is owned by Kath and a truly beautiful creature he is. Until the winter of 2001 he was a marvel at all the shows he attended and carried through all those complicated manoeuvres that we see on TV shows concerning competitive horsemanship. Kath worked very hard with him seven days a week and fifty two weeks a year and while she thought at that point that he might be somewhat lazy her work paid off handsomely.

That was until she decided to have a baby. Knowing that she would be unable to give him the same love, attention and training during her advanced pregnancy she took him to the stables of a friend who had agreed to look after Jake until things returned to a more usual state. After the birth of their baby, Kath felt that with a little bit of hard work she would soon bring her favorite horse back to his high state of competitiveness once more.

It was one of those things that was fine in theory but did not work out in practice. When he was at the other stables she visited Jake regularly although she was not in a position to ride him but others gave him plenty regular exercise. The link between this sensitive and beautiful creature and his mistress was close and due to that closeness Kath realised that the horse that she put out for temporary stabling was not the same horse, so-to-speak, that was finally returned to her. Oh yes, it was the correct horse, right enough but its personality had changed somewhat. It no longer seemed energetic: it no longer wanted to try to do its best and it no longer seemed to have an interest in any new challenges in which it once used to revel. It was not just a slightly changed horse: over these few months 'holiday' it had become a **very changed** horse.

Being a good and careful owner, Kath called in a vet and then a second vet and then a horse specialist vet and then finally she had Jake taken to the private stables of one of the best and costliest of veterinary colleges in the UK. That was a place that has at its disposal every x-ray machine and the like that man has invented. It didn't come cheap and Kath was probably £ 4,000 out of pocket at the end of the whole business but to her, Jake's well-being came before money.

Virtually nothing at all was found! And while the spending of all that money certainly gave Kath a clear conscience it had not brought back to her the lovely animal that she had had before her little baby girl was born.

It was an act of real desperation that drove this lady to call in one of those unusual people on the verge of the horse world …a 'horse-whisperer'. They were unscientific Kath had always thought and like healers of human beings no one was quite sure how much of the treatment was just 'mumbo-jumbo' and how much was true healing. Even that healer made little headway and it was quite by chance that I was sitting across a table from Kath and her husband at a charity dinner one evening. While a lot of money was raised that night for a lot of deserving charities, one of the interesting side events of the evening was that Kath and I got chatting and I found that both she and her husband were interested in the work I do with Francesca. That, in turn, led to the possibility that Francesca and I might be able to come out at some point to Kath's stables to have a 'chat' with the horse for, strange though it might seem, I knew that Jake might actually be able to transmit to Francesca what was the matter with him.

I must now tell you that, at that point in the proceedings, I knew virtually nothing of the above ….all I was told initially was that the horse in question had suddenly and mysteriously become a changed character and that vets and a horse-whisperer had been called in and had totally failed in the task given to them…..to find out what was wrong with Jake. I did not know, for example, that he had been boarded out at the stables of a friend. That, you will soon see, is one of a series of points showing that I could not have told Francesca things that I, myself, had never known.

On August 4th we found a gap in our timetable so we decided to see how we might be able to help Jake and his mistress. The whole thing was of an experimental nature and this I was very careful to tell Kath: even more so than with humans I said very clearly that we promised nothing at all. We *might* gain knowledge I said but it was also possible that the evening meeting in the field might shed no light at all on why Jake's character had changed.

Little was I to know that Francesca had one of her mysterious surprises up her sleeve for me…although neither of us realized it until a couple of days later. The stables in question were about 35 miles from Francesca's home and she had to get the train to the area and then I picked her up by car and took her the rest of the way. As we were moving towards our objective through a town we found ourselves passing down an avenue of dense trees in the town …so dense that a stranger to the area like Francesca would have no idea at all as to what lay beyond the trees. In spite of that I felt the lady stiffen and turn her head to the left,

"Is there a supermarket in that direction?" she asked, putting her arm out to signify the precise direction. "I feel one over there for some reason and I'm also feeling a car parking area next to it as well as a horsebox parked there and a dog."

Being quite used to Francesca's sudden (and often unlinked) statements I told her that there was indeed a supermarket there and while I once again marvelled at the accuracy of this lady pin-pointing something that she could not possibly see, I also said that I could see no connection between what she had just said and what we had set out to do that evening. The statement was therefore almost instantly forgotten.

We reached the lovely home and the stables about five minutes later and Francesca met Kath. The weather was glorious and so we went straight up the sloping field to meet Jake. He was indeed a lovely and a noble creature!

Up to her usual standard, the medium asked, as we walked up the field, if there had been a couple of dogs roaming in the area for she was sensing a spaniel and a dalmatian. I honestly cannot remember what was said about the spaniel but Kath told us that a dalmatian used to run around in the area but was now dead, having been put down the previous year.

"Well its still running around yet!" she said smiling but I'm not sure the horse can see it. I was glad that she added that for it might just have been possible that the horse was being spooked in some way by seeing a ghost dog in its field with it.

The electric fence was switched off and Kath brought Jake out of the field to be with us. Having had horses of my own many years before, I reminded Francesca not to go too close behind the creature as it did not know her and a rearwards kick from an agitated horse is something not likely to be forgotten easily. The medium did not seem the least afraid and put her head against Jake's. For quite some time the pair of them stood together like that and then finally Francesca drew her head back.

"He's telling me that he's spent time away from here ….at a place that he grew to fear and hate. He began shaking violently when we were thinking about it together. He had got several terrible frights and one of these was of such a catastrophic nature that he has never got over it. In fact he is in a state of complete nervous collapse! If he were a human being then we'd be treating him for a severe nervous breakdown."

I must have looked amazed and Kath looked shocked for that possibility had never crossed her mind and I think she might have had a conscience about the fact that she had been trying so hard to train him up again once she had taken up horse-womanship after the birth of the baby. The thought suddenly appalled her that she may have been attempting to overwork a horse that was at least temporarily disabled mentally due to a nervous breakdown.

It was at that point that Kath told us about the horse's 'holiday' at other stables.

"What could it be that caused such a state during the horse's stabling at another site?" I asked Francesca and she answered immediately for she had already been given the answer by the horse.

"He tells me that where he was there were people running along the back of the stables at night with shotguns of some sort...at least he is letting me feel and hear something of that nature coming from behind his stables. Whatever it was, it had happened on several occasions and each time I am being allowed to hear the same terrible noise that he heard."

But then Francesca went on to tell an even more horrifying story,

"But the thing that really caused all the mental damage occurred one dark night when someone came up to the front of the stables, opened the door and then there was an almighty explosion *inside the stables.* The flash was as horrific as the noise and the poor horse never recovered: its mental processes just shut down with shock there and then!"

I could see that Francesca was really considerably upset herself at relating the story and while the word was never actually used I visualized a *firework* of some sort being thrown into the horse's stable. How shockingly cruel! None of us know the truth even yet for even a couple of years later no physical damage has been found within Jake's body by further vets who were later drafted in to unravel the mystery. Certainly the area where Jake's temporary stables were is quite well known even yet for general vandalism but the friend who owned those stables swore to Kath that she knew of no such incidents involving either shotgun blasts or fireworks. Once again I don't think we will ever be able to unscramble the truth.

What I will say, however, is that Francesca is very much sticking to her initial story and that she feels that her sensing something about the car park of the 'unseen supermarket' is part of the answer. There is certainly a possibility that someone (perhaps employed by that supermarket?) living close to the stables area ...which is about a couple of miles away...got up to wicked nonsense at times at those stables. Did he let off shotgun blasts in that general area perhaps and on one occasion after the horse was shut up for the night, did he open the stable door and toss in a lit firework?

We will never know but understanding Francesca as I do, I am prepared to take a bet on something like that happening.

Three years and about £ 6,000 later Jake is still a very changed horse. Sadly, he has never returned to his former self.

CHAPTER 10

ODDS AND ENDS

Three for the Price of One
Windows on the Past
The Door Handle

Three for the Price of One

You my readers might expect, with a bit of justification, that I spend a lot of my time at seances and at spiritualist group meetings as a means of furthering my research but that is not at all true for several reasons. Firstly I have found from experience that that is not the most time-effective method of gaining information about the psychic world for the facts that come up are usually of a repetitive nature and are somewhat mundane. In other words, once you have attended several such public meetings you've seen all there is to see for it is mostly 'variations on a theme'. I feel that I gain much more from the research point of view when I go out to a dedicated case where some entity is loitering around someone's house or office and just won't go away until they make contact with you. Francesca and I can then get to grips with the entity on a one-to-one basis and that is what throws up considerable (and often fresh) research.

The tale I now tell is of a public spiritualist meeting and the information received during it and is, therefore, a somewhat exceptional account coming from me.

I don't often stay away from home overnight except for my annual holiday but friends in Glasgow persuaded me to come for a few days to visit them and I was pleased to accept. On the first evening of my visit the question arose as to what we were to do with our time and my host suggested that as he had seen a small advertisement in his local newspaper that morning for a spiritualist meeting we might consider attending it and then we could head for the local pub afterwards.

It transpired that the meeting was in rather a nice Victorian public hall just around the corner and we arrived with minutes to spare. The medium for the evening gave a little preliminary talk (which I found included several erroneous statements and quite a few presumptions) and thus at that point I was not too enthused about what might happen next. A hymn was sung and a prayer said which showed me that this particular group was still linked to some degree with traditionalist Christian Church methodology.

*(About 90% of spiritualist meetings still have such links but many are now leaving religion aside which is not only the correct thing, for **religion has nothing to do with the psychic world**, but it also allows other faiths in our multi-racial society to take part without feeling that they are letting down their own personal faith in some way.)*

Two messages came forth from the medium for two different people and then she looked towards my friends and I.

"I have a message from a well-built man who was once Chief Inspector of the Glasgow Tramways."

I pricked up my ears at the word "tramways" as my own maternal grandfather had been Chief Inspector of the tramway system in Kirkcaldy, in Fife which is seventy miles to the east. I looked at my two companions for they lived in Glasgow and so it was reasonable to expect that, by coincidence, one of their ancestors could also have been involved in the organisation of the once-large Glasgow tram transport system. They looked so blank that I was then forced to say to the medium,

"Well, I can handle most of that statement but not the "Glasgow" bit of it."

The lady then said somewhat sheepishly that as we were all sitting in a Glasgow hall, she had included the word "Glasgow" out of her own imagination. Not a good idea for a medium!

It now appeared that my grandfather was, in fact, attempting to make contact with me from the other realm. Naturally I was pleased, for this he had not done previously in any way and I certainly had not been thinking of him of late and so had not 'drawn him into my mind' so to speak. I waited patiently for whatever information he had for me but knowing the amount of trivia that often comes forward during such meetings I had not made up my mind to hear great things or earth-shattering statements. I was correct in taking up such a mental stance.

"The gentleman says that he is laughing at your attitude to something or other."

"I'm glad he's happy!" I responded, "But what exactly is he laughing about?"

"Oh dear," went on the medium, "This must sound very strange for he tells me it's all about broken bottles and your dustbin."

(That's what I mean by trivia coming from the other world! I get communication from my Grandfather for the very first time and does he greet me with words of comfort and great wisdom? Not a bit of it! He wants to discuss "broken glass and dustbins"!)

I must not 'make mock' however, for I was really quite astounded at what he said and the reason was this. My house lies in a little village and has a high wall around it: about nine feet tall in parts. There is a little pub close by and of late a few thoughtless clients (Summer visitors?) appear to get evicted from this bar at midnight still clutching their beer bottles in their hands. These they finish as they walk past my house and rather than throw the bottles down in the street (something to be commended I suppose) they toss them over my wall and into my garden. When they land on the grass I can just pick them up next day, which I don't really enjoy, but if they hit the concrete yard at the rear of my house they smash into a million little bits and my cat and her vet start complaining about matters. Naturally, I was close to the point of visiting the local publican, placing my cat upside down on his bar with her bandaged paws in the air and making a formal complaint of some kind but I had not actually done any of that by the time my grandfather made contact. **I had never told a single sole** about my 'bottle problem' and because of the high wall no one could possibly have seen me sweeping up broken glass every second day of late …..and yet my grandfather appears to have seen me!

I asked the medium why he had been laughing at my actions for I felt genuinely incensed that anyone, *dead or alive*, should laugh at bottles being broken and animal's paws put at risk. I then remembered the well-known fact from psychic circles that attitudes of deceased persons are exactly the same **after** their death as they were **before**. Could it be that as my grandfather lived in the late nineteenth and early twentieth century his attitude to cats was somewhat different from ours today? Did he see cats as creatures not worthy of compassion and care? I hope not but that was a common attitude in such far off days and one that still exists in some parts of the world even today.

Apparently his laughing, the medium said, concerned my over-serious attitude towards the whole affair. Perhaps he was really telling me to "lighten up!"

(Readers who are not used to such spiritualist meetings must wonder why some close relative whom I have not seen for fifty years, comes forward from the other world and, without any sort of formal greeting, merely wants to laugh at me concerning my sweeping up broken glass. On the face of it, it sounds ridiculous! Perhaps it is not so ridiculous if my grandfather already 'sees' me on a day to day basis without my ever knowing anything about it. Under those circumstances it might not occur to him to start any sort of formal communication for he'd just be having a chat with his grandson as if we'd been in the same room together in the same house. We don't, after all, introduce ourselves afresh to our family members each time we speak to them. That appears to be just another problem concerning the psychic world and its link with ours. Perhaps when we feel that a deceased person is around us somewhere .... they really are!)

****

If that had been the only message for me that evening I might not have written of it here ...or at least I might not have given it any sort of prominence. There were, however, another two messages that came to me from different people close on the heels of my grandfather's ridicule and those I initially found mystifying and then eventually very interesting. I use the word "eventually" for at first I hadn't a clue as to who was sending me the messages.

"I have a message for you from Jimmy who asks you to pass on his best wishes to friends you both have in common."

You would have thought that the name "Jimmy" would have instantly struck a cord with me as it is a common enough name. You might also have thought that such a message could be taken by almost anyone in the audience but I was told it was for me and me alone.

(This business of a message being linked to one person and that person alone is something that is borne out very strongly indeed by some very fine statistical research undertaken over the past five years by Professor A. Roy and Mrs. P. Robertson of the Scottish Society for Psychical Research).

I asked the medium for some further information regarding the identity of "Jimmy" for it was just far too vague a name for my liking.

"He has produced a gigantic postage stamp before me (she held her hands about three feet apart) and is telling me that that had great meaning in his life and he is also repeatedly pointing to the crown on the upper part of the stamp and saying that that too validates his identity."

I know it sounds sad but I had to tell the medium the truth, which was that I did not know the person she was talking about. She insisted that it was for me and indeed I believed her but at that time I was unable to link my mind with the deceased person. The lady then moved on to a third message for me,

"Lizzie is asking for you and for all her friends."

I knew quite a number of persons who were in the spirit world who had been christened "Elizabeth" but none had ever been called, "Lizzie" during their lifetime and think as hard as I could, no such individual came to mind. Naturally I was disappointed and the medium moved on to a new member of the audience leaving me feeling somewhat foolish.

For reasons that I do not understand my brain works best at a point somewhere between 5am and 5.30am. At that time and in my friends' house I sat bolt upright in bed with a jolt because something (or someone?) had just explained to me who both "Jimmy" and "Lizzie" were.

I'd had an acquaintance (rather than a close personal friend) in both my Curling Club and my Rotary Club and his name had been Jimmy Moyes. While not being all that close to Jimmy we were all sorry to see him sail his yacht south out of Scottish waters and towards Spain where he said that he intended to live. His being relocated to Spain was a loss to both clubs I'm sure and for about the last six years no one I know seems to have heard about him. Could this be the Jimmy mentioned?

Jimmy had been the postmaster of two local post offices: Pitlessie village and then Leslie town in Fife. What better to show me (per the medium) as proof as to who he was than a large postage stamp? He had also been an officer in the merchant navy prior to being a postmaster and, surprise, surprise, what is the main emblem of that calling? A crown …just like the one found on a postage stamp! I now had no doubt at all that the Jimmy who came through to me that evening was indeed Jimmy Moyes.

There was, however, a little problem here that could have knocked this whole business on the head and that was,

"Was Jimmy Moyes actually dead ?" for I know of two embarrassing cases where a medium relayed a message from a supposedly 'dead' person only to find out that he was still very much alive. I decided to find out Jimmy's present state, of course, for it takes a very fit man to sail a seven metre yacht single handed across the Bay of Biscay and then to the southern tip of Spain. He must have been a very healthy man when he was last seen in the U.K.

I talked with several Rotarians who had known him, as well as one or two of his former curling companions but no one had heard from Jimmy from that day to this and so I was forced to look more deeply into matters. Eventually I found someone who knew someone who knew Jimmy in his last days and I learned that he had indeed died two years previously! But there again I knew he had to be dead or I could not have got that message. I passed on his good wishes, of course, to some very perplexed Rotarians and Curling Club members.

(I hope it has occurred to you that this incident throws up some rather interesting research for it is often levelled at mediums that they are merely picking up and regurgitating information that the client or sitter has in his or her own mind at the start of the sitting…….and that could have been levelled at my account of my grandfather's message. Regarding Mr. Moyes, however, such a thing could not have been levelled at me. I could not possibly have given such information to the medium…even subconsciously…. for not only had I forgotten all about the existence of Jimmy Moyes but I had no idea at all whether he was alive nor dead. Wherever the medium was getting her information, it could not have come from MY mind.)

Then there was "Lizzie".

I now think I know who Lizzie is but in a less sure way than I know who Jimmy is for she gave me no clues through the medium. My knowledge of the working mechanisms of the psychic world had to be called upon in order to track down Lizzie's identity.

I explain the technicalities of it all in another book but take it from me that there is an enormous memory system 'out there somewhere' where all facts about everything are recorded. The best way of thinking about this information is that it is in lots and lots of little boxes and when one box is opened not only are there other linked things in that box but the act of opening one box also lifts the lids of other linked boxes allowing us to see into them also.

It was a natural thing that my grandfather came through to me for his 'memory box' and mine are continuously linked by virtue of my being born into his family but that is not true of either Jimmy Moyes or Lizzie Birrell. I believe, through my researches, that the answer is this:-

My grandfather chose to converse with me about the broken bottles lying in the area to the rear of my house in the village of Kingskettle. This triggered the opening of a memory box that might be entitled perhaps, "Kingskettle village".

Lizzie Birrell was a dear old lady who lived merely 100 yards from my house in the same village and in her latter days I learned that her father had been one of the last managers of the rather large linen-weaving mill here that shut down during the second world war. In its time it supplied tablecloths and napkins for many luxury liners like the Lusitannia. She told me, some years ago, that she still had in her possession many examples of the lovely linen work that had been carried out at the old mill that had long since been demolished to make way for housing. Interested in all local things, I determined to ask her to show me those items and she was very pleased to do so for she said that after she died there would be no one to cherish such fine pieces of linen cloth. To be frank I rather think she took me to her heart, as they say, for she gifted me a considerable amount of samples that I currently hold for posterity. Sadly, the lady was correct in her prediction for I heard that most of her fine linen samples were eventually disposed of after her death.

Jimmy Moyes' connection is also a very **local one** for he was the local postmaster as you might remember but I was also linked to him by our both being members of two clubs simultaneously. His bond with me would therefore be stronger than my bond with Lizzie and so he would come through to me first …which is precisely what took place. Yes, that chance evening in Glasgow threw up more than I had initially given it credit for and thus I've shared it with you.

(Regarding seances and similar: the more studious amongst you should note that there is a fine line to be drawn between the coming in of secondary entities like Jimmy and Lizzie…because they have some link with the primary situation (i.e. things that happen in Kingskettle village) …. and entities called "drop in communicators" who appear absolutely out of the blue at such times. Those latter spirit-beings merely realise that there is a connection between their world and our world and seize upon the opportunity to make contact. They cause some fun and confusion at times but do no harm otherwise.

There is always a chance of drawing in secondary entities for they belong to a pre-linked situation but drop-in communicators come forward in a totally haphazard way.

A good example of a drop-in communicator is described in Volume 1 of this series of books, on page 101 although even 'Dr Margaret' might be concluded by some to be a normal secondary entity who might have been expected to show up anyway. As I said, the dividing line is a thin one.

Another aspect to cause a researcher a lot of thought is the fact that Jimmy Moyes identified himself merely as "Jimmy" and surprisingly he made no attempt whatever to use his second name. Instead he chose to play games with us and show giant postage stamps and crowns in order to let me know who he was. I'd love to be able to tell you why he didn't just say straight out who he was but I do not have the answer to that. If he could pass the name "Jimmy" and knew that he had once been a postmaster and a merchant seaman why didn't he just say that?)

I often come across spirit people who don't seem to know their own names or can't project them through the medium correctly...and in fact some don't even know that they are dead! Such are the problems that psychic investigation throws up and difficult as such things are, we at least know the questions we'd like to ask...which I suppose is one stage closer to getting to know the answers.

I have a very sensible friend called Anna who takes a greater interest in the activity of mediums and spiritualist meetings than I do and we discussed the above cases. She reminded me that of the several methods by which mediums gain their information clairsentience is currently the most common. That is, information is passed to the medium by 'innate feelings' rather than by senses of hearing (claireaudience) or seeing (clairevoyance). She suggests that the first name of "Jimmy" may have been given to the medium by allowing her to feel the presence of someone she already knew and who was called "Jimmy" also. Unless she also knew someone called "Moyes", Anna says, the surname was unlikely to come to her easily and so the spirit person, realising her inability had to resort to clairvoyance. That is why she was **shown** an image of a large postage stamp.

Anna drew to my attention a story about another medium who had difficulty in getting a surname but kept getting images of ducks: ducks on farms, ducks on ponds and even china ducks on tables. The client was unable to accept any part of that until it became apparent that the man's surname was "Mr. Drake", then all was clear. Pictorial imagery seems to pass to most mediums much better than lettering but that still does not explain why Mr. Jimmy Moyes could not have shown an image of the spelling of his surname as printed on a sheet of paper. That is an image is it not? I also refer you to page 251 of Volume 1, where a young entity man did not know his name until we suggested that he listen to his mother calling to him across the fields to come home for his meal. Only then did he remember that he was called "Toby"!

A Prophecy that Evening?

While this account is not given to you in order to start you thinking about 'prophecy' that does actually come in as a completely side issue so I'll merely touch upon it now for the medium lady of the above meeting did make a prophecy to me.

I don't like prophecies, I don't trust prophecies and I tend to shy away on the few occasions when Francesca makes one. I take those actions because I feel that I do not understand (yet) the psychic mechanisms behind such mysterious things and so I am still 'sitting on the fence' here. And that in spite of the fact that on many occasions my medium associate tells me, when we are out on a case, that we will find certain things at our goal hours beforehand and when it is still fifty miles away. She's always correct too!

Anyway the medium in Glasgow that evening told me, before a public audience, that, "You will be making a visit to a hospital soon!"

Now we all know that such a statement has many different meanings which range all the way from, "making a delivery of some sort at a hospital", to "visiting a sick relative", to "ending up in bed there after a traffic accident". I therefore was not unduly alarmed although I was watchful of the situation, given that this lady had already given me a message from someone who was undeniably my grandfather.

Ten days later the answer may have come out of the blue for I got a letter from my local hospital asking me to take part in a second round of tests as part of an area mass-screening to detect colorectal cancer. I was reminded in the letter that I had already taken part in the voluntary community round one tests in the year 2000.

I did, in fact, take the medical authorities up on their offer and was left wondering if this event was the one 'seen' by the medium. I suppose in a way she was correct for although I, as a whole and entire person, did not visit the hospital at least the 'samples' I supplied did and thankfully, proved negative.

Perhaps, in hindsight, that medium would have been better to have said,

"You will soon be strongly connected with a hospital," or similar (if indeed that is what she meant). Perhaps she was just a mentally/verbally careless medium? You will remember that she had to confess to me early in the proceedings when my Grandfather came forward that she "had made up" the reference to Glasgow.

****

Windows on the Past

Here are two interesting snapshots of the past written as if from my diary.

"July 7th 2004, Visit One

Written at the end of rather a tiring day both for myself and for Francesca who I delivered back to her home in the late afternoon.

I never get over the marvel of knowing that as I watch Francesca in some of her trances I am truly watching a snapshot of the past, for her body often takes upon itself the positions and responses of the body of the spirit person whom she has allowed to take her over …whether that person lived a year before or several centuries before.

Today's visits to two very different clients more than fifty miles apart showed just such a thing but in different ways.

The first visit we made was at 10 am in Dunfermline, Fife after I had picked up Francesca from the rail station. For maximum efficiency, the young man concerned met us at the station and we followed Graham and his car to his comparatively new house that had been built on the site of an old hospital which had been demolished not so many years before. It had been called "Miles Mark Hospital" and that had been replaced by a fine, new and modern building but on the other side of town and was now re-named the "Queen Margaret Hospital". The family who had invited us in had been reasonably prosperous and outgoing initially and had been so proud of their new home but sadly, death took one of their children away from them not so long ago and now leukaemia looked as if it was about to deprive them of a second child. No wonder they asked themselves if the house that they lived in had brought them such dreadful bad luck.

At the end of an hour's mental and spiritual searching the case itself brought forward nothing of help to that poor family but during our search for a possible psychic element to all of this Francesca stumbled across the presence of a rather unpleasant and mentally disturbed male spirit entity.

His 'spirit self' had locked itself onto the space that the house now occupied upon the land surface in the time-honoured manner and was reluctant (or unable) to move on and to be totally absorbed into the spirit memory system where most of us will end up after death.

The man had apparently attempted to take his own life on quite a number of occasions (he told us*)* and thus he had been committed to a ward in the now-demolished hospital for his own safety.

(No doubt the records will establish that there had been such a ward there.... actually I feel that it was an entire external building in its own right and not just a sub-section of a main building. Once again I feel badly that I just do not have the time to research the situation further for the few facts that came forward today must be quite easily confirmed surely.)

Probably the most noticeable thing of the visit was that while Francesca was vocalising to us all the details of the poor man concerned, her body was taking up poses that were completely alien to her normal posture positions. Initially, when in trance, she had her arms firmly crossed over on her chest for most of that time and her fingertips pressed *tightly* against her opposite shoulders. When she was not in this strange pose I noticed that she was sitting *bolt upright* with her arms in a rigid *vertical* position and, once more, she had her fingertips tightly pressed against the respective shoulders.

Because of her unusually twisted bodily positions, her glasses slipped unnoticed from her knee and were temporarily lost under the easychair upon which she was sitting.

I have no doubts at all that what we were witnessing in the clients' main room was the mental patient as he had been when he had been secured in two different forms of 'straight-jacket'! The emotion generated at such times by this unfortunate mental patient must have been so understandably overpowering in his earthly life that it is little wonder that he had taken it into the spirit memory system with him. I felt it so terribly sad that such action had been considered necessary for him and yet in those past times I suppose such forms of restraint had been thought to be for his own good. In fact he said, through Francesca, that he had led a worthless and meaningless life and cared nothing for anyone as nobody cared for him but he understood why he had to be restrained for his own benefit.

Realising that while all this was interesting no doubt, it neither helped nor reassured the unfortunate family in whose home we were sitting. I myself felt genuine and very considerable compassion towards this poor spirit man whom we had stumbled across and I felt too that the others in the room felt likewise. I wanted to use this compassion in a creative way and knowing what I knew from past meetings with spirit persons, I spoke quietly to Francesca. I asked our medium if she would transmit the feelings of love and pity that we all felt to the man from the spirit world that we had momentarily stumbled across, so that he could move on into the system that exists to hold all spirit entities.

(Recognition of a past problem and compassion towards it, is enough to 'move on' probably 90% of entities....provided that they are willing to use that mechanism.)

The lady's head bowed and then came up again after about a minute and she told us that she believed that he had, in fact, moved on from the site of their house.

None of this did the slightest good for the sad family of course...except that it may have reassured them that their house was completely clear of all spirit entities although I stressed to them that the spirit man we had encountered had nothing at all to do with their bad luck ...or rather, neither Francesca nor myself felt any connection whatever between the bad luck of this family and the mental patient.

****

Matters might have rested there except that just as Francesca was about to get up and make for the door she hesitated and said that a single word had come into her head and appeared in her mind as very large and bold capital letters. It was the word, "MEMORIAL". While we discussed its possible relevance … mostly concerning the older and now dead little girl ….we came to no final conclusion as to why the word came forcefully to our medium. She did say, however, that the family should keep the word in mind and she was very definite when making that point.

I must now tell you that Graham phoned me two days later with two bits of news: firstly that the family had found Francesca's glasses under the chair where she was sitting and that ……surprise, surprise!… a lady doctor of international note who works wonders with child leukaemia cases was about to fly from a hospital in the United States to visit their sick little girl at their local Queen Margaret Hospital. The hospital where this American doctor usually worked was,

"The **MEMORIAL** Hospital of XXXXX"

****

July 7th 2004, Visit Two

On the second visit of the day and about 50 miles to the west, we found ourselves in the home of a young woman in her mid thirties who had concluded that she had been psychically possessed by several spirit beings for the past seven years. The case had, in fact, been passed to me by a London-based group called the "Spirit Release Foundation" who specialise in dealing with persons who are "possessed". This young woman, Jennifer, had apparently phoned the S.R.F. and claimed that she had been suffering 'overshadowing' by several entities for almost seven years. She had tried countless things and had contacted countless people in order to rid herself of the nightly traumas that overwhelmed her....which currently took the form of her being poked, pushed and violently shaken by some unseen force as she lay in her bed. She believed that the force actually lived within her and as there were several aspects to her misuse by the force, she had concluded some years previously that several entities might have taken up residence in her mind and/or her body.

*(In actual fact the girl **could have** been correct, for when entities invade a victim' the fact that the mind and body of the host is in a receptive state to receive one entity that also means that it is in a state suitable for receiving more than one entity. Being host to multiple entities is not at all uncommon in the bizarre world of possession. However, I must take this opportunity, I feel, to correct the Hollywood impression that there are 'body-hunting ghouls' out there somewhere, lurking in the bushes just waiting for young women like Jennifer to pass by, ready to be leapt upon and overpowered. Not true!*

Possession can take place for a whole host of reasons....like during physical or mental illness, like being in the wrong place at the wrong time or even putting one's mind into a receptive state and actually 'inviting' passing entities in.

"Who would do such a foolish thing?" I hear you say. And the answer is, people who play around with ouija boards, planchettes and the like or people who take part in seances without the correct guidance and who open up their minds to spirit entry and yet have not the knowledge to close their minds down again at the end of the whole mental process.)

We listened for a very long time to Jennifer's sad story.... certainly for well over a hour. Convinced that she was possessed she had, over the years, called in a large number of mediums of all sorts of qualities and I could see that she was becoming more distraught with each medium she was telling us about. Finally when I heard her tell us about a male 'ghost-buster' who was meant to have caught two of her three (claimed) entities in a bubble and sent them on their way I thought, "Enough is enough"! Francesca and I glanced meaningfully towards each other and I asked the medium in all honesty if she felt any sort of spirit entity in or around Jennifer's body or mind.

This talented lady slowly shook her head and said that she felt nothing at all in or around the girl. Like all mediums, Francesca has her stronger points and her weaker points but she is excellent when it comes to detecting the *presence* of a spirit entity. Some of those entities (the more unpleasant ones) attempt to hide or to lie low until the medium is due to leave the property but Francesca knows immediately of their presence, quite independently of whether she is able to engage them in conversation or not.

There was no doubt in Francesca's mind…there was NO entity in or around Jennifer! At that time in the afternoon, therefore, I was on the point of giving up the quest for missing entities and returning to the car and (with some reluctance) leaving the weeping girl to her own devices. What else could I do?

It was then that I noticed Francesca unexpectedly sliding into a trance and I could see that she was going unusually deep. I realised immediately that I should be keeping a very watchful eye on her psychic and physical welfare. Knowing that something was about to happen I suggested to the client that we just sit still for a bit longer and watch what was about to take place. After a considerable period of silence the medium sat stiffly upright and then we saw her head tilt back, hard back. There was then a quick jerking action to the head and neck area and then a second lesser jerk of the head. We continued to watch in silence and then after about four minutes Francesca's eyes opened slowly as she looked around herself to see where (and in what century) she was. I smiled to reassure her but she was far, far away mentally and I don't think she saw me at all at first. She said nothing while she moved her head about gently in order to relieve the stress that had formed in her neck muscles. What she did finally say astounded both Jennifer and myself for she told us that she had just been hanged by the neck on a public gibbet in the city of Glasgow!

We had actually witnessed the public hanging of a noted thief from another century and you can't get history much more real than that! What a privilege …albeit a frightening privilege… to be present at a hanging in 18th century (?) Glasgow.

This is the astounding explanation of what we had both witnessed and as the medium and I worked away at 'untangling' the story that was coming forward, we were pleased to hear Jennifer chime in every now and again saying that what Francesca revealed blended exactly with her own recall of various incidents seven years ago.

The man had been John McAlister (spelling?) and he confessed that he had been a "pick-pocket and foot-pad" in the city of Glasgow although he did not seem to be able to say in what century he had lived. He had been caught and was hanged for his crimes on a gallows that was almost permanently on-site in the Gallowgate area of that city.

One evening in the summer of 1997 several coincidental things took place in that area of Glasgow. Jennifer, who was a member of a spiritualist circle that met regularly in that part of the city, had been using her mind (along with others) during the indoor meeting to carry out some sort of communication with the spirit world. As the girl was a comparative novice to this sort of thing she had to mentally work away at 'opening up her mind' and at the end of the evening she would be expected to do the reverse before she set off for home: she would be expected to know how to 'close down her mind'. Apparently this shutting down procedure was not carried through because (Jennifer told us) she had never been taught such a mental practice.

Jennifer therefore walked out into the night air and she did as she always did, she slung her handbag with its short strap over her left shoulder and headed for home. What she did not know was that, in some mysterious way, the spirit of John McAlister was around.

(Spirit entities have 'high' and 'low' periods of cycles of some sort. At least some of those appear to be linked to past earthly high points like birthdays and times of death or traumatic situations. I wondered if that summer evening was, in fact, the anniversary of the man's hanging but I have no factual evidence to back that up.)

Anyway, the bold John McAlister told us that he could not resist doing in death as he had done in life...... he saw Jennifer's bag hanging upon her shoulder and it was just asking to be robbed. He never actually said whether he managed to riffle it or not but he did say that he had come home with Jennifer to her house. He somehow took up residence with the girl in her bedroom and enjoyed shaking the life out of her on a nightly basis as well as putting grotesque images into her mind for reasons best known to himself.

Jennifer was NOT a 'possessed' person but she was very probably a perpetually 'haunted' person. That is, the entity had not taken possession of her mind and body at any point but he was perpetually getting at her in various other ways.

The question that was uppermost in the mind of both Francesca and myself at that point was,

"Can we now get this man to move away from Jennifer in spite of the fact that he seems quite happy to be perpetually associated with her?"

Francesca once more moved herself into a deeper than usual trance. Incidentally, it is **not** she who sets the depth of trance: it is rather set for her by the system through which she works.

*(I must tell researchers truthfully that I do not understand why, in some cases great depth of trance is needed while in other cases a shallow trance seems to be sufficient to make contact with the entity involved. I know it is **not** merely to do with the number of years the entity has been deceased or it would have become apparent to me a long time ago that when we talk with monks from the 12th century, for example, that would tax Francesca's emotional energies a great deal more than when she makes contact with someone from the 19th century. The process just does **not** happen like that!*

It might have to do with the resistance the entity generates 'around himself' in order to retain his anonymity: it might require additional energy from the medium to overcome this. It might even have to do with the devious nature of the entity's mind, for some spirit people are simple and straightforward while others have been (and still are!) bitter and twisted by nature. Perhaps it takes more energy from the medium to penetrate such a barrier.)

I am pleased to tell you that once Francesca had moved out of her very deep trance she said that she thought she had persuaded John McAlister to move on to where he should rightfully be. Our medium was very flushed and tired indeed I could see and I was very sorry for her but Jennifer was immediately elated and was almost jumping around saying that she felt as if a load had been lifted off both her mind and her body.

For that I was very pleased and it was a good note to depart upon.

****

It would be very easy indeed for some psychologist or psychiatrist to declare that this young woman had been on the edge of some sort of mental breakdown for the past seven years and was blaming it upon the spirit world... perhaps to attract attention and sympathy.

When we asked Jennifer about her interaction with the medical world she said that,

"They basically said that I should get a grip on myself and handed out tranquillisers of various types and sort of walked away from the situation."

How pleased I am to tell you, therefore, that the *Spirit Release Foundation** membership is rising in number because more and more psychologists, psychiatrists and doctors are now joining its ranks and beginning to understand that the psychic world really does exist and really can influence our earthly world and all people on it. The necessary mental changes required of those professional persons will take a long time to become apparent of course but in the fullness of time change *will* take place so that 'chemical coshes' and straight-jackets will finally be a thing of the past for those people seeking help with their mental illness.

* *The Spirit Release Foundation* exists to enhance the understanding of what psychical possession is and to alert the medical fraternity in particular to the fact that such a thing can have a bearing upon the mental well-being of a patient under their care.

****

The Door Handle

Door handles, for the most part, are of one of two types. Either they are ball-like and allow the human hand to mould over them to turn them and so gain entry to a room or they are long and lever-like so that the hand can grasp them and push one end downwards. It is this latter type that forms an early part to the account you will now read.

Jan and Ian were a delightful young couple and on the threshold of life and were fortunate enough to live in a small but comparatively new home in the town of Showergate in Central Scotland. Everything was going well for them except for something that they felt they could not mention to anyone else…. they felt that they were not alone in the house for they sensed the presence of others who were there but invisible. There was no sense of badness or evil but things just were 'not right' somehow and as time went on, this feeling whatever it was, was beginning to cast a blight over their hitherto happy lives and togetherness.

They were sure that at times their dog would see something that they did not and, of course the young couple put this down at first to their overactive imagination. It happened, however, with such regularity that sooner or later they had to accept that perhaps the dog really was seeing something that they could not sense. This was coupled with other things. Small items either moved positions within the house or even at times disappeared altogether, only to reappear in their initial position as if they had never gone in the first place. This business, each of the pair put down to the over active imagination of the other or their lack of attentiveness…which did not help in their relationship as you can imagine.

It was only when the internal doors in the upstairs part of the house began opening and closing by themselves that they decided to put a bit more mental effort into solving their problem. Ian was clever enough to come up with a foolproof method of testing a theory that they were forced to develop which indicated that the doors were actually being opened from their closed positions without resort to the lever handles being used at all. Ian's idea came into being because of the possibility that the dog was using its paws to jump upon the handles to open any door in the house. However, on several of these 'door-opening' occasions it had been an impossibility that their dog was concerned in any way, for either it was not on the property in the first place or was shut in a room in such a manner that it would have had to open a series of doors and then shut each one after its escapade in order to escape detection.

Ian decided to check the door that opened by itself with most regularity with regards to the correct working of the catch. "Yes", it was working beautifully! It shut nicely into position each time with a very satisfying click. He then cleverly hung a small length of metal chain with a little weight attached on the lever door handle that was on the outside of the door. He tested his device over and over again and it worked each time. There was no way that anyone could get into that room...dog or human...without that chain device being tipped off the handle and rattling onto the floor.

You can guess the rest, I suppose. The door was opened wide in their absence and the chain was still hanging in position on the handle! The only conclusion was the correct one...that the door had been opened by a means that was not normal!

Even then Ian could not bring himself to believe what his own eyes and test were showing and so he closed the door and pushed forcefully against it to see if vibration could in some way open the door. In fact he pushed the door so hard during this testing procedure that he actually snapped the catch right off. The end result was the same of course and the couple decided to call in someone who know more about psychic things than they did.

I got an initial phone call from Jan and then a subsequent call a little later telling me two further things that had just taken place. She told how Ian had been asleep when he was poked in the back of the neck as if by the point of a finger and a female voice had simultaneously called him by his name. This disturbed him to quite a degree and was followed by a final but small incident that could not be explained. A heavy and flat metal key-fob with a bunch of keys attached had been placed centrally on the internal window ledge in the most effected room by Ian at the end of a certain day and almost as a challenge to whatever strange power 'lived' in that room. At some point during the night those objects had not only moved to the extreme left hand end of the windowsill (and behind the curtain) but had flipped completely over so that the lower surface of the heavy metal fob was now uppermost. That did it for the young couple and they phoned again and asked me to visit them and explain to them what might be taking place.

Francesca and I drove out to Jan and Ian on the second day in April 2004 and after a little trouble in finding the house amongst a maze of other properties we stood outside it in the Spring sunshine. It was built near the top of an area of sloping ground and by rights should have had some sort of amazingly fine view down a valley but because of the built-up state of the housing this was not something that was true. Regretfully, because of other properties being in the way, there were no beautiful views over a valley or the like. Francesca, however, picked up on this 'height business' as soon as we got out of the car…almost too much so in my opinion for I know this lady's expressions and attitudes having worked with her for about five years. For a second time within minutes, and as we walked up the path to the door, she once again referred to the 'height' of the place and its possibility for views and yet there were no such views. Even then I realised that this medium was already in a sort of twin mental situation: she was beside me in 2004 and yet I felt she was also there looking over a valley from a prominent hillside position *as if in some earlier period of time*. This later proved to be exactly the state she was in.

Jan and Ian told us their story again in a face to face way and said, in all honesty, that of late matters seemed to have quietened down. In fact they said that matters quietened from the moment that I agreed with them on the phone that we would come out and visit.

(Such a thing is only to be expected for almost all experiences that family homes have placed upon them by the psychic world is caused by that world…or rather by 'the inhabitants of it'…. wanting to make contact to let we living humans know that they once existed on that site in the past. Spirit entities both see us and hear us as they choose and so they would know that Jan had made that important phone call to me and that it was only a matter of time until Francesca and I visited. They would know too that through the clever mediumship of Francesca it would be highly likely that they would be able to put over more of their story to the people who lived in the property in question. That is one of the main aims of spirit people…to tell their story to we humans.)

We went up to the upstairs room that seemed most effected and which seemed to be the locus of the majority of the strangeness. Jan had left the heavy key-fob untouched at the left end of the windowsill and I looked down at it. I suppose that it was only a silly human feeling but I felt it was almost daring me to touch it and move it. I decided not to!

"You wouldn't happen to know what stood on this site prior to the houses being built here?" I asked and the young couple both shook their heads.

Francesca did not shake her head but quietly bowed it and went into a mini trance.

"There was a small building with two floors here once: right on the side of the hill," she said and then went on to describe the people who worked in it for the downstairs seemed to be some sort of area where workers clocked in while upstairs was a true office where the paperwork of the company was carried out."

The medium seemed to be describing the general office of some sort of a quarrying, mining and trucking business that was taking place at a lower level on the hillside below. There had been windows at the front of the upstairs office and from them there had been a considerable view over the valley. An ideal situation one might think and a scene that I truly believe Francesca was seeing from the moment she got out of the car. That is why she was so insistent in talking about the elevated position of the site in spite of the fact that in 2004 there was **no view**. Sadly, while the view was magnificent, the ambience of the office was not and tension ruled day in and day out apparently. When I asked Francesca if she could identify the source of the ongoing tension that finally brought the whole business to a standstill she said that the company had been called, "Wallace and Sons" and that the quarrelling had been so great between the sons that the whole business had finally collapsed. The business had disappeared many years before but the tension had not and it was that that the young couple were feeling around them.

Having discovered the basis of the problem Francesca went on to ask Ian if he had ever known his grandmother. The man was obviously puzzled by being asked such a question but answered in the affirmative.

"Well, said Francesca, "It was you grandmother who was attempting to gain your attention. It was she who poked you and called your name in your ear!"

(I then explained to the pair that once a reasonable bond has been made between the spirit world and our world (as by the mining 'ghost' people in the quarry office), others in that world who might know us take advantage of the situation and use that connection to further their own ends. So it was that Ian's grandmother took advantage and made contact.)

Our medium told Ian that his grandmother was often close by him and the young man was, quite understandably, overcome by the thought that she still cared for him and loved him as she had done when he was a child. Grandmothers are very special people!

I told our hosts that further activity or an increase in activity was now unlikely although I did say that sometimes after a visit like this there was a sort of final 'blip' of activity almost as if the psychic world was saying a last goodbye. They were two sensible young people and decided jointly not to seek any formal 'exorcising' of their home. They would happily coexist with the past …if it ever made itself known again.

Saying our own "goodbyes", Francesca and I set off for our second case of the day which was back in central Edinburgh.

****

The second case was in no way remarkable so I'm not going to waste my time recording it with you or your time reading it. I will, however, mention something connected with it that most people might call 'coincidental' but which I know has meaning for I have worked with Francesca for many years.

As we were driving through central Edinburgh to get to that second case we passed, by chance, a garage that I noticed was called, 'Sunnyside Garage'. Francesca too was looking at it I noticed and then she said,

"Oh I once knew the owner of that 'Summerfield Garage.'

I corrected her sentence in as much as the premises was definitely 'Sunnyside' and not 'Summerfield' garage and to this the medium replied that she did not know why she had used the incorrect term for she knew perfectly well the correct name of the garage.

All was forgotten about that name business until we were at the house of the second case where the lady of the house eventually told us that she felt that most of her problems arose because she had been foolish enough to marry for a second time and take a new husband. When I enquired about the name of the man she had married and who was the origin of her problems I was told that it was, "Summerfield, Mr. John Summerfield".

Ten years ago I would have put such a thing down to coincidence but knowing Francesca as I do, I now know that she somehow picks up on psychic things many hours before we ever find out details of a case through the usual method of question and answer techniques. Was this 'Summerfield' name business some sort of chance event, an initial slip of the tongue or had Francesca's able psychic mind already picked up upon something in the house we were about to visit?

CHAPTER 11

SNIPPETS

The Lost Share Certificates
Feuding Miners

The Lost Share Certificates

Have you ever gone to a cupboard to get something and then left the cupboard carrying something else having completely forgotten what you went there for in the first place? This story is a bit like that except that the jar of jam is a folder with share certificates in it to the value of about £ 25,000 ($45,000) while the cupboard can be equated to an accountant's office.

This lady who I know …let's call her Muriel… had, for many years left her shares in the safe-keeping (joke!) of her accountant but as the stock market drifted relentlessly downwards after Sept. 11th 2001 she had had enough and thought that she'd at least re-appraise her whole share-holding situation. To that end she asked for her share certificates to be forwarded to her by her accountant who she knew at personal level. They never came and unfortunately she seemed to let time slip by before she asked a second time for them to be forwarded to her. Then there was a third time but once again, no share certificates appeared. Getting desperate, and as she was a personal friend, she made an appointment with the man at the end of his working day so that she could have a bit of social chit-chat and perhaps a little meal or a visit to a local pub and then finally come back home with the items that she sought.

Well, it didn't work out like that! The chat was fine, although a bit stilted Muriel thought and after it was all over she began to drive home. Yes, you've guessed it …she forgot to ask for the certificates! Too late then to turn the car around for the man had 'shut up shop' and gone home. The next day one final letter was sent to him and a curt reply came back saying something to the effect that he no longer had the certificates but had passed them on years before to a stockbroker at Muriel's request. The whole situation was a mess and a costly one at that because it was going to cost many hundreds of pounds to have these lost certificates re-issued. Naturally this lady wanted to know what *had* happened to her certificates because they were certainly not with her stockbroker as far as she was concerned. While she was merely telling me her story on the phone she had completely forgotten that I am closely associated with some people like Francesca who have unusual psychic abilities. I told Muriel the little story about the lost dog that occurs earlier in this book and said that I'd have a word with Francesca on her behalf to see if she could locate the whereabouts of the lost share certificates.

(Researchers should realise that there is no difference, from the psychic point of view, between finding a lost dog and finding misplaced documents; the information for each is stored in precisely the same way in the Great Universal Memory System. What may well differ is the route by which that information is accessed. For example, does the medium move towards the information via contact with some physical object or does she work through the memory system of some deceased (or living) person or does she attempt to go straight into the Great Universal Memory System in a direct manner?)

The long and the short of the matter was that Francesca did come up with information but information that was in no way helpful in an immediate way. She told of how a junior member of the accountant's company had been told, a year or two before, to put the contents of certain old files in the skip and when that junior had queried the correctness of the directive given to him he was told to obey his boss's orders and to get on with the task in hand and to *leave the thinking to the boss.* Francesca told me how she felt the office junior agonising mentally as to what to do about the matter for it did not seem right to him to throw out certain current and valid share certificates, Muirel's included.

The files at that point seemed long gone and that was thought to be the end of the matter!

Addendum

That last sentence was correct when it was typed but in early December 2004 I received an interesting phone call from Muriel which updates matters for us.

The lost share certificates have been found!

They were discovered, amazingly enough, amongst *dental records* in a local dental practice and were eventually returned to Muriel, the rightful owner!

What appears to have happened is this:-

Due to a shortage of storage space in the accountant's office that company was allowed to keep some of their records in an adjoining storeroom owned by a dental company where they also kept their own records. When the (wise) office junior had been ordered to throw out Muriel's share certificates by his boss I reckon that he knew positively **that he was in the right** …..and the boss in the wrong. Instead of dumping these valuable documents as instructed, this clever and far-seeing lad merely took them to the other side of the storeroom and slid them in between existing dusty dental records from a previous period, in order to hide them. He guessed correctly that the boss's error regarding their dumping would sooner or later be discovered. He knew too that when that time came he would merely go to the storeroom, withdraw the certificates from between the dental files where he had hidden them …….and no doubt get a big 'pat on the head' by the boss for being so far-sighted. The trouble was that the office junior had moved on to another company at the other side of the city by that time and so these documents were stumbled across quite by chance by the dental company in a tidying out process and were then handed back to the (amazed) accountant and thus to Muriel.

All's well that ends well! And I believe that Muriel, with some justification, is suing the accountant to recover the costs of having to get a complete set of duplicate certificates.

I have placed that little account before you so that you can compare and contrast it with the details of the "lost dog" story. True researchers will enjoy making such a comparison no doubt.

****

Feuding Miners

Till Hell Freezes Over!

"Love thy neighbor!" is a phrase that we hear so often and yet there are many times when neighbors loathe neighbors and some do so to excess. Who would have thought that a feuding neighbor could go on fighting the folks next door fifty years beyond the grave but this case shows that it did happen: while the man died, his wrath did not.

Most of the cases I go out to are personal to me in as much as the worried householders have found *my* phone number and have made contact in order to ask for help with some psychic problem that is effecting them and their families. Technically this case was different in as much as it fell into my lap in my capacity as Case Coordinator for the Scottish Society for Psychical Research. As that society had few members in eastern Scotland my initial problem was to find sufficient members in that area who would be willing to go out to the case which was in a small town about 30 miles east of Edinburgh. Wanting to leave myself out of the situation altogether in order to give others the experience of organising a visit to a probable paranormal case I initially managed to get a team of three organised ...or at least that was what I thought at first. Unfortunately, in the finality of things, the team-leader allocated to the case backed out prior to the event and so I had to reconstruct the team by using myself as a replacement. As I find Francesca a fantastic help at such times I took it upon myself to ask her along for I wanted to use the situation as a sort of a 'tutorial' for two new members of the team who were both dedicated students of the paranormal. One of those already held an degree in psychology and was now undertaking a masters degree in parapsychology, which must be considered an interesting 'psychic addendum' to her degree. The experience of being in the presence of a world-class working medium would be something of importance to this girl I felt sure.

Anyway, on a rather dark, blustery March evening in 2004 I drove my car around the streets of Edinburgh and collected my investigation team from their homes. I thought it wise to make the very level-headed graduate girl, Christie, the 'recorder' for the evening and I was pleased to see that she had brought along, not only a notebook but also her camera to record matters in a thorough manner.

As usual I had the postal address of the family concerned as well as their phone number but as they lived in a town that I did not know at all, I also had some scribbled instructions as to how to reach the house once we had entered the town itself. It was Anna, my passenger, who attempted to read my scribbled notes by the internal car lights as I drove carefully through the steady drizzle and into the town. I edged the vehicle into the street that seemed logical but Anna thought that we should go one street further east and so I drew back out of the first street and headed for the second. It was at that point that Francesca and her marvellous abilities came to the fore for we had hardly got the length of the second street when she spoke from the rear seat.

"Archie, I got the feeling when you drove into that first street that we were actually heading in the correct direction. I felt the psychic world telling me that we were getting closer to what we were looking for and that it really was at the end of that first road we turned into."

As not one of my companions in the car knew anything about that little town, including Francesca, I knew that she could not be speaking from any knowledge of the layout of the town. And so it proved, for the second street led to a very different area and we were eventually forced to return to the first street which led us to…surprise, surprise…the very house we were seeking. Once again I faced the problem that Francesca keeps placing before me on our cases: how can she possibly know if we are heading in the right direction if I've told her NOTHING AT ALL about the case in advance? She did not know the house or the householder or the address or the phone number and YET she knew the direction in which she was being mysteriously drawn.

(Researchers will be pleased to know that I deal with this strange question at length in another publication which is given

over totally to explaining the mechanics of the psychic world….
"Anatomy of a Ghost".)

Upon our arrival we were made most welcome by both Mr.
and Mrs. Holmes as well as their young seven-year-old son,
Mathew. The team and I noted that the house, while not being in
the best part of town, was tidy and clean and well organised.

Mrs. Holmes told our team what she had already told to me
on the phone, namely that their family had experienced quite a
wide range of strange phenomena. She cited these,

1) Feeling her hair being touched by some invisible
   hand when she lay in bed.
2) Hearing the noise of heels walking across the floors
   of some rooms.
3) Seeing "little lights floating in the air".
4) Hearing considerable and loud banging on the wall
   that separated their house from their neighbor's
   home.
5) Seeing the apparition of "a man coming up the
   stairs".
6) Feeling a sense of presence within the house
   sometimes.

As soon as Mrs. Holmes mentioned the banging on the
intercommunicating wall her husband agreed totally with her, as
indeed did their young son…although neither of those two were
in a position to back the mother up regarding some of the other
things. This banging seemed to exist at two distinct levels: the
first being a sort of hammering behind the fireplace in both the
main room and the upstairs bedroom above it (both of which
backed onto the corresponding rooms of the house next door). It
was as if the occupant of the house through the wall was banging
away at their fireplaces in some manner. The second type of noise
was upstairs and consisted of one almighty and horrendous bang
that could be heard from time to time in the bedroom. It sounded,
apparently, as if the ceiling had collapsed….yet not a single bit of
damage was ever found to account for the gigantic noise!

It must be obvious by now that if the majority of the
mysterious noises were taking place close to (or even 'within')

the intercommunicating walls then the next door neighbor might also be hearing such things. This was indeed discovered by the Holmes family at a very early stage in these events. Both families were mystified and initially each was, understandably, blaming the other for the loud sounds.

Mrs. Holmes began discussing the idea that perhaps, because she and her neighbor used an ouija board in the house every now and again, that something had 'come out of the woodwork' so to speak to haunt them both. I told the lady that while such a thing was possible because of a voluntary opening up of minds to psychic things I thought that we might be dealing with some 'leftovers' from a previous time in the history of the property.

Such a history was obviously not a long-standing one for the house had only been built about fifty years earlier.

Now was the time to include Francesca into the conversation for up till then she had just been listening attentively.

"The noises are definitely of a psychic origin," she said, "And are the psychic remains of neighbors feuding in the past. My how they must have hated each other!"

As the conversation and the knowledge moved forward it became apparent that the adjoining houses both held members of the local mining community. There had been an older man in the property now owned by the Holmes family and a younger but larger family through the wall.

When one of the team asked Francesca to give a date she gave both a date and names. The goading of one family by another concerned a Harkness family and a Williams family and took place around 1951 and 1952. Apparently one group would hammer a heavy metal poker again and again against the back of their fireplace in the noisiest way possible and then the second family would respond in a similar manner. On one occasion the old man concerned, Mr. Williams, got so overwrought that he grabbed his own bookcase and overturned it, flinging it to the floor in a total rage. That is probably the origin of the tremendous crash that is sometimes heard by Mr. and Mrs. Holmes. Francesca told how things had suddenly come to an abrupt end in May when the old man had died of a heart attack which overtook him as he stood on the top landing of his stair. Hardly surprising I suppose!

In the upstairs bedroom, where the great crash had been heard, I am pleased to say that Francesca told the team that she had made mental contact with the deceased man and had informed him that she understood the highly unpleasant times he had to endure at the hands of his neighbors. She reassured him that all that was now in the past and that new people whom he did not know now lived in the house that had once been his. She asked him to acknowledge the presence of this new family and to leave them in peace.

Perhaps he heard her pleas for it has been almost a year now since our visit and I have had no second phone call from the Holmes family for further assistance.

It was a minor case for us, I suppose, but an unpleasant interlude in the lives of Mr. and Mrs. Holmes and their neighbors.

THE END